The Economic Revival of
Modern Britain

The Economic Revival of Modern Britain

The Debate between Left and Right

Edited by

David Coates
Senior Lecturer
University of Leeds

John Hillard
Lecturer
University of Leeds

EDWARD ELGAR

Published by
Edward Elgar Publishing Limited
Gower House
Croft Road
Aldershot
Hants GU11 3HR
England

British Library Cataloguing in Publication Data

The Economic revival of modern Britain: the
    debate between left and right.
    1. Great Britain—Economic conditions
    —1945–
    I. Coates, David   II. Hillard, John
    330.941′0858   HC256.6

    ISBN 1-85278-001-0
    ISBN 1-85278-000-2 Pbk

Printed and bound in Great Britain
by Billing & Sons Limited, Worcester.

Contents

Acknowledgements

The editors gratefully acknowledge permission to reproduce the following:

Chapter 1 reproduced from N. Lawson, 'Britain's Economy: a mid-term report' (Conservative Political Centre, 1985), by permission of the Director, Conservative Political Centre, 32 Smith Square, London SW1P 3HH.

Chapter 2 reproduced from a speech by Rt. Hon. Edward Heath MP at London Business School on 27.11.1985, by permission of the author.

Chapter 3 reproduced from an open letter from Rt. Hon. David Steel MP to Trade and Industry Secretary, January 1986, by permission of the Press Officer, Parliamentary Liberal Party.

Chapter 4 reproduced from a speech by Rt. Hon. David Owen MP to the Industrial Society 10.3.1986 (and updated specially for this collection), by permission of the author.

Chapter 5 reproduced from a speech by Rt. Hon. John Smith MP at University of Sussex on 10.2.1986, by permission of the author.

Chapter 6 reproduced from Sir Keith Joseph, *Conditions for Full Employment* (London, Centre for Policy Studies, 1978), by permission of the Director, Centre for Policy Studies, 8 Wilfred Street, London SW1E 6PL.

Chapter 7 reproduced from *Employment: The Challenge for the Nation*, CMND, 1985, by permission of HMSO.

Chapter 8 reproduced from J. Lester and D. Grayson, *Jobs: Bringing Hope* (Tory Reform Group, 1986), by permission of Tory Reform Group, 22/23 Gayfere Street, London SW1P 3HP.

Chapter 9 reproduced from SDP/Liberal Alliance, *Budget Priorities 1986*, by permission of SDP/Liberal Alliance, 4 Cowley Street, London SW1.

Chapter 10 reproduced from John Prescott, *Planning for Full Employment* (Labour Party, 1985), by permission of the author.

Chapter 11 reproduced from A. Glyn, *A Million Jobs a Year* (Verso, 1985), by permission of the author, and Verso/NLB, 15 Greek Street, London W1V 5LF.

Chapter 12 reproduced from Ecology Party, *Jobs for Keeps* (1982), by permission of Green Party, 36/38 Clapham Road, London SW9 0JQ.

Chapter 13 reproduced from Charter for Jobs, 'We *can* cure unemployment' (Employment Institute, 1985), by permission of the Director, Employment Institute, Suite 107, Southbank House, Black Prince Road, London SE1 7ST.

Chapter 14 reproduced from House of Commons, first report of the Employment Committee, session 1985–86. 'Special employment measures and the long term unemployed' (1986), by permission of HMSO.

Chapter 15 reproduced from House of Lords Select Committee on Overseas Trade: *Report* (House of Lords, Session 1984–85, 238-I), by permission of HMSO.

Chapter 16 reproduced from Department of Trade and Industry: Balance of Trade in Manufacturers (CMND 9697, December 1985), by permission of HMSO.

Chapter 17 reproduced from Ashbridge Lecture, given on 20.11.1980 (and published in Quarterly Bulletin of Bank of England, December 1980), by permission of Economics Division, Bank of England, Threadneedle Street, London EC2R 8AH.

Chapter 18 reproduced from Institute of Directors: *Job Creation Without a U Turn* (November 1984), by permission of the Institute of Directors, 116 Pall Mall, London SW1Y 5BD.

Chapter 19 reproduced from CBI: *Unemployment: A Challenge To Us All* (summary of first report of the CBI steering group on unemployment 1982), by permission of CBI, Centre Point, 103 New Oxford Street, London WC1A 1DU.

Chapter 20 reproduced from Popular edition of 'Faith in the City' (Christian Action, 1985), by permission of Board for Social Responsibility and Christian Action, Church House, Dean's Yard, London SW1P 3NZ.

Chapter 21 reproduced from TUC *Economic review 1986*, by permission of TUC, Congress House, Great Russell Street, London WC1B 3LS.

Chapter 22 reproduced from NALGO, *Alternative Economic Strategy*, by permission of NALGO, 1 Mabledon Place, London WC1H 9AJ.

Chapter 23 reproduced from P. Minford, *Unemployment: Cause and Cure* (2nd edition) (Oxford, Basil Blackwell 1985), by permission of the author, and Basil Blackwell, Publishers, 108 Cowley Road, Oxford OX4 1JF.

Chapter 24 reproduced from Christopher Huhne, paper for the Tawney Society, 1986, by permission of the author.

Chapter 25 reproduced from B. Stafford, *The End of Economic Growth* (Oxford, Martin Robertson, 1981), by permission of the author, and Basil Blackwell, Publishers, 108 Cowley Road, Oxford OX4 1JF.

Chapter 26 reproduced from F. Cripps et al, *Manifesto* (London, Pan 1983), by permission of the authors.

Chapter 27 reproduced from *Socialist Economic Review 1982* (London, Merlin 1982), by permission of The Merlin Press.

Chapter 28 reproduced from a longer version of an article originally in *Marxism Today* (February 1986), by permission of the author, and the editor, *Marxism Today*, 16 St John's Street, London EC1M 4AY.

Chapter 29 reproduced from K. Coates (ed.), *Joint Action for Jobs* (New Socialist/Spokesman 1986), by permission of the author, and Spokesman Books, Bertrand Russell House, Gamble Street, Nottingham NG7 4ET.

Introduction

One of the virtues of liberal democracy is that it offers voters a regular though intermittent opportunity to choose between alternative solutions to the pressing issues of the day. Sometimes the issues and the choices are minor—and in reality little is at stake. In other times and places just the reverse is true. So deep are the problems, so major the choices, and so much is at stake, that there can be no guarantees that the result will be accepted peacefully by everyone. In this way, elections differ in their seriousness and significance; and by these criteria at least British elections now are more significant than they were two decades ago. The problems under discussion are severe ones; and the choices on offer, though limited, are real and distinct. To make an informed decision, voters need to understand these choices and be able to compare and evaluate them. But here lies the paradox: that at the very moment when the electorate needs to be well-informed, the sheer scale and complexity of the issues involved makes it progressively more difficult to gather and assimilate the necessary information. It is at times like this that a concise but comprehensive collection of material may be of greatest value, and it is just such a collection which we have attempted to gather here.

There are immediate and longer-term considerations in all this. We have already tried to gather a representative sample of the arguments surrounding Britain's long-term economic decline in our *The Economic Decline of Modern Britain* (Brighton, Wheatsheaf Books, 1986). That first collection focused on the processes of the past, and had very little directly to say on what ought to be done immediately if the situation is to be retrieved. Indeed, when we began to pursue more immediate policy solutions, we were struck first by how few academic articles and books were being produced in this area. Academic scholarship—however politically committed it might be—is apparently happier working on things which happened long ago than on things which could happen tomorrow, and is stronger on the specification of problems than on the drafting of solutions. So we turned instead to practitioners of all sorts, asking them for the solutions they canvassed; and we met a surprisingly large, generous and high-quality response. There is a lot of work being done by various individuals and institutions (including, of course, the government itself) on how to strengthen the economy and return to full employment. Our files here at Leeds are now full of the lectures, speeches, pamphlets and conference papers of our respondents; and two things at least stand out from the replies which we received. The first is that they are coloured by a series of political disagreements of the usual Left–Right variety, a set of disagreements on underlying causes and long-term remedies which manifest themselves in a consistent way at every level in the debate. The second is that the debate does go on at different levels, or if you prefer, in different arenas: between politicians on the hustings, between the political parties which these politicians represent, within the pressure groups which surround them, and amongst the commentators who observe the interplay of politicians and the lobby. So we have decided to organise this collection around those two dimensions: taking you from the most immediately available mani- festation of the policy debate (in the speeches of prominent politicians) to the more reflective pieces of those who commentate upon them; and within each section, moving from positions sympathetic to current government policy to positions highly critical of it.

Not everyone, of course, was willing to play ball. For some, the pursuit of solutions is beyond them. One of the most treasured posses- sions in our collection of replies is a two-line letter from the editor of a well-known right-wing weekly journal which said simply, 'Thank you for your letter. I am afraid I have no solution to Britain's economic decline.' Yet others doubted that there really was a problem to which solutions were necessary. This, for example, is the bulk of a letter from the deputy director of a well-known economic think-tank:

> You refer to economic decline in Britain and to the poor performance of the British economy. When you do so are you thinking of the performance as measured by the balance of payments? Just from memory I seem to recall that in the first thirty or so years after the War there was a balance of payments crisis almost every other year which led to damaging, ad hoc, stop-go restrictions and to special measures to protect the pound. I believe I am right in saying that for the last six years the balance of payments has remained steadily in surplus and the pound has surprised the pundits by having failed to drop below the one dollar mark. This doesn't seem to fit the general interpretation of the UK as an economy in decline.
>
> The obverse of all this, of course, is that the UK has once again become the largest, or certainly the second largest, international investor in the world. The portfolio has leapt from about £10 billion in 1978 to over £70 billion last year—hardly a poor performance. This tremendous benefit to our foreign exchange earnings has also, of course, been reinforced by the outstanding performance of the financial services sector. In brief, whatever happened to the dollar shortage and the balance of payments constraint?
>
> These are the important tests, it seems to me, of the success or otherwise of the economy, but it is also worth noting that inflation is down to its lowest level for many years and is still falling. The Stock Exchange certainly seems

to have taken the view over the last eighteen months that the outlook is not altogether desperate. And the value and volume of retail sales are at record levels—surely an important indicator. Retail sales are after all some measure of the satisfaction of consumer wants which is the objective of any economy. I would guess, though I haven't looked, that if one were to compare the saturation of all kinds of domestic appliances in the UK with other European countries we should be at least as well placed.

P.S. You no doubt have in mind the level of unemployment as recorded in the rather controversial figures. What is much less controversial and rather striking is, of course, the increase in employment which has taken place, leading, as you know, to there being a higher proportion of the UK population of working age in gainful employment than in any other European country.

So it may be that the whole exercise is misconceived, addressed either to a problem which does not exist, or to a solution which can never be found. But we remain unconvinced. It simply is the case that the strength of the British economy *relative to its major competitors* has diminished over the last forty years on a number of crucial performance indicators, including the share of world trade, rates of economic growth, levels of investment, productivity and wages. It is also the case that the performance of British industry *relative to its own past* has also dwindled, on indicators as vital as unemployment levels, inflation rates and degree of import penetration. The result of both those things is that Britain now faces a situation in which unemployment is massive, job insecurity for those in work is severe, and previously accepted levels of welfare provision are no longer attainable. The incidence of all this is, of course, unevenly distributed. It is possible to feel that things are rosy if you concentrate on finance rather than industry, if you focus on those in work rather than those who are not, if you look at the South-East and ignore the suffering of workers in the North and Midlands, and if you concentrate your attention on the suburbs to the exclusion of the inner city. It is also possible to draw some comfort—particularly if you are not yourself personally involved in losing your job—by pointing out that the decline of old industries, cutbacks in welfare provision, and rising levels of unemployment are happening across Western Europe as a whole. But that last observation, though it may make finding solutions more difficult, is not a denial of the problem. At least 11.5 per cent of the working population are now unemployed. The size and competitiveness of British manufacturing industry has diminished; and it is appropriate to ask of politicians the question they repeatedly ask of each other— what are you proposing to do, what are you proposing to stop doing, and what would you have other people do, to create a situation again in Britain where employment is secure for all?

In responding to these questions, there is clearly no space for glib replies. There are major structural obstacles to the achievement of full employment in the 1990s. Demographic and social factors leave politicians with an ageing population to sustain through taxation, and a labour force made larger by the return of women to paid employment on an increasing scale. The decay of old industries, the development of new technology, and the emergence of a new international division of labour with powerful industrial nations on the Asian rim, all combine to make economic restructuring a vital prerequisite of any return to full employment here. The domination of industrial production on a world-scale by multinational corporations, and the less buoyant conditions of world trade and finance which have prevailed since 1973, mean that governments trying to restructure the local economy face companies who are quite capable of shifting their base of activity abroad if political conditions here are too demanding, and face too more and more pressure from producers abroad to sell their goods in Britain—with an ever greater adverse impact on the trade balance. Britain is now a net importer of manufactured goods. The Conservative government can preside over the creation of 600,000 new jobs, and still see the underlying trend of unemployment go up and up. Political programmes for economic reconstruction therefore now have to be judged by their ability to counter international trends of sluggish world demand, multinational corporate power, unstable exchange rates and intensifying competition, and by their ability too to engender industrial restructuring and rising productivity in the local manufacturing base. Those are very tough criteria indeed.

The sources of economic decline go deep into British society and history, and we shall do well to be wary of analyses which place *all* blame on the policies of any one particular party. The weakness of British industrial capital relative to finance capital, the defensive strength of British trade unions, the world ambitions of Britain's political class, and particular patterns of class power, privilege and attitudes, helped to create industrial decline, and will continue to reproduce it unless altered (as was argued at length in *The Economic Decline of Modern Britain*). Options will need to be tested against that background too, and against the track record of their implementation in office. The Alliance at least is free of that test, but Labour is not, and nor now are the Conservatives. There can be no doubt that the first 18 months of Conservative rule after 1979 precipitated a massive capital export, price inflation and collapse of 20 per cent of British manufacturing. But whether that was bad or good depends on interpretation, assessment and wager. Was it a vital cleansing out of dead wood, or a serious weakening of Britain's economic base? Is it safe to plan for a future where oil revenues and the overseas earnings of the City compensate for a deficit on our balance of trade in manufactures? Is it the case that investment is low now, and employment levels still inadequate, because wages are still too high or because demand levels in the economy are still too low? And what criteria/performance indicators are we to use to measure success and failure: financial ones (inflation rates, balancing the books, overseas earnings) or material ones (the trade balance, labour productivity, levels of employment)? These too are questions to bear in mind as we explore the alternatives on offer. For it is quite clear that in 1987 the financial indicators may be positive, but the material ones are not.

The Prime Minister has claimed, quite properly, that things are much better now than they were in 1981: 'output as a whole is up by 13%, exports are up by 20%, investment is up by 20%, manufacturing productivity has risen by 24%, and profits have soared by £30 billion' (to the CBI, 22 May 1986). But those figures obscure more than they clarify. 1981 was a particularly bad year, where all these indicators were low: and if 1967 or 1974 had been chosen for comparison, the sense of progress would have been less. If oil production is extracted too, again the performance indicators drop significantly: and in those figures there is no mention of the 11 per cent unemployed. In any case, official figures have to be treated with particular care: 'Records achieved by economic indicators which habitually grow are as irrelevant as they would be for the heights of children or trees. It is rates of growth which matter for such indicators and it is disconcerting to read the stark claim in Cmnd. 9697 that manufactured exports reached a record high last year particularly when they also reached a record *low* when expressed as a share of world trade' (K. J. Coutts *et al.*, *A Cambridge Bulletin on the Thatcher Experiment*, Cambridge, March 1986, p. 1). To quote just one of the Prime Minister's many critics:

> we shall argue that almost all these claims are inappropriate. Although inflation has fallen since 1979, this has been achieved at the cost of virtual stagnation in total output and a decline in manufacturing output. Unemployment has risen by at least 2 million since 1979, probably reaching $3\frac{3}{4}$ million at the beginning of 1986 if the pre-Thatcher way of counting is used. And it is still rising . . . while most industrial countries have suffered from recession over this period, Britain's performance as regards output and employment has been worse than most others despite the rapid growth of North Sea oil production, and even our record on inflation is not outstanding. (Ibid., pp. 1–2)

So the question still remains: how to regenerate the British economy, how to generate work on a large scale? Here then are the answers currently on offer.

PART I:
The Politicians

This section gathers together recent statements of policy by leading representative political figures. The speeches reproduced here are intended to indicate the tone and character of the political debate on industrial regeneration, and to capture, in their complexity and detail, the major policy options currently on offer.

The debate focuses primarily on the form and scope of government intervention; so it is appropriate to begin with the Chancellor's defence (in July 1985) of seven years of Conservative policy. In his mid-term report, Nigel Lawson insisted that policy now is qualitatively different from policy before 1979, because now the control of inflation is at its core. Lawson distinguishes between macro- and micro-policy, giving the task of price stability to the first, and job-creation to the second. His critique of previous policy is that governments before 1979 reversed that relationship: using macro-policy to affect employment directly, and micro-policy to head off the inflationary pressures which resulted from their willingness to 'overspend' at the macro-level in the pursuit of full employment. Lawson contends that this is what all the government's critics are proposing to do again. But he will not. The central concern of this government, according to its Chancellor, is to keep money supply growing in line with 'the natural growth potential of the economy', whilst pursuing a series of discrete reforms (changes in trade union law, privatisation, and a general reduction in the cost and scale of government activity) to leave market forces and private enterprise free to raise that growth potential and to create jobs once again. It is also Lawson's claim that this is already happening: that new jobs are being created (600,000 since the last general election), essential welfare provision has been protected, inflation rates have been reduced, and productivity and growth enhanced. The Chancellor here is making in more measured tones the claims heard in more strident form from other ministers, that there is no crisis, that growth is now happening, that for the employed at least 'the country has never had as good a time as it has today' (Lord

3

Young, *Guardian*, 27 May 1986, p. 32), and that so long as 'we' do not relax (particularly by paying ourselves too much) economic growth will continue.

The government's critics are less sanguine. Edward Heath, for example, does not accept that we are in a period of economic prosperity. Nor does he find the Chancellor's characterisation of macro- and micro-policy adequate or accurate. Instead two things concern him. The first is the level of demand in the world economy: how its absence blocks economic recovery here, and how a different, more enlightened form of international economic cooperation could provide it. The second is the lack of adequate levels of demand within the British economy—the need to inject demand here to stimulate competition and productivity. Quite contrary to the Chancellor's claim, Edward Heath's fear is that this government lacks a coherent industrial strategy, beyond a preoccupation with privatisation. In his view this is just dogma. Instead it is necessary 'to forget all this 19th century liberalisation and get down to forging a relationship between government and industry' (*Guardian*, 13 March 1985, p. 11). As he put it: 'the cry is always inflation, inflation. And this is the . . . myth. This fear has paralysed us. Yet it is groundless. What I propose is not inflationary. It is counter-deflationary'— government action to stimulate capital expenditure in manufacturing industry and industrial training, action by the government 'to invest in people' and to improve 'our roads, railways, sewers, gas, electricity and water supplies—the basic infrastructure on which industry depends' (ibid.). It is Heath's concern, which he shares with many others, that this Conservative government is squandering the opportunity provided by North Sea oil, using its revenues 'to pay the £16 billion cost of unemployment, made up of the direct costs of unemployment, other benefits and lost tax revenue' whilst allowing manufacturing output to remain low (11 per cent below its 1979 level, and 14 per cent below its 1973 peak), and not facing up to the looming problem of what to do when the oil revenues are no longer there to cover the weakness of the economy's manufacturing base.

Edward Heath's sense of unease is echoed and developed in the letter which David Steel sent to the Industry Secretary to mark the beginning of Industry Year, and in David Owen's 1986 speech to the Industrial Society. Like Heath, the Alliance leadership is appalled by what it sees as the complacency of the government in industrial matters, and by its apparent refusal to recognise the need for systematic action in a number of crucial fields. The training of labour in the skills of the new technology is one of these. Research and development in the new technology is another. David Owen in particular calls for 'the prioritising of industry's needs' by government, for changes in government policy, and for greater government responsiveness to the requirements of the manufacturing sector. Critics of government policy simply fear that any future exploitation of easier economic conditions by British industry will be blocked by a shortage of the necessary skills; and that in any case new opportunities will not emerge here unless government acts now to fund research, development and investment in the new technologies. Nor does the Alliance leadership accept that trade union reform of the Conservative kind is enough to facilitate joint action by managers and workers in industrial reconstruction. They are prepared to concede that much of this Conservative legislation is valuable; but they want to supplement it by extensive profit-sharing schemes, and by an incomes policy underpinned by an inflation tax and by widespread arbitration. Existing government policy, in their view, leaves Britain too short of skills, too deficient in research and investment, and too vulnerable to wage explosions in any expansion to come.

The speech by Edward Heath which is reproduced here combines international and national concerns. David Owen's does not. But this should not be taken to indicate any lack of internationalism in the solutions proposed by the Alliance leadership. David Owen in particular played an important role in the joint authorship of a pamphlet produced by the Trilateral Commission (an international body of Right and Centre politicians and other public figures set up in 1973). His co-authors of the pamphlet *Democracy must work: a trilateral agenda for the decade* (Trilateral Commission, New York, 1984) were President Carter's National Security Adviser, Zbigniew Brzezinski, and a former Japanese Foreign Minister, Saburo Okita. Together they called for coordinated international action (a series of economic summits) to initiate and oversee a six-point programme to:

1.   reduce the US budget deficit,
2.   strengthen competition in Europe,
3.   increase Japan's world role, commensurate with its economic power,
4.   achieve a 4 per cent annual growth rate in the OECD,
5.   spread the cost of defence more equally between NATO members, and
6.   devise a method to solve the international debt problem.

However, these international dimensions do not figure centrally in the current public debate on economic alternatives, and certainly have not been at the heart of the Labour Party's formulation of solutions to economic decline. The final entry in this first section of the collection is a speech by Labour's principal spokesman on industry and trade, John Smith. Labour's alternative to Thatcherism, as described by Smith, involves government action on both the demand and supply sides of the economy: on the demand side, to stimulate job-creation and investment; and on the supply side, to regenerate industrial competitiveness and guarantee sufficient levels of skill and finance to sustain industrial recovery. The key term in all this is 'planning'. The Labour Party's route out of the recession gives an even greater role to the state than that canvassed elsewhere in the political spectrum, sharing with more moderate critics a commitment to government spending on infrastructure and training, but adding too a government bank to finance industrial investment and a public purchasing policy designed to encourage home-based producers, lessen imports, and strengthen job-intensive sectors. An incoming Labour government would create new institutions of intervention and consultation, and extend public ownership in new and less bureaucratised forms.

Quite what that new form of public ownership will be is not clarified in the speech by John Smith, and is, in fact, still a matter of contention within the Labour Party. The Party is in retreat from the radicalism of its 1979–83 period. Public ownership is being downgraded again, and Conservative concerns with inflation are no longer being pushed to the margin. As Roy Hattersley told an LSE audience in January 1986, a future Labour government would 'only proceed as quickly as inflation constraints allow. If we have not constructed a mechanism which allows us to expand at maximum speed with minimum inflation,' he said, 'then the speed of our reflation will have to be reduced' (*Guardian*, 31 January 1986). But Labour obviously feels that such a 'mechanism' can be created: in the guise of new forums of consultation with industry and labour, and new agencies of economic intervention (a revamped National Enterprise Board and a new National Investment Bank). In other words, what the Labour Party has to offer is what Roy Hattersley chooses to call 'planned Keynesianism', a planned increase in aggregate demand within the framework of extensive consultation with both sides of industry. And Hattersley at least wants that consultation to start now, with Labour-controlled local councils being told to begin work immediately on schemes to rebuild their local economies and to form partnerships with private enterprise, so preparing themselves for the return of a Labour government which will require them to respond quickly to government offers of money. As Roy Hattersley told *Marxism Today* in October 1986, under a future Labour government:

> A substantial increase in demand will be inserted into the economy. But it has
> to be directed in such a way that the multiplier which we all learned about 30

years ago doesn't operate in Tokyo and Stockholm more than it does in Birmingham and South Wales. Therefore we'll direct the new spending power in three phases. The first, because it's the quickest, is the job-creation measures. I have to tell you that I personally am extremely sceptical about such measures because I believe we are much better served by genuine jobs. We'll try and make sure that direct job creation is as much related to real jobs as possible.

The second phase is public investment in the infrastructure and the capital sector. Now, we'll do our best to get that working quickly as well. I propose to tell local authorities that they'd better start preparing for this in anticipation of a Labour government. They'd better start deciding what it is they want to build, and who's going to build it, because when I'm chancellor I'll have somebody who goes to Birmingham, Sheffield and Leeds saying 'we'll provide you with money quickly if you can ensure that there are jobs waiting to be done as long as the money is there'. While all that's going on we can start on the third phase, the process of reinvigorating manufacturing industry and creating the new jobs there, which is a longer term and in one sense the more important operation.

It is Labour's claim that Nigel Lawson 'has written manufacturing industry off', so creating a self-fulfilling prophecy of industrial decline. They offer instead 'new forms of autonomous social ownership, new investment institutions, new partnerships between workers and owners' (LSE speech, p. 22); and it is this offer which Conservative ministers continue to dismiss as a return to policies which have already been tried and found defective. In the debate between the politicians, each continues to insist that their opponents' solutions are in fact part of the problem itself.

1. Britain's Economy: A Mid-term Report*

Nigel Lawson

There are two strands of policy, each of fundamental importance. On the one hand a macroeconomic policy designed to conquer inflation. And on the other, a microeconomic policy, indeed a whole range of microeconomic policies, designed to improve the operation of markets so that the economy can perform better and generate more jobs. These two policies have to progress in parallel; they are complementary. It cannot be repeated too often, that, except in the very short run, there is no trade-off between inflation and unemployment. To imagine otherwise betrays a fundamental misunderstanding of the way the economy operates, a misunderstanding indeed of the events of our own past. A misunderstanding, however, which is based on decades of mis-education by politicians and commentators.

For what we have had to learn, and to learn the hard way, is the exact opposite of the conventional post-war wisdom. The post-war consensus implied that it was *macroeconomic* policy which controlled the level of output and employment. Budget deficits were manipulated in an attempt to maintain full employment. At the same time governments used microeconomic policies—usually prices and incomes policies of one kind or another—and other devices to buttress those policies, in order to try to control inflation.

That misguided approach was already creaking in the 1960s; it collapsed altogether in the 1970s. What happened was this. Most of the cash pumped into the economy in an attempt to increase output and maintain full employment, generated not real output at all but what economists call 'nominal' output. In other words, between 1973 and 1979 total output measured in cash terms trebled. But over 95 per cent of that increase was dissipated in higher and higher prices and less than 5 per cent turned out to be a real growth.

At the same time, the other policies which were being pursued—

* 'Britain's Economy: a mid-term report' (Conservative Political Centre, 1985).

8

interference in industry, and in wage bargaining in particular—had produced debility and demoralisation throughout much of industry and the economy. Management's ability to manage was undermined and employees lost any sense of realism in their wage demands. Market disciplines, which are essential to a free economy and a free society, almost ceased to operate.

We have had to pay dearly for those mistakes. We shall pay again if we return to them.

The opposition—in all its manifestations—still believes that the old system will work. It is this old, discredited approach that they are peddling now in a variety of guises. Their memories are short. But it is up to us to ensure that the memories of the British people are not so short. We have to remember the chaos of 1978–79, the 'winter of discontent' and all that went with it. It was a grim period. Constant destructive strikes, relentlessly declining competitiveness, an atmosphere of despondency and almost a routine acceptance of national decline.

We have turned our backs on that. This is widely recognised overseas. Britain's reputation is now higher than it has been for many years. Of course, we still face very considerable problems. But we have to see them in proportion.

THE GOVERNMENT'S PRIORITIES

Our first priority was the reduction of inflation. That is the first duty of government in the economic sphere and can be achieved only by creating and sustaining sound financial conditions. That does not mean holding the economy back. It means guaranteeing that there is sufficient growth in the money supply to sustain the economy's natural growth potential while not pumping more cash into the economy than the natural growth rate justifies. All *that* produces, and again this is the lesson from our own past, is inflation.

At the same time we are engaged in reducing the share of public expenditure in the economy as a whole, pushing back state involvement in the economy, in order to expand the productive and wealth creating sectors.

It is vital to emphasise—many people misunderstand the point—that it is not a question of choosing lower inflation as a primary objective when inflation is high, and then switching to jobs and employment when unemployment is high. We are concerned about both, and have policies for both. As I said, we have consistently to pursue complementary parallel courses to deal with both. . . .

INTERNATIONAL SUPPORT

I can understand why there is some confusion amongst the electorate, and even amongst many of our own supporters. For the approach we pioneered when we came to office in 1979 does run counter to conventional postwar wisdom. Many interpreters of the economic scene, many so-called opinion-formers, are still anchored to the old ways of thinking. But I have to tell them that our approach is now internationally accepted throughout the world. If you read the communiqués of the OECD, if you read the speeches of the Managing Director of the International Monetary Fund, you will see that. Even the leading Socialist and Social Democratic governments in the world today accept our way of thinking about economic policy.

It is only our own Socialists and Social Democrats who are out of line. They are the true little Englanders, and a very little England indeed it would be if they were to have their way.

When we first took office we inherited very considerable economic problems, problems in many cases worse than those of our major competitors. We suffered from higher inflation, from lower growth, from widespread overmanning, from particularly backward-looking trade unions. But because we did pioneer the new approach to economic policy, we were the first country to emerge from the world recession, and since then we have experienced stronger growth than our Common Market partners. Our productivity has risen more too. And the number of new jobs that have been created since the last general election, over 600,000, is more than in the whole of the rest of the European Community put together.

INFLATION

Now to what extent can we say, in this mid-term report, that the policies we have been pursuing for the past six years have succeeded? There is a worry, I know, that inflation is once again rising, so let me say a brief word about that.

First, even at 7 per cent it is lower than at any time under the last Labour government. But given their appalling record that alone will be small comfort. What is more important is that inflation is set to head back towards 5 per cent later this year and to get back below 5 per cent next year. Nevertheless this temporary check is unwelcome. I make no bones about that. The lesson is that we must always remain vigilant. We cannot take the conquest of inflation for granted, ever. It takes a long time to eradicate the psychology of inflation which built up in this country, as in some other countries, over many many years.

MONETARY POLICY

Now the key to success against inflation—and let us not forget the extent of that success, under the Labour government the average rate of inflation was over 15 per cent—has been firm control of monetary conditions.

This is an extremely complex matter. There is no automatic pilot that will do the job for you. But just because it is complex that does not mean that it is any less important: it remains vital. And for all its complexity in practice, the essence of the medium-term financial strategy is simple and straightforward. What it means is a commitment to financial discipline. It is needed in every practical walk of life and it is needed in the conduct of economic policy. Those who wish to abandon the medium term financial strategy are effectively arguing for no financial discipline whatever. At present, regrettably, that financial discipline requires high interest rates which have an effect on mortgage rates and a short term effect on the retail price index, an effect which we are seeing at the present time. But I have to say that I am not prepared to take any chances with inflation.

What about the other leg of the strategy? The policies designed to make the markets work better, to increase the growth potential of our economy and so to create even more jobs than we have been creating since 1983?

PUBLIC EXPENDITURE

The first aim here has to be to reduce the burden of the public sector on the economy. This will improve the economy's productive potential and is also an essential prerequisite for the reduction of taxes, which itself improves efficiency. In every country public expenditure has tended to rise inexorably as a proportion of the economy as a whole. We were determined to turn back that tide. It was a difficult challenge and in some areas expenditure was bound to go on rising, indeed it had to rise.

For example, we accepted the NATO commitment to 3 per cent annual real increases in defence expenditure from 1979 up to this year. Again, as many of you will remember, we inherited the massive post-dated cheque of the Clegg public sector pay awards. Then again we have protected the living standards of pensioners as a deliberate act of policy, at a time when the pensioner population has been growing quite fast.

But despite these and other claims on the public purse, we have managed since the end of the recession to hold overall public expenditure as a steadily declining share of national output (setting aside a very small rise last year as a result of the coal strike). But in that total we have made some shifts of priority, consciously and deliberately. We have provided less cash for the nationalised industries, in part due to privatisation and in part due to improved operating efficiency, and we have put an end to indiscriminate industrial subsidies. Industry needs low inflation and a benign tax regime far more than subsidies.

Again we have made lower provision for public sector housebuilding, because there is a healthy private sector alternative which is what most people want. Over 800,000 council homes have been sold to tenants. And a smaller bill for the Common Market as a result of the agreement which the Prime Minister succeeded in negotiating.

But there have also been increases where these were justified. On health, where expenditure is up 21 per cent since 1978–79 in real terms. And more important perhaps than the money, big increases in the numbers of doctors, nurses and patients treated. 11 per cent more family doctors, 15 per cent more district nurses, 11 per cent more home helps and 12 per cent more patients treated in hospital. We have also—to take another example—spent a lot more money on roads. Capital investment on national roads is up 30 per cent in real terms since 1978–79.

We must recognise, though, that it is not what you put into public spending programmes that matters. It is what comes out. And that depends on the efficiency with which the money is spent. There again our record is a good one. We have brought about real improvements in the way these vast sums of money are spent. Among other things there has been a large reduction in the number of civil servants. 133,000 fewer since 1979. The very positive way in which civil servants have responded to this reduction, and to the need to increase efficiency and productivity, is a tribute to their skill and professionalism—a tribute which I gladly pay.

Now these achievements are important and we have to ensure that people are aware of them. Our record on public expenditure has been one of steady but carefully limited and targeted increases. That could not be in greater contrast to the Callaghan years. The Harold Wilson government which took office in 1974 went on a reckless public spending spree, and Wilson then passed the buck to Callaghan just as they were getting into deep trouble as a result. So the Labour government were then forced to cut back very sharply when the IMF came and ended that Rake's Progress. The true public expenditure axeman—although he was told to do it by the IMF: I admit he didn't do it on his own volition—the true public expenditure axeman was Jim Callaghan. While he was Prime Minister he cut public expenditure in real terms by 8 per cent in one year. No Christmas bonus for the pensioner, deep cuts in our defence capability, a wide range of other cuts across the board. We don't want to go back to that. What we want to do is to maintain firm control over expenditure, which with a growing economy will lead to more scope for lower taxation and greater incentives for a healthier and more robust economy. Because that is the route, the only route, to more jobs.

TAXATION

We have made some progress on the tax front. By next year we shall have at 35 per cent the lowest rate of corporation tax in the western world. We have abolished three taxes altogether, the National Insurance Surcharge, the Investment Income Surcharge, the Development Land Tax. We have cut income tax at the top rates, raised thresholds at the bottom, up by 20 per cent in real terms and of course brought the basic rate down from 33 per cent to 30 per cent.

But personal taxes are still too high. Even if you take no account of North Sea oil revenues at all, the total tax burden during our period of office so far has in fact risen as a share of GDP. We cannot be satisfied with that. Nor is it good for the economy. We are therefore committed to doing more on income tax and we shall. Because lower taxation means a more dynamic economy. You only have to look at the United States and Japan, the two most successful economies in the modern world, and see that they also have the lowest proportion of taxation as a share of GDP. That is no coincidence.

MAKING MARKETS WORK

The government's microeconomic policies are varied and wide-ranging. But the clear objective is to make markets work better, and in particular the labour market. We have addressed that in a number of ways. First and foremost, perhaps, through trade union legislation, which is only now beginning to have its full impact: the requirements for ballots, the curbs on the closed shop and a number of other reforms. . . .

Privatisation is an essential part of this policy. We have moved a very sizeable chunk of state-owned assets into the enterprise sector. No fewer than twelve major industries and companies, representing 20 per cent of what was the state sector of industry when we took office in 1979, have already transferred to the private sector and there are a lot more still in the pipeline. Linked with that, wider share-ownership, which has been achieved spectacularly through British Telecom but also through every single one of the privatisations we have carried out, is a boost to the identification and commitment of employees to the success of their companies. It will have more impact than any other measure could on the 'them and us' mentality which has been so damaging in British industry.

We have introduced, too, a range of deregulation measures all aimed at increasing efficiency and removing burdens on business. One indicator of progress is that we have abolished more than 15,000 government forms.

We have also made major improvements in education where we have switched the priorities to science and technology, and in training. There is no doubt about the success of the Youth Training Scheme, a massive and unprecedented scheme which will remedy a major defect in our economy and offers great hope for the future.

What we have sought to do in all these ways is to create a new and healthier atmosphere, one where enterprise and success are rewarded, where ambition is valid and profit is not a dirty word.

UNEMPLOYMENT

These policies are all firmly in place. But their success at the present time is obscured in the public mind by the high level of unemployment. Does this mean then that we should change our priorities? I believe the answer is, clearly, 'No: we should not.' It is a fallacy that changing policy would help employment. What we have to do is to look and see why it is that unemployment is so high rather than simply shout the odds as the opposition does. Unemployment, as we all recognise, is a major human and social problem, and also a grievous waste in economic terms— although with the social security system we have in place now it is not right to compare our present position with the 1930s. But we have to ask ourselves what is it that has caused the high rate of unemployment, not only in this country but also in many other countries, indeed in almost all European countries?

All countries have had to make adjustments in the last decade but we have been particularly badly affected. When the Conservative government came to office we were faced with the need to make a number of different adjustments at the same time, which made it particularly difficult. There was the second oil shock which upset the equilibrium of the world economy and pushed it into recession. Then there was North Sea oil, emerging for the first time as a major element in our economy, pushing up the exchange rate with consequences for other industries. At the same time, new technologies were changing the shape of many markets and the newly industrialised countries of the Pacific basin in particular were embarking on a major competitive challenge.

All these were changes to which we had to adjust, all of these changes had a particular impact on our older heavier industries, the so-called smoke-stack industries, requiring a painful process of adjustment and slimming down.

Throughout Europe the consequences of these shocks (apart from the North Sea oil factor, which was peculiar to Britain) has been high unemployment. For us it has been a little worse than for many others. Not a great deal worse, but a little worse. Partly because of our particularly obstructive trade unions with their restrictive practices. Partly because of inadequate training, which we are now making good, and of problems in our labour markets. All these are powerful factors slowing the industrial process and holding up the creation of new jobs. We look to the United States to see how, through having freer markets, they have succeeded in creating many many more jobs than all of us have done in Europe, not just recently, but consistently over the past 10 or 15 years.

We have also had demographic trends against us and a higher participation of women in the labour force than in most other countries. Indeed the proportion of people of working age actually in jobs in this country is still higher today, despite unemployment, than in France or Germany. And then we suffered too in the past from the problem of widespread overmanning. Everybody knew this was a problem of British industry—everybody knew it had to be dealt with—but in the short run there was bound to be some unemployment as a result.

What we have not suffered from is a shortage of demand.

Indeed Britain's total turnover in cash terms this year will be twice its 1978 level. To seek to solve the problem of unemployment by injecting more cash into the economy is rather like assisting an alcoholic who has given up drink by giving him just a small drink to help him on his way. That is the worst possible thing you can do.

The opposition like to pretend that we are still in recession. That is clearly nonsense. While unemployment remains a serious problem, output, investment, productivity, profits and exports are all at record

levels and all are growing. The plain truth is that we have made
substantial progress.

THE FUTURE

What of the tasks that lie ahead? We are tackling many of the more
difficult problems at this moment. Norman Fowler's major reforms of
Social Security will have an important impact on the unemployment and
poverty traps. There is more privatisation to come. Further deregulation
of various parts of our economic life, such as bus services, where an
important Bill is now before Parliament. And further big strides in wider
share-ownership and employee share-ownership.

All these changes will help to make a freer and more robust market
economy and a freer and more responsible society. And that, I repeat, is
the only sure route to more jobs. The strength of our policy is that it is
based firmly on an understanding of the successes and failures of the
past. On an understanding, too, of the basic instincts of our people, the
instincts for ownership, and for a sense of belonging. For thrift and for
honest money, for hard work and for just rewards. It is vital for us at this
juncture to stick to what we know to be right, and not, as other
governments have done, to allow ourselves to be deflected by mid-term
by-election reverses. We are discharging our duty to the British people.

In conclusion let me say this. There has been a lot of talk about public
expenditure. . . . How much should the government take of people's
incomes to be spent on public services? The opposition, of course,
choose the easy option. Spend more on everything.

Labour and the Liberals, with their junior partner in tow, vie with
each other for the title 'the last of the big spenders'. Labour, given the
chance, would spend until they were forced to stop.

That was the story of the last Labour government. Spend, spend,
spend until the IMF bailiffs come in. Then slash, slash, slash. For them
winning an election is like winning the pools. And just about as likely!
When the cash runs out there are savage cuts. Boom and bust.

The Liberals—true to their Lib-Lab ancestry—are now on the same
course. They say they will increase spending everywhere: a cheap way to
win a by-election: a disastrously expensive way to run a country. They
try to pretend that we are at the other extreme, that we have cut back
everywhere. Not so. We have made savings. We spend less on council
house building—because more and more people want to own their own
homes. We spend less on handouts to the nationalised industries,
privatising some and getting the others to become more efficient. We

spend less on the Common Market budget, having negotiated a fairer share where Labour failed. And we have cut red tape.

But we do spend more where it is needed. On doctors, on nurses, on each pupil at school, on the police, on defence. Our public spending record is a good one. It is the middle way. Governments have to be careful about how and where they spend other people's money. To govern, as someone once said, is to choose. Unlike an irresponsible opposition, a government has to recognise that there is a limit to the nation's capacity to pay. That is what governments are elected to do, that is what we are doing and will continue to do.

2. The Need for Expansion Here and Abroad*

Edward Heath

What causes unemployment in Britain? Self-evidently lack of demand for the goods and services that our industry and commerce produce: that is a truism. We must look behind it to the cause of demand deficiency. There can be only two explanations for lack of demand for the goods we produce: first, that the goods we produce are so unattractive and uncompetitively priced that we cannot either sell them abroad or maintain our share of our own domestic market; or secondly, that there is insufficient purchasing power in the British economy and the world economy of which it is a part.

It is demonstrably the case that there is a deflationary bias in the international economic order: this has been so for the whole of this decade so far. It must be corrected.

Why is it demonstrably the case? Because there are over *25 million* men and women unemployed in the OECD alone. The number of unemployed in the rest of the world is not quantified. I think we can accept, in part at least, that uncompetitiveness is the cause of unemployment in Britain. If we are not competitive, there is less demand to buy British goods, not only in export markets, but in our home market too. But uncompetitiveness cannot be the explanation of the high international level of unemployment: for after all, by definition, we cannot *all* be uncompetitive.

The answer is that there is a lack of demand in the international system. People say that international trade is at a record level. And so it is. And this is an indication that demand has grown. But demand cannot be seen in isolation. If employment is to be preserved, demand must keep pace with productivity. For if the demand for goods remains stable and rising productivity means that it take less labour to produce these goods, naturally unemployment will rise. Demand may have grown, but it has not grown fast enough.

* Speech to the London Business School, 27 November 1985.

18

It is difficult to quantify the deficiency in demand. That is an area for detailed economic research. Full global figures are not available, but let us look at the OECD Big Seven, the countries for which we have the fullest data. If we take final expenditure upon the gross domestic product as an indication of demand, graphing it against productivity (defined as output per man-hour), we have a rough picture of the situation. It shows that since the end of 1980 or the beginning of 1981 growth in productivity has exceeded growth in demand.

If we look at the position for the United Kingdom alone, the pattern is similar, although rather more marked. I strongly suspect that the global picture if it could be sketched out would be the same.

What then are the causes of that insufficiency of demand which is the only plausible explanation of world unemployment and the present fragile position of the international economy?

It does not seem that net saving by households is detracting from demand internationally. In the United States, for example, in spite of exorbitant real interest rates, the savings ratio remains relatively low. The latest figures last month showed it to be only 2.7 per cent of disposable income.

The answer lies in the incorrect management of the international financial system by private sector institutions, by national governments and through them by the international agencies themselves. This has manifested itself in the inept recycling of the OPEC surpluses by the private sector in the 1970s, the failure of national governments to coordinate their economic policies to offset cyclical factors in the 1980s, and the debt crisis of the developing countries to which no effective solution has yet been agreed. All these factors are linked. And it benefits us not at all to try to apportion blame. We are all in this situation together and our common purpose must be to get out of it together. How? By a return to the policies of cooperation, coordination and consensus that characterised those successful decades after the Second World War.

What I am urging is a return to international demand management. Yet I would stress that it is not, nor has it ever been, my view that demand management alone is sufficient. Demand management is a necessary, but not a sufficient element of economic policy, whether at national or international level.

I do not accept the Chancellor of the Exchequer's claim made in 1984 in his Mais Lecture that he had effectively reversed the roles of macro- and microeconomic policy. His analysis is an oversimplification, indeed a caricature of the views of those of us who have advocated demand management. We have always known that macroeconomic policy alone would never be sufficient to produce real growth: but if we accept that competitiveness and productivity are also vital factors, it is clear not only that demand must rise alongside productivity gains, but also that the type of supply-side reforms that encourage competitiveness are far, far easier to achieve when our managers can carry out investment confident that there will be a market for the extra goods that high productivity will permit them to produce.

Nor have I ever believed that inflation could be controlled by micro-economic policy alone. Money supply and monetary theory were taught as part of Modern Greats even when I was at Balliol! But I am also quite sure that our high unemployment is part of the cost of the failure to use micro- as well as macroeconomic tools to control inflation. So the proper roles of macro- and micro-policy are far less distinct than the Chancellor would have us believe. And their proper relationship is a complementary one in a balanced economic policy.

How are we to implement 'demand management' at an international level? We can treat this question in either the short or the long term. In the long run, we shall have to develop the roles of the World Bank, the International Monetary Fund and the GATT to provide them with more adequate resources, structure and power for the purpose. In the short run, we must tackle the key problems in international finance today: the debt crisis, the US budget and trade deficit, interest rates, the level of the dollar and the question of who will assume the job of being the locomotive of the world economy when the US upturn runs out of steam.

Let us begin with the debt crisis. It is as good a place to start as any, and we shall see that all those key questions are inextricably inter-linked.

The essentials of the debt crisis are that, taken together, the non-OPEC developing countries owe the developed world an amount of about $800 billion, and that they are unable to service these debts. Why? This is the result of a combination of factors. Since much of the debt was incurred interest rates have risen sharply (partly as a result of the US budget deficit), the price of the oil they import has increased dramatically and the price of the commodities they sell to pay for what they buy has fallen. They are thus squeezed from all sides.

What is the consequence of this for us? First, that our banking system and the whole system of international trade on which we depend is placed in jeopardy. Second, that the inability of the debtor nations to buy what they need to continue their development means that we in the developed countries are not needed to supply them. The demand is not there to sustain employment.

It is not the fact that these countries have debts that is important. Industrialising countries almost always have debt. This was true of the United States, Canada and Australia amongst others during the nineteenth century. It is the ability of the countries to service these debts that is important. For it is upon their ability to service debt that their ability to gain new credit to finance new projects rests. And this depends not only upon earning a positive rate of return for individual projects, but also upon access to the required foreign exchange to satisfy repayment obligations. The satisfaction of repayment obligations is crucial to confidence. And it is upon confidence that the system rests. This confidence has broken down and this is the explanation for the most extraordinary reversal in the direction of capital flows.

Bank for International Settlement's figures show that in the first quarter of 1985, for the first time since records were kept, there was a decrease of lending to the non-OPEC developing countries. During that period there was a net overflow of $1.7 billion from these countries compared with a net inflow of $2.4 billion during the equivalent quarter of 1984.

Mexico's rescheduling in August 1986 was billed as way of paving the road for the resumption of normal borrowing. But this is easier said than done. New voluntary extensions of short-term trade credit have been more than offset by net repayments of existing loans. Banks have curtailed new lending even to developing countries that have avoided debt problems.

Because of their exposure to Third World debt risks, banks are reluctant to increase still further their lending to debtor nations. Any new money has been largely involuntary: the IMF has threatened not to put up money to help debtors service their debts unless the banks accepted the need for new money for new projects to earn rates of return and thus facilitate repayment in the future.

It is now clear that many debtors see that they are being forced to choose between funding the service of debt and funding growth. This is a highly dangerous situation.

Take Latin America, for example. According to some estimates, the net transfer of capital out of the region averaged $25 billion per annum between 1982 and 1984. This is roughly equivalent to 25 per cent of regional expenditure. The magnitude of the transfer and its implication both for the economies of Latin America and of the developed world have not been fully perceived.

The truth is that it is a major element in introducing a deflationary bias in the international system. According to the figures in the latest Inter-American Development Bank Report, the ratio of investment to

GNP declined from 26 per cent in 1981 to 20 per cent in 1983. Similarly, per capita GNP has declined dramatically after thirty years of uninterrupted growth. And this represents a great deal of goods not purchased by *them* and output not produced by *us*.

But where has the money gone? Much of it has fled to Wall Street to finance the burgeoning US budget deficit. The $200 billion budget deficit, which is mirrored in the trade deficit of $150 billion, has caused enormous damage to the international economic order. It is true that it has administered some boost to the US demand for consumer goods and this has to some extent ameliorated the deflationary bias in the system. But at the same time, the combination of the deficit and the extreme monetarist doctrine of the Federal Reserve Bank has produced exorbitant real interest rates and an overvalued dollar. These factors have acted to redouble the burden upon the debtor nations: it is estimated that for every point increase in interest rates, the annual interest burden on these unfortunate countries increases by between $3.5 billion and $4 billion.

A large element in the growth of the US budget deficit has been the arms build-up under President Reagan. The proposed defence budget for 1986 is $313.7 billion which is 29 per cent of the budget, while expenditure in the current year will exceed $284 billion. Yet according to the Mitsubishi Research Institute, infrastructure spending is at least 1.6 times higher in its economic effects than military spending.

We have always believed that the multiplier effect of spending was much stronger in Third World countries. So the diversion of spending from the build-up of infrastructure in the Third World to spending on armaments in the First World can in itself be said to introduce a deflationary bias into the international economic order.

Equally worrying is that the present US upturn is unlikely to be sustainable, in the medium let alone the long term. Worse, the trade deficit that is its concomitant is prompting increasing pressure for protection in the United States. We saw the consequences of that in the 1930s.

In the 1985 UNCTAD report it is estimated that one third of exports from developing countries are affected by some form of protectionism and that 65 per cent of their manufacturing exports are restrained by non-tariff measures. If these barriers were dismantled and the developing world allowed preferential access to industrial markets, their export earnings could be increased by $34 billion annually. The present value of a $34 billion increase in earnings is calculated to be $700 billion, in other words, 85 per cent of Third World debt.

UNCTAD goes on to assess the impact of the debt crisis upon the OECD. It has estimated that about 8 million jobs have been lost in the developed world over the past three years as a result of reduced imports by the major debtors in Africa and Latin America. About 90 per cent of this effect would seem to have fallen on Europe, which has suffered a loss of 6.8 million man-years since the debt crisis broke in 1982: more than 2 million jobs in each year.

What is the prospect that faces us now that the slowdown in the US economy has begun. Even leaving aside the threat posed by protectionism, we face a difficult situation. Not even the Keynesian Aunt Sally of monetarist demonology would urge the continued application of fiscal stimulus to the US economy by allowing a continual escalation of the budget deficit. This represents a misallocation of resources on a global scale, for which we shall all suffer. In such a situation, the public sector in the United States would continue—because of the vast scale of the American economy—to pre-empt a lion's share of available international capital, starving more worthwhile prospects and ventures.

Yet while the rest of the world will continue to be deprived of badly needed capital that it can use to better economic effect, if US policy remains unchanged, high interest rates will continue to hit the Third World long after the partial compensation of expanding US imports of their products has ceased.

Already, on the back of slowing US growth, the economies of the Far East have started to slow. Europe has had only slow growth throughout the present 'recovery' in the international economy.

Now at last, belatedly but none the less welcome, governments have begun to realise that this situation must be 'managed'. The Group of Five meeting in New York in September (1984) and the IMF meeting at Seoul (in 1985) heralded a major change in the balance of opinion about management of the international economy. At the Group of Five, the US Treasury Secretary on behalf of the administration explicitly recognised that the dollar was 'overvalued', and that action was necessary to ensure a 'soft landing'. This was a major change in the rhetoric of an administration that had previously recognised no values but those of a market, the omni-competence of which was completely unqualified. It was echoed by our own Treasury.

Even more dramatically, Mr Baker's initiative on Third World debt announced at the IMF Annual Conference in Seoul represents an abrupt *volte face*. Belatedly, the Reagan administration has recognised that deflationary adjustment policies are unlikely to re-establish the creditworthiness of debtor nations. Having long downplayed the purpose of the World Bank, the United States is now recognising the importance of its proper role in assisting in the implementation of long-term policies.

This is undoubtedly a step in the right direction, even if the $30 billion package is clearly insufficient when compared to the scale of the problem. In 1982, when we published the second *Brandt Report*, we estimated that at least $75 billion would be required. Since then, there has been improvement in the balance of payments situation of many debtor nations, but at the same time, it is recognised that the resources Mr Baker hopes will be made available will permit only fifteen countries to be included in the proposed scheme. Further, Mr Baker has conceded that it will be impossible to deal even with all fifteen at once. He wants to start with a 'reasonably major debtor'.

In outline, Mr Baker's plan is a three-part initiative. It recognises that reliance on IMF adjustment or austerity programmes linked to short-term loans, though necessary, are insufficient. I am glad that the Reagan administration has realised this: it was, of course, the reason why the World Bank was created in the first place. Thus, alongside 'a continued central role' for the IMF, Secretary Baker attaches new priority to a second element, the World Bank and other multilateral development banks in supporting the debtors in pursuit of 'market-oriented policies for growth'. Thirdly, he proposes increased lending by private banks in support of comprehensive economic adjustment, as guided by the IMF and the World Bank.

The aim is to promote economic growth now that many of them have carried out more or less successful external adjustments. As well as continuing with IMF-type fiscal, monetary and exchange rate policies, they would be expected to adopt 'supply-side' policies of a type long advocated by the World Bank. These include liberalisation of foreign trade, inward direct investment, reform of tax and public expenditure arrangements and moves towards a rational structure of relative prices by withdrawing subsidies and ending controls.

Mr Baker has suggested that the commercial banks should advance an extra $20 billion over the next three years to support supply-side strengthening measures. In return he advocated an increase of 50 per cent in lending by the multilateral development banks, from the expected level of $6 billion in each of the next three years to $9 billion a year. As there are to be about $2 billion a year repayments, the net increase in credit outstanding would be about $20 billion over the three years, or about $10 billion more than had been expected. This represents an annual increase of about 17 per cent a year on the $34 billion of multilateral development banks' credit outstanding to the fifteen 'Baker countries'.

Nevertheless, the $20 billion in new money from the commercial banks would represent an annual growth in loans of only 2½ per cent in each of the next three years. This is, of course, negative in real terms, and is certainly slower than the rate at which banks generally expect to increase their capital. Even so, it does represent an improvement on the present situation in which lending is shrinking in nominal as well as real terms.

Thus, the exposure of commerical banks will decline, while the exposure of the World Bank will rise by 50 per cent. At the same time, the exposure of the IMF is likely to remain roughly steady at $15 billion: it is just about at the limit of its resources.

Our hope must be that this will allow the World Bank and the IMF to exercise greater leadership, notably through co-financing of loans, which in the medium term will restore confidence and therefore allow a resumption of new capital transfer to the developing world by the private sector.

My own feeling is that much greater resources will be required by the World Bank and the IMF to enable them to carry out the role of restoring confidence to the extent where the Third World's requirements of funds for adjustment and investment can be met.

Mr Baker's plan does have one striking political advantage, however. It is that a general capital increase to finance the higher rate of activity of the World Bank can probably be put off until 1987. This means that it need not go before Congress (and other national legislatures) until after the November 1986 mid-term election.

In a sense, therefore, we are still paying the price of Poujadiste sentiments about international economic management. The Reagan administration has begun to recognise the direction in which it must go, but is held back by the spirit in Congress, which the administration itself did so much to foster.

What is needed is reserves on a sufficient scale for both the IMF and the World Bank to enable them to get properly to grips with the debt crisis. Rather than just fighting fires and nudging countries back when they get too close to the brink, we could begin to construct a long-term solution. And the sooner we do that, the sooner we shall be able to put our own people back to work in the developed countries.

The World Bank should be given a substantial capital injection as soon as possible to finance not only structural and sectoral adjustment loans, but also project loans. Equally, the IMF now almost at the limit of its resources, has no spare capacity to permit it to deal with the balance of payments consequence of a world trade downturn in the developed countries. It seems likely that its role in the foreseeable future will be little more than rolling-over existing credits: this will give it substantially less economic influence and leverage than if it had the resources to assist.

Finally, alongside a further increase in IMF capital, I would welcome a new issue of Special Drawing Rights. There has been none such since 1981, and the time has come to give a boost to world liquidity and demand. This would have the effect of relieving upward pressure on interest rates. I can already hear the cries of 'inflation, inflation', but this is to misunderstand. Such an increase would not be inflationary in present economic conditions (though I recognise that there are circumstances where it would be). It would be counter-deflationary, not inflationary. It would play some part in offsetting the deflationary bias in the present international order.

It seems that, at best, the two-pronged Baker initiative through the Group of Five and at Seoul will keep the world economy afloat. The scale of the proposals is insufficient to boost the world into a new phase of growth.

Since the Group of Five meeting, central bank intervention to engineer a sustained but orderly decline in the value of the dollar has scarcely materialised. And while I believe strongly that the central banks have a role in smoothing currency movements, I do not think that they can override market forces. In the end it will only be a reduction in US interest rates, partly the result of the deficit, but also the product of monetary extremism at the Fed. that will allow an orderly reduction in the dollar rate. Otherwise, we can expect the dollar to continue to ride high, until there is a change—most likely an abrupt one—in market sentiment, leading to the feared 'hard landing'. This will happen when the markets realise—as they realised in the 1970s in the wake of Vietnam—that even the United States cannot sustain endless borrowing. So, however much I welcome the signs from the Group of Five that cooperative management of currencies is to be resumed, I regret that without an agreement by the US to cut its interest rates and begin to reduce its new borrowings the action will be largely ineffective.

A reduction in interest rates would of itself provide some stimulation to the international economy. It would relieve pressures in the Third World, fostering investment there as well as in the industrialised countries. But the counterpart of the Group of Five decision to resume economic cooperation in currency management, must be a wider agreement within the OECD to renew wider coordination of fiscal and monetary policies. The aim of this exercise must be to avoid a new recession in the world economy as US growth slows, bringing with it the risk of a slump precipitated by sharp deterioration of the debt situation with all its concomitant risks for the banks.

At long last, pressure is now mounting for a convergence of economic policy in the leading industrial nations. Perhaps coordination would be a better term than convergence, since the prescriptions advocated are not identical in the case of each economy. Germany and Japan, for example, are urged to relax their emphasis on tight fiscal and monetary policy and to become more expansionary. At the same time, the United States should pursue a much tighter fiscal policy, perhaps coupled with a slightly looser monetary regime.

This is the first time since 1978 that the body of opinion has shifted behind a coordinated approach to world economic management. The long 'U' turn is now almost complete.

Few people any longer put faith in 'supply-side' means *alone* to reduce unemployment. There is still dispute about whether US superior economic growth in 1983–84 was due to the enormous fiscal stimulation of the budget deficit or to supply-side flexibility. No doubt the robustness of the supply side was important and we in Britain must put every effort into the strength of our industry and commerce, but the emerging consensus puts emphasis on the crucial part played by the fiscal stimulus in circumstances when the supply side was in a strong position to respond to the challenge of a boost to demand by raising output rather than prices.

Of course, inflation will be the charge levelled against me by the monetarists and the neo-classicists. These fears are misconceived and rest on misunderstanding of the nature and causes of inflation. In particular, they rest on a misreading of the French experience of 1983–84. In France it was not reflation *per se* that caused inflation, but the way in which reflation there was achieved, directly increasing industry's costs, and the context in which it was carried out, against the background of contraction by her principal trading partners.

Why has not the much stronger US reflation led to inflation? Because it did not increase costs. And also because the reflation in the United States was not accompanied by fiscal stimulus in the rest of the OECD, which would put pressure on raw material prices. It was a bottleneck in the supply of raw materials—especially but of course not only, the 'political bottleneck' of the OPEC cartel in the case of oil—that caused the inflation of the 1970s. Which brings us back to the debt crisis: for there is another risk in the massive reduction in investment in the Third World. Unless we get the investment in the extraction of commodities, the risk of renewed inflation as we get a proper international recovery will be increased. The bottleneck in supply of raw materials may, as a result of neglect, be far worse than we experienced in the early part of the last decade. So, here too, in our own interests, we must look to a solution of the debt crisis.

What can we in Britain do as part of an internationally coordinated strategy? Our present fiscal policy is hardly to be described as expansionary. The ratio of debt to national income in the UK is 55.5 per cent, which is close to the OECD average. It has been falling steadily, though there can be no justification for a fall at a time of high unemployment. A stable debt:gross domestic product (GDP) ratio would permit public sector borrowing of about £15 billion.

Still, I am wary of placing too much faith in the Public Sector Borrowing Requirement (PSBR) as an indication of fiscal stance. We all know that it is distorted by asset disposals. It is less appreciated, however, that PSBR is not adjusted for inflation; it makes no distinction between current and capital expenditure—the basic principle of financial accountancy. And no allowance is made for the phase of the trade cycle. I am in favour of making such adjustments in order to establish a more reliable guide for fiscal policy: I am not disposed to pick and choose between adjustments, which would be more likely to distort the picture still further.

But why is a more expansionary fiscal stance necessary? First, as our share of an internationally coordinated strategy; secondly, and of no less importance, as a *sine qua non* of a British strategy of strengthening our industry and commerce—our supply side.

We all understand how much easier it is to restructure our industries when the economy is expanding. We all know how difficult it is to restructure without investment. We all understand how great a disincentive to investment our present high interest rates are.

And this must be a further element in our internationally agreed package: a reduction in interest rates and a slackening of monetary policy. Again, we in Britain have room for manoeuvre here too.

Again, I hear the charge of my critics: 'He says he wants lower interest rates yet he calls for greater public borrowing.' In the simple mechanistic world of the rigid monetarists and neoclassicists, more borrowing means higher interest rates. The picture is much more complex than that, and the upward pressure on interest rates occasioned by high borrowing can be compensated for by increasing liquidity in the financial market, or in other ways.

So a slackening of fiscal and monetary policy is a prerequisite of strengthening our 'supply side'. Personally, I think it is one of the saddest features of present government policy, that it lacks a coherent strategy for industry. We have the ironic spectacle of a so-called supply-side government, without a policy for the supply side. Except, that is, for privatisation: this is the apology for a policy which we are offered. And will it increase competitiveness? In some areas perhaps. But the bulk of the policy has involved shifting the ownership of natural monopolies between the public and private sector. And there is an obvious danger that this will not improve competitiveness by one job.

Still worse is what has happened to the proceeds of the disposal of state industries—Lord Stockton's 'family silver'. They have been spent not on new investment, but on consumption, including benefits for the unemployed. And the next batch seem to have been earmarked for tax cuts. I can predict with great confidence what the result of tax cuts will be—a new surge in imports of consumer durables from abroad. Not a lasting boost to British capital stock and British industry.

A year ago, I said that tax cuts would be an insult to the unemployed. I still believe that. More than that, however, in present circumstances, tax cuts would be an insult to the employed as well as to the jobless. They would be an insult to the intelligence of the British people and an affront to their integrity. In a very real sense, one man's tax cut might mean the loss of another man's opportunity of employment.

Indeed, I strongly suspect that privatisation has mopped up a good deal of the capital from our capital markets, which would otherwise have been seeking worthwhile investment projects. And the money released to the Treasury has been used, not to invest in the nation's future, but for jam today. This strikes me as a financial profligacy which ill befits a government which in its rhetoric sets such store by fiscal and monetary rectitude.

Yet this is not the only false note in the government's current rhetoric. We are told we are in the middle of an economic miracle. I sometimes wonder whether government ministers who made that claim live in the same world as the rest of us. Do they ever travel outside the prosperous and privileged quarters of London and the stockbroker belts of the South-East. They talk about the fifth successive year of growth at an average of 3 per cent a year. But let us look at the true picture. Between 1979 and 1982, the economy fell dramatically, by over 4 per cent. We did not regain the 1979 level until 1983. The economic miracle therefore amounts to growth of $2\frac{1}{2}$ per cent in 1984, $3\frac{1}{2}$ per cent in 1985. But if we take the average growth rate of the life of this government, it is about 1 per cent per annum. This is the worst record for any period since the Second World War.

So the instincts of the British people are not wrong. They know that Britain is far from booming and no publicity or propaganda, however slick, will convince them that it is.

Manufacturing output has not yet reached the 1979 level, let alone the level of 1973: so also investment in manufacturing. In real terms manufacturing investment is still £4 billion below its peak in 1979 and still further below the all-time high in 1973.

I have already danced gladly upon the grave of monetarism. It is now time to lay to rest another dogma that has damaged our economic future: economic liberalism. This is the dogma that forbids us to emulate the successful relationship struck in the United States, in Japan, in West Germany and in many other of our more successful industrial competitors, between government and industry. It is the doctrine that prevents us from pursuing the proper supply-side policy to regenerate our industries that I believe is so vital.

I hope that we shall be able to strangle this extreme liberalism more quickly. The fruits of North Sea oil have given us a breathing space in which to restructure our industries. We have already reached and passed the peak of North Sea oil revenues. So far, we have wasted much of the reserves to pay unemployment benefit rather than using them to put the unemployed back to work. We must not squander the rest on tax cuts. By 1992, the oil revenues will have fallen drastically. As the House of Lords Select Committee have pointed out, we have only that time to generate the new industries that will pay our way in the world once we have no surplus oil to export. We can no longer afford delay.

In the past, I have praised the role that the Scottish Development Agency plays in the Scottish economy. This is not an instrument of heavy-handed socialist intervention. Instead it pursues a market-oriented strategy, ensuring as far as possible that Scottish industry capitalises upon its strengths and seizes its commercial opportunities. This is an approach which I favour most strongly: we would do well to extend it to other parts of the United Kingdom with severe economic problems.

I have urged the creation of a national training scheme to invest our young people with the skills they and we shall need for the future. Not a cosmetic exercise to massage the unemployment figures.

We in the Conservative Party cannot continue to pretend that unemployment will go away of its own accord. Or that it is the product of special factors that will disappear. It will require deliberate action. Nor is it any good to claim that we are creating new jobs: we must remember how many we destroyed in 1980–82 and that there are still fewer jobs today than in 1979. Demographic figures are no excuse: every government has faced a rising working population, at least since the Industrial Revolution, and probably since the Black Death.

We have got to begin a concerted drive to tackle unemployment, or it will tackle us. I see no evidence of such a drive at present. The White Paper, 'Lifting the Burden', contained no proposals that would affect significantly the level of unemployment.

The government must begin to construct such a strategy. We face a situation not far short of a national emergency. The government must recognise this. It must take the British people into its confidence and initiate a debate on tackling unemployment. And on the basis of the widest possible consensus, it must begin the urgent task of putting Britain back to work. I do not underestimate the scale of the task.

We can no longer afford trench warfare. That is the easy answer for politicians bent solely upon power and unmindful of the national interest. I believe strongly that the British people will show their contempt for those that simply cling to their ideologies with no heed to reality or to the nation's vital needs.

Those of us who have the good fortune to travel abroad know the seriousness of our nation's plight. We know how far behind we have fallen. We know that this must not be allowed to continue. We know the urgency of the task.

This is the challenge that confronts us.

3. A Ten-point Industrial Strategy*

David Steel

There could be no greater mistake on the government's part . . . than complacently to represent a minor consumer boom, fuelled by inflationary wage increases and tax cuts, financed by the once and for all sale of assets and fed by a flow of foreign imports, as economic recovery. It is nothing of the kind, as over three million of our fellow citizens out of work can testify.

I urge the government to adopt a positive industrial strategy, with a concerted programme of measures to help rebuild our capacity to create wealth and employment. If you do not do this in 1986, the next government of Britain, no matter of which party or parties it is formed, will face a bleak prospect of decline and degeneration.

Our share of world manufacturing is half what it was twenty years ago. Indeed, under the Thatcher government Britain is a net importer of manufactured goods for the first time in its history. The deterioration is not just in sectors of traditional strength, such as engineering, but also in new sectors such as information technology.

The relative, and now absolute, decline in manufacturing has taken place under both Labour and Conservative governments. It is now accelerating as we pay the cumulative price for past mistakes: poor industrial relations, patchy marketing and design excellence, under-investment in new plant and technology, and resistance to change within industry. These have been coupled with, and exacerbated by, disastrous and wildly shifting government policies in regard to the economy and industry, particularly the neglect of education and training in recent years which has led to the progressive deskilling of our workforce.

Over the years, the contribution of successive governments to the plight of industry has been negative rather than positive. Labour seems to have learned nothing from the past and is still committed to the same old state socialist remedies of expropriation, central direction and

*Open letter to the Trade and Industry Secretary, January 1986.

control. Your own government appears to believe that its role is confined to the Chancellor's dubious manipulation of the macro-economy, first through the money supply and latterly through interest rates and the exchange mechanism. As the Westland helicopters crisis well exemplifies, the government has no consistent industrial strategy.

The Liberal Party, and the Alliance as a whole, believe that the proper role of government in relation to industry is neither to attempt to take over, as with Labour, nor to stand negligently by, invoking the ghost of *laissez-faire* in justification for indifference, as you and your colleagues do, but rather to roll up its shirtsleeves and give industry as much practical help as possible. That is what our major European and Japanese competitors have been doing for years.

If you would follow our lead in adopting the concept of a positive partnership between government and industry, in which the role of government is to do everything in its power to enable industry to succeed, you would find a ready response not only from our benches in Parliament but from the whole country.

1986 is Industry Year, and we welcome the attempt to improve communications and understanding between industry and the wider community, but it is time the government stopped being a spectator of industry's struggles. The following ten measures are the main elements of the new industrial strategy which the Alliance is proposing in what we believe should more properly be called 'Save Industry Year'.

First: A major expansion in, and commitment to, education and training, not just within schools and universities but, on a matching funds basis, in industry itself. It is a grave indictment of government policy that, at a time of record unemployment, there is also a widespread shortage of skilled labour. Every young person should receive a basic education that fits him or her for the new age of innovation and then, after school, the chance to acquire specialised skills, knowledge and capacity through further education, training and apprenticeship.

Second: Government backing for the development and introduction of new technologies on which our competitive future depends, not only in new industries but in our traditional industries, with grants and tax incentives for investment and training.

Third: Major new government involvement in research and development through the Research Councils, through universities and polytechnics, and through direct help to selected industries.

Fourth: Encouragement to industrial investment by lowering interest rates, which are so high at present that they discourage both construction and capital investment. If, as is likely, the exchange rate falls as a consequence this would not only help our exporters but enable us to enter the EMS and stabilise the damaging fluctuations in the value of the pound.

Fifth: A boost to construction, with consequent spin off benefits throughout the economy, by up to £2 billion investment in repairing and rebuilding the infrastructure. Housing starts could be stimulated by more encouragement to housing associations, co-ops and municipal partnership schemes, with an expansion of housing improvement grants to repair and renovate old stock, and permission to local authorities to spend the substantial funds locked up in their capital accounts on new housing. This should certainly be a higher priority in the Budget than tax cuts.

Sixth: A new partnership between public and private finance, using the incentive of central government cash on tax relief to unlock the vast amounts of private capital for long-term investment in plant and construction. Industrial Development Bonds on the US pattern could stimulate new investment in Britain rather than abroad.

Seventh: A major and concerted export assistance programme designed to give British exporters a comprehensive back-up service of intelligence, contact, credit and support easily available from one source to assist their overseas marketing.

Eighth: A total commitment by government departments and nationalised industries to give every opportunity to British companies to supply their orders on a first and last quotation basis. This would also serve as an example to large private companies to encourage and develop the smaller companies with whom they deal by paying their bills on time and working closely with them on the Marks and Spencer pattern.

Ninth: A new programme of assistance to regional and local enterprise agencies to enable them to contribute to the regeneration of the economy at the grass roots, with practical encouragement and help for local entrepreneurs starting up.

Tenth: Incentives for companies to introduce profit-sharing throughout industry and commerce, so that every employee becomes a partner in his or her own enterprise, with an interest in its success and reduced pressure on wages and unit costs.

This programme is by no means exhaustive but it provides the basis for an industrial strategy which is well within the grasp of your government if you are prepared to discard dogma and adopt practical and commonsense measures which industry needs, and which would help secure our prospects and employment into the next century.

I do not believe that the alternative of a flashy high street boom, paid for by the electoral bribe of tax cuts, will hoodwink the people of Britain or help industry. This is a time for looking to the future and for the government to do anything else would be a cynical abdication of its responsibilities.

Please unite the country and give our wealth creators a real chance by making 1986 Save Industry Year.

4. Industrial Regeneration and Industrial Partnership*

David Owen

Britain has to earn a living in international markets. Much of our success in securities, banking, and insurance, comes from our being the third financial centre in the world, along with New York and Tokyo. What is needed and what successive British governments have particularly lacked is an industrial strategy firmly international in outlook, that bolsters the British economy through the expansion of companies and industries capable of competing on a global scale.

The evidence is now overwhelming that the government is sacrificing the long-term competitiveness of British industry for a short-lived pre-Election consumer boom. The Treasury's own figures show a 1.4 per cent growth in gross domestic product (GDP) in the past twelve months, compared with a 5 per cent rise in consumer demand. There has been an explosion in private credit demand, both for house purchase and consumer goods. Household debt, for example, is rising at an all-time high of 15 per cent per annum. The harsh reality is, however, that excessive personal liquidity and fiscal relaxation is also resulting in rising imports and driving the balance of payments into deficit.

The present level of demand is high. The public sector financial deficit (PSBR + asset sales) is on course to rise to £13 billion this year, no less than £5 billion up on 1985/86. This is exactly the fiscal stimulus which the 1986 SDP/Liberal Alliance Budget argued for, but instead of channelling it into wealth creation and jobs, it has been squandered on the candy floss economy. It is being frittered away on consumer spending and imports. Instead, it should have been channelled into higher output and industrial exports.

The SDP was founded as an internationalist party. However tempting it might be to score temporary party points, we will not cease to remind this country of the realities of its serious industrial and economic decline to nineteenth in the industrial league table and to warn that we will not

*Speech to the Industrial Society, 10 March 1986.

stop this decline, let alone reverse it, by turning in on ourselves. Industrial chauvinism is no answer to our problems.

As the Confederation of British Industry (CBI) pointed out in 'Change to Succeed', to dispute whether Labour or Conservative have had the superior approach since 1945 is irrelevant 'since either would have been better than a policy which vacillated between them, as governments changed'. British industry has been bewildered to see both 'bigness' and 'smallness' in fashion at different times. Institutions have come and gone, and there have been frequent changes in the value and types of financial assistance to industry.

The Government no longer regards even manufacturing industry as a critical part of the economy. Since 1979 our factories have shed 1.5 million jobs, as many as in the previous twenty years. Although new jobs are being created in the service industries, the rate of job losses in manufacturing is forecast by the CBI to continue at 8,000 a month in the medium term.

Regional industrial spending reached a peak of £1.5 billion in 1975/76. It will be one-fifth of that by 1988/89, both measured in 1982/83 prices. Successive governments have been forced to make reductions in regional assistance because of immense difficulties in controlling the growth of total public expenditure. To put the needs of industry first, as we should, then we have to face the implications of this decision for other areas of public expenditure.

Far from this government putting industry first, it is industry, energy, trade, transport, housing, and employment budgets that, taken together, have fallen by nearly 36 per cent in real terms over the last seven years. These are the biggest losers and they reflect an ominous development: because total public spending has consistently overshot its targets since 1979/80, the government has been mainly obliged to squeeze capital programmes, in some cases quite drastically, to get back on course and stay in line with inflation. The harsh reality is that in future, if extra resources for industrial recovery and higher employment are to be found, on present trends this must mean not promising generalised increase in the rates of growth in big spending programmes such as health, social services, and local authority services. Industrial competitiveness depends critically on reversing the decline in capital spending and improving the quality of our capital infrastructure. But to achieve this we must recognise that there will be a price to pay elsewhere.

More fundamentally, we need to restructure the predominant role of central government in economic decision-making. The success of economic federalism in both the European Community and the United States offers a proven way forward for us in the UK. It would be a practical way of evolving towards a system of regional government and as in the case of the European Community, the initial building blocks would be economic, industrial and commercial. An important lesson from the US is that despite the free-market economics of the Reagan administration at the federal level, a large number of state governments have actively pursued an interventionist strategy to develop their local economies and create employment.

In Europe, where distances are more similar to those in the UK, the diversity in the German *Länder* and other countries' regions has allowed for experiment and innovation. In England, the mechanism for achieving similar results, in light of the successful experiences of the Scottish Development Agency (SDA) and the Welsh Development Agency (WDA), already exists. Both are helped by the existing sense of nationhood and, particularly in Scotland, a tradition of national banking and financial institutions. The efforts of the Mid Wales Development Board and the Highlands and Islands Development Board, primarily in the agricultural sectors, have also been effective in reversing rural depopulation, encouraging inward investment and stimulating a rapid rate of new-business formation. With their proven record of success, they provide further lessons as to the appropriate structures for the different regions in England to build.

The SDP/Liberal Alliance Worksearch Campaign in the nations and regions of the UK has devised employment strategies for the micro-economy from the grass roots up. It shows the enormous potential for reinforcing a macro industrial strategy with local initiatives at the micro level.

In the UK, the decline of industrial capacity has gone further and faster than in virtually any other member of the OECD in the last fifteen years. Our manufacturing sector now represents a smaller proportion of national output than in any other western industrial country, except the United States. Apart from Norway, Britain is the only OECD country whose factories are producing less now than they were a decade ago.

Apologists for this situation claim that the advent of North Sea oil meant that there was bound to be some deterioration in the non-oil trade balance, but this can be expected to go into reverse as oil output gradually declines and the premium on sterling's international value disappears. The acceleration of manufacturing decline was influenced by sterling being a petro-currency. They argue that the decline in manufacturing does not matter greatly in the long-term because, once North Sea oil revenues fade, so exports of services and the income from oil-financed overseas assets will help to plug the gap in the balance of payments.

The decline in oil prices, even if offset by a decline of the pound against the dollar, will undoubtedly leave a large hole in the trade balance that manufactured exports and services will have to fill. Since only a quarter of services are tradeable, the services sector will remain highly dependent on the manufacturing sector. The key question is: in a climate of faster world economic growth, stimulated by lower oil prices, will the UK's manufacturing industry respond or grow as fast as its competitors?

According to estimates by the London Business School, as much as 17 per cent of the pre-1980 manufacturing capacity has been scrapped and not replaced, whilst the boom in new business formation has scarcely touched the manufacturing sector. Forecasts for the growth of manufacturing output are being revised downwards. Our relative competitive position continues to deteriorate. Simulating the SDP/Liberal Alliance Budget on the Cambridge econometrics model shows that a 1 per cent improvement in competitiveness hopefully brought about by the Alliance's industrial strategy shows that a £1.5 billion improvement in the current account would be achieved. This would be crucial for success because the current account deficit on all econometric simulations for expansion could well be the critical limiting factor.

Restoring the strength of manufacturing industry must therefore be an overwhelming priority. The present burden of high interest and exchange rates adds to business costs by a bigger margin than money wage rises. The government's strategy of trying to price British products back into lost markets, by lowering both selling prices and real wages, is the wrong way to tackle the problem of poor competitiveness. The future lies in higher value added products with an international market, where the accent is on design and quality and on the company's ability to respond rapidly to market requirements. The UK cannot rely on cheap labour and low skills to reduce industrial costs. The emphasis instead should be on achieving higher productivity from a better-paid and better-skilled labour force through the introduction of new technology and innovative production methods designed to develop a stream of new and more competitive products.

Employment and technological changes are going to be substantial in the future and this must mean that education and training will be a critical factor in Britain's economic performance. This is particularly true in those parts of the manufacturing and service sectors which are exposed to international competition. The increasing impact of automation and competition from newly industrialised countries with low wages will mean fewer unskilled jobs.

We need to alter the in-built bias in British education against applied science and technology. At lower levels skill shortages are now acute, and may well explain why in many of our industries there is lower productivity per man-hour even in factories using the same capital equipment as that used in other European countries. We need to move forward to a system of skill training which is based on standards achieved rather than time served, which can be built up bit by bit on a modular basis, and which is open to adults as well as school leavers. A remissable tax system is required under which each company spending more than the standard percentage for its industry on training would have all its extra expenditure rebated from public funds, while any company which spent less than that percentage would have to pay a tax equal to its underspending. As a result, the system would be self-financing in the long term.

Not all new jobs in the service sector will be high-skilled high value-added, high-wage jobs. Along with the professional jobs and the jobs in information technology will also be a lot of traditionally lower wage jobs in areas such as fast foods, retailing and health care. It is imperative not to prevent these jobs emerging by minimum wage legislation. Also, if we generate sufficient wealth in the tradeable manufacturing and service sectors, the country can then afford to expand jobs in the public services to improve standards of care and service.

It requires leadership of a far higher quality than we have yet seen to convince this country that technology does not destroy jobs and that there can be enough jobs to go around in the future. Admitting our decline does not mean accepting the mood of defeatism. The reality is that the faster British industry adapts to the skills and opportunities of technological change, the more likely we are to be able to achieve a higher level of employment in the future.

Improvements in the private sector pay bargaining environment are also essential. Pay increases which are not matched by productivity remain an intractable problem in the British economy. Removing labour market rigidities, increasing genuine competition and breaking down monopoly pricing arrangements are vital for reducing the growth in unit labour costs and improving industrial competitiveness. So also is the need to retain collective bargaining in the private sector and in the commercial public sector. The new trade union legislation is proving itself and it would be folly to repeal it. As it settles down, we can look at a system of positive rights for trade unionists, but to open up the whole of trades union law to the partisan feeling and vested interests of either a Labour or Conservative government would be to risk lurching again to an unbalanced situation. Probably only a coalition government could tackle such a major reform and it would not be their highest priority.

Whatever the failings of existing collective bargaining procedures, they alone have some hope of reflecting, at decentralised level, market realities. Companies that are doing well and in profit can pay their workers more generously so that they share in the success. Companies that are doing badly with low or non-existent profits cannot and should not pay their workers above the inflation rate and at times will have to ask for sacrifices in terms of paying less than the inflation rate to their workforce—*in extremis* involving an absolute cut in pay. To succumb to the pressures for some sort of overall centralised statutory pay policy with fixed payments or percentage increases, or a combination of both, is to follow once again the path of unreality, create distortions and increase inefficiency.

The challenge is to work with the grain of the market and retain collective bargaining, but to ensure that the overall outcome is non-inflationary, thus allowing more room for real growth and higher employment. To achieve this, we need more widespread arbitration procedures—particularly 'pendular' or final offer arbitration—wider employee share ownership, more generally agreed consultative procedures and open information. But it will be some time before all of these factors in combination can give the British economy sufficient market realism to ensure that the collective bargaining process does not fuel inflation. We have not reached that situation yet and there is a temptation to relinquish that objective and advocate again rigid and formalised statutory incomes policies, or to believe we can continue to use the discipline of high unemployment.

The chief lesson from the experience of countries with centre-left governments, such as Australia, New Zealand, Spain, and Italy, is that incomes strategies can work effectively to restrain inflation when placed in a framework of incentives and market-oriented devices not normally associated with governments of the centre-left. Market-liberalism and incomes policies can it seems work together to promote greater competitiveness in the labour market and other parts of the economy.

In the UK, the effect of high earnings and lower productivity growth in recent years has been to steadily push our unit labour costs out of line with the major OECD countries, our principal competitors. British unit costs in manufacturing are continuing at more or less the same pace as last year—6.8 per cent in the year to February 1986, and 6.1 per cent for 1985 as a whole. According to IMF estimates which adjust the figures for cyclical effects, 'normalised' UK unit labour costs in manufacturing rose about 7.5 per cent in 1985, whereas the average increase in OECD economies as a whole was only 2 per cent. The fall in the retail price index thus owes little to our own self-discipline. Britain is benefiting from a happy coincidence of external events—the fall in oil prices and the fall in other commodity prices which, together with a lower dollar and lower inflation in other industrial countries, is permitting some fall in nominal, though not real, UK interest rates.

Unit labour costs are a much better guide to underlying inflationary trends than the RPI. The government can go on trying to soften the inflationary impact on the RPI of spiralling pay by maintaining a higher exchange rate than would otherwise be necessary. But that has a heavy permanent cost in high unemployment and, as we have seen in the decline of our manufacturing sector, is particularly savage due to the higher exchange rate of 1981.

A policy of counter-inflationary discipline through sole reliance on the exchange rate leads to a loss of market share and a gradual erosion of employment opportunities. The decision to maintain a strong exchange rate in the wake of the sterling crisis in the first few months of 1985 may well be responsible for the present fall-off in manufacturing output and the fact that the downturn in unemployment predicted for this year has not yet occurred. Such a policy also imbalances the economy to an alarming degree. It cannot be sustained and a readjustment of the exchange rate, downwards, is now inevitable.

The SDP/Liberal Alliance is committed to an efficient market economy. Our incomes strategy would seek first to change the climate of voluntary pay bargaining to achieve greater market realism. If this can be achieved and unit labour costs reduced, then statutory powers would be unnecessary. It would, however, be wrong to count on such an outcome.

In present circumstances, our strategy would be as follows. We would seek to change the climate of voluntary pay bargaining. First, a payroll incentive—through a rebate on employers' National Insurance contributions—could be given to companies which awarded pay increases below a unit costs target based on average productivity growth. This would be linked to longer term pay settlements, over a period of at least two years, which would bring about greater bargaining stability and reduced inflationary expectations. As part of this incentive, companies would be able to offer their employees benefits in the form of share options which, if they retained them, would accrue tax concessions.

The payroll incentive would, therefore, help companies which sought to contain unit costs. First, it would also encourage them to achieve a better balance between improved earnings and higher employment. This would be a transitional measure to encourage firms to move towards longer-term reforms in their pay bargaining, involving new forms of arbitration and a higher profit-sharing element within their earnings. It would help widen employee share ownership in a way which would promote much greater awareness among employees of the potential of improving competitiveness and expanding markets.

Second, if companies failed to take advantage of these new incentives and continued to award inflationary increases, the stand-by mechanism of an inflation tax would be used. The tax penalty would only cover increases in average earnings in excess of the declared unit costs target. But it would not seek to penalise success. Companies who genuinely sought to share profits with their employees through registered profit-sharing schemes or approved share ownership schemes would be exempt from the tax. This would apply only to companies with over 100 employees, just under 20,000 companies encompassing three-quarters of the total workforce. Since small businesses and new firms would be outside the scope of the tax, most of the fastest growing high technology and service firms would not be affected.

Moderating pay pressure in the private sector will help to lower claims among groups in the public sector. The steady widening of the gap which has taken place in the last five years is increasingly likely to fuel discontent and disputes. A quarter of the workforce and half the trade unionists in the country still work in the public sector. Some groups like the police, the armed forces and the nurses are covered by one-off pay reviews or review bodies. This has nurtured the feelings of resentment among those who have been removed or left out of such arrangements. They deserve greater justice.

We therefore propose a new system of comparability for the public services as a whole. A single and independent Pay Information Unit covering the whole of the public services would develop comparisons with jobs outside. This material would be made available to negotiators, but would not be binding on unions or government. A yearly efficiency audit of the public services would be undertaken by the new body to secure accurate comparisons between productivity in public and private industry. Greater synchronisation of pay dates would help to prevent pace-setting settlements and allow for a more rational determination of comparisons. A system of pendulum arbitration linked to no-strike agreements could be established in key public services.

In the longer term, we would introduce more widespread arbitration in pay determination in the context of more decentralised pay nego-tiations. This would avoid the rigidity which characterised previous pay policies. Building on our payroll incentive proposal, much greater support would be given to profit-sharing schemes for the whole work-force.

If there is to be a sustained recovery in the manufacturing sector however, the other engines of growth on the supply side of the economy, apart from technical innovation, need to be running smoothly and strongly. We need more private investment, better exchange rate management, focused and relevant research and development, and effective export promotion. Together they would form the type of coherent industrial strategy called for in the House of Lords Report, which recognised above all the length of time which such a recovery will take. The 1986 SDP/Liberal Alliance Budget proposes a well designed industrial credit scheme operating through the market and the existing banking and venture capital system to reduce the burden of interest rates on new investments. For instance, at a cost of £100 million per annum over five years, it would be possible to release £2 billion for loans at 5 per cent below market rates. That would be of real benefit to companies currently paying above 11 per cent—an all time high—on such loans.

Achieving a consensus on exchange rate management should not be beyond the capability of UK politicians. The Exchange Rate Mechanism of the European Monetary Sysem (EMS) offers us a way of reducing exchange rate volatility and uncertainty, essential if industry is to plan long-term. The critical Sterling/Deutschmark rate has to be maintained at a competitive level if export-lead growth is to be achieved. The EMS provides a disciplined framework to mainta'n that competitive position. Continuous depreciation simply adds to inflation. The EMS is not a soft option but provides an important external way of imposing a greater degree of internal consistency on the way successive UK governments would approach monetary policy.

Despite all that is said about the importance of industrial research and development, the size of intramural R&D expenditure in manufacturing—financed by government and private industry—at current prices has fallen slightly from £1.56 billion in 1978 to £1.48 billion in 1985. The priority must be both to increase the funds allocated to industrial R&D, and to aim them more specifically at the commercial exploitation of new technology and the development of prototypes.

A sustained and successful export drive is essential to increase Britain's market share of world trade. Time is not on our side. Bluntly, the Department of Trade and Industry allocation of £42 million for 1986/87—the same in money terms as the out-turn in 1985/86—to be spent on export services overseas trade promotion is insufficient and extra resources are needed.

There are many ingredients—attitudinal and mechanistic—to industrial regeneration at both the political and economic levels. Choosing 1986 as Industry Year offered a new opportunity to demonstrate the importance of manufacturing industry to our economy, but it has to be sustained as a national priority for two decades. It has been said that for the Japanese and the West Germans, every year is Industry Year. Changing our political structure and introducing proportional representation is supported by many in industry because they see other countries' political systems and voting arrangements and they know from their own practical experience on the ground that in those countries, industrial success and wealth creation are helped not hindered by the broad approach of their governments. The motivation for both wealth creation and creating employment can exist side-by-side. Without a readiness to adapt and regenerate, we will fall even further behind and our relative economic decline could easily become absolute decline.

5. An Industrial Strategy for Britain*

John Smith

I believe the central failure of the Thatcher government has been a failure to confront the long-term *strategic* problems which face the British economy. We must therefore develop and get our industrial strategy right. The Labour Party sees the way forward as involving active demand management to raise the overall level of activity and investment, combined with an active supply-side strategy involving a coordinated use of industrial and trade policy to address the regeneration of manufacturing industry which is now rightly regarded as central to the long-term recovery of the UK economy.

The UK's manufacturing tradable capacity must be restored in such a way as to allow a resumption of economic growth at socially acceptable levels of unemployment and output. The first problem is therefore how to raise the volume and quality of investment that producers are willing to undertake. The second is how to ensure that sufficient financial, human and other resources of the right amount and quality are available for the programme of investment and innovative activity required.

The first and overriding requirement in raising the volume of private sector investment is to raise the level of effective demand for domestic manufactured output. Although the public sector may itself embark upon a programme, for example, of public works projects, it is the private sector which must provide the bulk of the investment effort required. Tinkering via investment subsidies or other means to alter the relationship between the cost of capital and the rate of return on investment, has noticeably failed to alter the UK's chronic low investment performance. Private sector investment will not be forthcoming without the prospect of a period of sustained buoyant demand. Ensuring a high and sustained level of demand by raising capacity utilisation (and as a consequence raising profit margins) is therefore a necessary requirement for industrial investment revival.

This will require the adoption of a trade and exchange rate policy to

*Speech to the University of Sussex, 10 February 1986.

handle the transitional period before a regeneration programme can have such an effect on the competitiveness of the UK economy. In this connection two points are worth emphasising. First, although it must be the case that in the last resort the UK should be prepared to go it alone and adopt whatever individual trade policies are required to sustain expansion, it is infinitely preferable that UK recovery should be part of a coordinated programme involving the European economies. The promotion of such an expansion should be a priority for UK international economic policy. Second, in the context of the vital policy for expansion and recovery of manufacturing, the extra degree of freedom offered by the existence of substantial stocks of assets overseas as a result of North Sea oil revenues being invested there cannot be ignored. The phased repatriation of overseas assets, with institutional tax privileges being made conditional on meeting specified asset portfolio, or net investment flow guidelines could provide a significant proportion of the resources we need. Policies which limit overseas portfolio investment are nothing new. They have been pursued in Japan, France and the US, as well as many other industrialised economies for many years. Restrictions on overseas investment stocks and flows have, of course, featured in the policies of Japan, the US and other industrial economies.

Necessary though demand expansion is, it cannot by itself be sufficient. For, although it is obvious that there is much to be gained in terms of raising the level of investment by a reversal of the macroeconomic policies of the recent past, the efficiency with which that investment is allocated and used is also of great importance.

It is in this connection that an active industrial policy as part of a planned domestic reflation can make a contribution. It can do so in two main ways. First, by helping to ensure the efficient allocation of scarce investment resources. Second, by helping to raise the efficiency of each investment project through the promotion of innovative schemes for product and process development, the reorganisation of the production process and the transfer and diffusion of technology between defence and civilian uses, academia and the commercial world, and between the firms in individual sectors. Planning can help meet both these objectives by improving the flow of information upon which investment decisions in the public and private sector are based, and by the coordination of policies designed to make investment effective. I believe we can identify four principal planning functions.

First, a central informational function to identify the capital requirements of the overall output and employment growth targets of the recovery programme, its manufacturing and industrial requirements, and within that to identify the key areas in which expansion should most effectively occur, and to indicate the broad types of investment required. We should be able to identify, as other advanced industrial economies have done, the opportunities and threats which face the various industrial sectors of our nation. We need to select priority areas in terms of potential comparative advantages, but also in terms of those areas where it is essential that the UK maintain industrial sectors to ensure that we have an industrial future at all.

The second main planning function would be by consultation and negotiation to discover the likely investment plans of public and large-scale private sector enterprise in relation to the investment plan framework; and thus consider the main impediments if any to the scale and type of investment desired being undertaken.

This will lead naturally to the third planning function, the provision of a framework for the negotiation and design of packages of support to encourage the private and public sector responses desired, for the evaluation of specific projects submitted for support and for the auditing and evaluation of the effectiveness of the support programmes. In this respect I think we have a lot to learn from the system of French planning contracts.

Fourthly, and finally, planning must also involve a framework for ensuring the provision of the sorts of resources required for the packages including provision where necessary for direct state funding or ownership stakes in enterprises and a coherent role for public procurement.

It is important to emphasise that the design of support packages and the provision of resources for them can go far beyond the usually emphasised need for financial resources in the form of subsidised loans, grants or the taking of equity, but could and should, where appropriate extend to training and manpower requirements; and the specification of standards or regulation for products. For instance any attempt to build up technological strength in advanced information technology, where the trade deficit increased tenfold between 1980 and 1984, must involve a collaborative effort in view of the scale, complexity and diverse location in the private and public sector of the resources and know-how required. . . .

The evolution of a framework to implement these planning functions requires a number of institutional developments. We already have NEDO, the forum around which government, the unions and management formulate sector working policies and report to government on their operation and effectiveness. A Labour government would require a greatly strengthened planning organisation on the NEDO model to be the fulcrum of communication and implementation of industrial policy.

Sector working groups in the present NEDO structure have done a great deal of valuable work but sadly they have been largely ignored by this government. I strongly believe that the core of our industrial strategy depends on a strong working relationship between all sides of industry and the government. This would not mean a return to the ideas of the 1960s, nor a French-style 'Le Plan', but a new partnership to establish a firm basis for industrial recovery. Priorities will be set for investment and development within the NEDO sectors, whether it should be the motor industry, electronics or any other which needs urgent assistance. . . .

Ultimately the responsibility for the central planning function must reside with the Secretary of State for Trade and Industry, working closely with the planning organisation. Although the overall policy framework has to be formulated centrally and its implementation be coordinated within centrally approved guidelines, the process of formulation, the setting and revision of guidelines, and the detailed negotiation, implementation and assessment of individual projects must involve the use of decentralised institutions working at sectoral, regional and local level. A Labour government will need local authorities to play a major part in its new economic strategy and this will involve councils in new regional planning bodies to ensure that public and private investment decisions are made more accountable to the regions.

The Scottish and Welsh Development Agencies, set up by the last Labour government, have a proven record of intervention and investment which has helped to alleviate some of the worst effects of the recession in both these countries. We believe that new regional bodies for England should have powers to invest in local industry through Enterprise Boards, to invest in training programmes and to back local employment campaigns and develop new technologies. These new agencies could cover, as a start, the key geographic areas of the North-East, North-West, Midlands and Yorkshire, all areas which have suffered during the past six years from the government's lack of an industrial policy.

The public sector which has made a signal contribution to our economic success in the past has been greatly reduced in size and scale by the ruthless privatisation policies of the Thatcher government. The Labour Party is giving careful consideration to the development of new policies for an enhanced public sector. . . .

I would like, however, in the context of innovation and the consideration of industrial policy-making, to draw attention to one important policy initiative which is finding support, not just within the formal ranks of the Labour Party, but also among a wider audience. We need a new and flexible forum of state intervention in the industrial economy. The Industrial Re-organisation Corporation of the first Wilson government, many of whose then young members now hold prominent positions at the head of British industries, pioneered the concept of creative intervention until it was foolishly destroyed in 1970. In later years the National Enterprise Board did valuable work, although it was diverted from its principal functions by its absorption in the British Leyland rescue. The time has come, I believe, for the founding of a new organisation, perhaps named British Enterprise, organised and funded by government, to be able to establish new industrial ventures on its own, to enter into joint ventures with the private sector, and perhaps most importantly to act as a catalyst for innovation. There is so much that needs to be done that I believe that a powerful new organisation along these lines will prove to be essential. It is a form of public ownership and intervention which offers the possibility of flexible and direct action, with or without private sector cooperation, which could command wide support within industry as well as be an effective agent in the planning of our national industrial recovery. . . .

I have sought to indicate some of the crucial elements in our approach to industrial policy. Each area of our actual and potential industrial effort needs particular consideration. Clearly, some will need more attention than others. In areas where we are already successful, there is obviously less need for a government to have to concern itself apart from ensuring that the potential of our existing success is maximised. In other areas, there will clearly be the requirement to have proposals for reconstruction and redevelopment which can be formulated through the planning process.

But in every area we must sustain three engines of recovery. These are investment, research and development, and training. I have already indicated some of our ideas on the first two, but the third is probably the most crucial. As we have seen industrial training progressively being dismantled, and as we have with horror observed our educational system diminishing at all its levels, it is clear that we have no hope of recovery unless we make a completely new and sustained commitment to education and training. Our aim—and it is a perfectly possible one—should be within, say, a ten-year period, to attain the best trained and educated workforce and management in Western Europe. Our future success depends on our capacity to develop to the full the skills of our own people. It is not just a matter of offering new scope for individual development as an end in itself—desirable though that is. Education is now a crucial element of a successful industrial policy. Far too many of our young people leave school at sixteen, poorly equipped for a world in which personal skills are the key to economic success and individual fulfilment. Far too many of our young people are unable to gain access to higher, further and continuing education which alone can offer them the opportunity to adapt and retrain in a world where change is swift and relentless.

PART II:
Political Parties

Behind the views of politicians lie distinct party positions. Debates on the nature of Britain's economic decline, and on policies to reverse it, have gone on within and between political parties here for at least two decades; and that debate intensified in the 1970s as the post-war Keynesian consensus disintegrated. The terms of reference of that debate were increasingly set by intellectual developments within the Conservative Party, and this domination was accentuated by the return in 1979 of a Conservative government committed to the implementation of radically new policies. One of the key protagonists in these exchanges was Sir Keith Joseph, and we reproduce here extracts from an important pamphlet published by him on the eve of the Conservatives' return to power. Alongside that we have reproduced part of the 1985 White Paper on employment, to show how consistently the government has stuck to its basic position through seven years of office. As we have seen, its critics within the Party (particularly Edward Heath) fear that ministers have no industrial strategy. It is clear however that they do, and that they have stuck to it throughout. As the Department of Trade put it to the House of Lords Select Committee investigating Britain's trade imbalance:

> The Government's policies aim to create the conditions for profitable and non-inflationary growth and for the encouragement of enterprise. An adequate level of investment is dependent upon the prospect of attracting real rates of return on capital. This is the only framework within which industry can improve its competitive performance, competitive design, technology, product quality, reliability, delivery and price. The Government believes that competition is the best spur to efficiency. The Government's commitment to the open trading system is the international counterpart to the promotion of competition in the domestic economy. . . . The Government also seeks to stimulate innovation in industry, for example through various forms of selective assistance, and to foster the introduction of new technology. But the longer-term exploitation of this technology—and the identification of market opportunities—is a matter for industry itself. . . . The Government believe in

the importance of a healthy and efficient manufacturing sector to the economy and the essential thrust of Government policy is to reduce market barriers and, by providing a favourable climate, to enable industry to respond flexibly to the requirements of the domestic and world markets. (House of Lords, Session 1984–85, 238-II, p. 5)

When challenged by the Committee on the existence of a certain complacency in governmental circles, the Permanent Secretary at the Department gave this description of the attitude of his ministerial superiors. In his view, ministers were concerned, but they remained convinced that their proper role ought to be a limited one:

> I think the Department would like to say that the trend in the trade deficit in manufactured goods is a matter of concern to Ministers. It is, I think, a symptom of a long-standing worry about the competitiveness of British manufacturing industry—of course, with shining exceptions. . . . I think it is true that at any rate of official level we do *not* regard the emergence of a deficit on manufactured goods as in itself tremendously worrying. We *are* concerned by the evidence which it provides of a failure of competitiveness in manufacturing. Therefore I think we would say—and I believe Ministers would say—that the action which the government should take in this area is the same as their general action to improve the effectiveness and efficiency of the British economy and of manufacture within it. . . . One of the themes of current Ministerial policy, of which you will be well aware, is that there is a limit to the role of the Government in this area. The main contributions from macro policies, notably getting down inflation and stimulating competition. These are familiar themes in Ministerial speeches, and they are certainly themes which are central to the objectives which have been set by Ministers for my own Department. On top of that, there are certain measures which are directly related to helping manufacturing industry: there are various schemes promoted by the Department, and there is the continuing operation of the export promotion activity through overseas posts and through the BOTB. (Ibid., p. 35)

In this spirit too we are told (both in the White Paper and by Sir Keith) that employment levels are not directly within the control of government. What government has to do is to set the framework (particularly of stable prices, but also of the free movement of resources, both capital and labour) within which market forces and private enterprise can then generate output and jobs. Overspending by the state must be curbed. Capital must be free to move to its point of optimum return; and barriers on the optimum allocation of labour must be removed. If unemployment persists even when all these things have been done, then pay levels must still be running ahead of rates of industrial productivity; and that is the case now—in the Treasury's view—as is indicated in this extract from its *Progress Report* of January 1985.

> *How pay affects jobs*
> The basic link between pay and jobs is clear. If people cost less to employ, more of them will be employed.

There are two elements to this. First, slower growth of pay would produce more jobs for any given growth of output. That is because it would slow down the process by which work comes to be done by machines. Labour-intensive activities would become cheaper relative to capital-intensive ones, and there would be more jobs on that account.

Second, a slower growth of pay would result in a faster growth of output. Costs would be lower, so companies would find it more profitable to produce goods and services. They would want to produce and sell more. To do that, they would on average set their prices lower than otherwise, and find it profitable to do so.

Lower prices would stimulate the economy in several ways. For example, unless the Government were to take offsetting action, lower prices would feed through to lower interest rates. Savings would be worth more, so people would tend to save less and spend a higher proportion of their incomes. Companies would invest more. There would be an improvement in international competitiveness, which would encourage exports and discourage imports. The public sector would be able to buy more goods and services for a given level of cash expenditure.

It is sometimes suggested that these mechanisms would be blocked. If people had lower pay rises, they would have less money to spend; demand would be lower, and we would end up with no more jobs than before. But the companies for which people work would have larger profits. Some of those would be returned to consumers through lower prices, as just described, and higher dividends. Some would be invested, and would create jobs in that way. Some would be spent directly on extra employment. The empirical evidence suggests that the net effect would be to increase demand.

Certain sections of the Conservative Party are no longer totally convinced by all this. The views of Edward Heath have already been cited; and he has never been alone in his unease. In fact, veiled critiques of government policy from inside as well as outside the Cabinet became a feature of political life after 1979. Peter Walker, for example, had this to say about market economics:

The unfettered market economy is only a partial view of freedom. The market economy idolises people as consumers and, providing the market mechanism is working, it gives consumers a wider freedom of choice, an important and essential advantage. But people are more than just consumers. They are workers, householders, students.

We should, when thinking of the future we wish to create, include the freedom from humiliation and the restraints of poverty, freedom from unfair discrimination, freedom from the dehabilitating effects of slum housing. We need to have a concern for the quality of life so that progress is measured not just in GNP or motorcars but new parks, leisure centres, artistic endeavour, the joy of living (*Guardian*, 1985)

Michael Heseltine seems to have become a later convert to a similar view, as his own sensitivity to industrial difficulties grew. Not for him a 'hands-off' relationship between government and industry. On the contrary, as he put it, 'the relationship between capitalism and government now appears very different and more complex' than once he thought. Governments have things to do in support of market processes: 'no one seriously questions the regulatory role of government in safety and health, in working conditions and planning', and very few 'now question the need for government support for research, training, start-up guarantees, launch and development costs, credit, regional aid and high technology subsidies'. What concerned him was 'the decline in our industrial base', 'the drift of resources and power from the old manufacturing centres of the Midlands and the North to an ever-growing and seemingly remote concentration in the City of London'. The Heseltine conclusion seems far removed from that of Joseph. Not, as he had once thought, 'that the most constructive thing to do with the Department of Industry would be to close it down', but instead that 'Trade and Industry should be reorganised as a strategic department. Its Secretary of State should be one of the most senior members of the Government, and should chair a Cabinet committee charged with the responsibility for the health of British industrial and commercial activities' (*Guardian*, 21 February 1986. p. 11).

Peter Walker is President of the Tory Reform Group, another important source of pressure for policy change within the Conservative Party. The group issued a pamphlet in February 1986 calling for what they termed 'a comprehensive strategy for jobs', a coordinated series of measures to 'increase infrastructure spending, open up the European internal market, strengthen European co-operation in the high technology field, increase competition at home, [generate] a national industrial strategy, [give] further stimulus for small firms, and [take] job creation and work sharing initiatives'. These are still calls for reform within a basic commitment to the broad thrust of Conservative strategy. The pamphlet's authors explicitly reject 'the demon Maggie myth', as they put it, that the government has deliberately caused mass unemployment. But nor will they accept either the 'Scargill myth' that old jobs can always be saved, or the ultra-Right argument that the government can do nothing to alter unemployment levels fixed by market forces. Though they are keen to stress the complex interplay of factors with which policy has to deal—including demographic changes, new technology, and changing patterns of work and employment—the pamphlet's authors insist that the government has already done much to create jobs and growth, and wants to do more. Though, as they put it, 'inflation has been brought under control', exports are at an all-time high and rising, trade union law has been reformed and we have 'record retail sales, output, business investment and GNP', they still want 'relatively modest increases in government spending both on capital investments and to fund further training and job creation projects'. Because without them, 'the situation will worsen further. That is unacceptable.' In fact, the Tory Reform Group told the Chancellor in 1986 that they 'fundamentally disagree[d] with the prevailing orthodoxy that . . . resources must be used either to cut the basic rate of income tax or to raise the personal tax allowance to a much higher level', believing instead that 'any extra resources should be used to cut unemployment by spending on direct job creation through essential public investment' and other measures. As they put it:

> There is much real work to be done on improvements to basic services and utilities for which our economy has urgent need. The jobs created by public spending of this nature are as 'real' as any. We are convinced that our society will benefit more in terms of both jobs and welfare from increased spending on housing, on education, on health and on the needs of both inner cities and shire counties, than from cuts in taxation—cuts which may cost a billion in lost revenue but benefit low income families by only pence per week.

> *Public investment creates jobs*
> We believe that public investment and spending are important in the creation of employment and, more importantly, in the creation of an efficient economy in which jobs can be created by private industry. A great deal of present public investment is being financed by asset sales. We believe that if pressure on oil prices reduces the Chancellor's scope for generosity, a strictly limited increase in the PSBR—now at a low level set against GDP—would be justified. The fact that extra public expenditure is being financed out of increased sales of assets is perfectly acceptable, so long as such privatisation brings about greater efficiency and competition; and so long as it is not allowed, like North Sea oil revenues, to disguise the reality that our economy is still not productive enough to provide for our needs. (Tory Reform Group, *The 1986 Budget*, p. 1)

The content of the Tory Reform Group pamphlet brings them towards the policy suggestions of the SDP/Liberal Alliance. The Alliance critique is, of course, more strident than the TRG can undertake, namely that:

> Britain is becoming a low growth, low productivity, low skill economy. One which cannot create enough wealth to renew its infrastructure or improve its social services. An economy where unemployment in the North is half as high again as in the South. An economy which is frittering away what remains of our oil revenues in a short-term consumer boom and unemployment benefit, rather than investing for the future. And, more ominously, an economy where the falling oil price is seriously undermining the balance of payments position and limiting the Government's room for manoeuvre.
> Our share of world trade has halved in the last thirty years. We have lost a fifth of our manufacturing industry in the last five years. Our industry has become less competitive and our productivity still lags behind that of our principal competitors. (SDP/Liberal Alliance, *Jobs and Competitiveness*, 1986, p. 1)

The Alliance calls for what they term an 'industry rethink', or 'a new partnership for success between government and industry'. Seven policy initiatives in particular are singled out.

1. a reduction in business costs: through cuts in National Insurance contributions and the provision of subsidised credit to industry,
2. tax incentives for firms to invest in new technology,
3. increases in the science budget to strengthen industrial research and development,
4. a fully comprehensive industrial training programme,
5. a £2 billion programme of public sector capital investment, concentrated mainly on construction,
6. comprehensive government back-up service to exporters, and
7. entry into the European Monetary System at a competitive rate.

The heavy emphasis in all this—and in the supporting documents drawn up by both parties—is on actively encouraging and assisting local firms to compete successfully in world markets, with the government 'intervening selectively to encourage industrial competitiveness: to create a highly skilled, high productivity, high value-added economy' (SDP: *The Only Way to a Fairer Britain*, 1985). The industrial credit scheme, a new training initiative, and the revitalisation of the British Technology Group (to provide selective aid for high-risk projects, and for research and development) are central elements in the Alliance strategy, as is a Cabinet committee on industrial policy 'chaired by the Prime Minister, to ensure that the needs of industry become the top priority of government policy' (ibid.). The tone of the Liberal Party documents are slightly less directional than those of the SDP, and more sensitive to ecological issues, decentralisation of decision-making, and profit-sharing. But they too are committed to a programme which includes:

*   capital investment in the repair and modernisation of the infrastructure;
*   the introduction of an incomes strategy in the context of profit-sharing and a more equitable distribution of wealth and incomes;
*   investment in people through a substantial extension of education, training and retraining;
*   renewed public investment in research and development.

The Labour Party has been equally active in planning an alternative industrial strategy, one in which government action is likely to be even more extensive than the Alliance would have it. The Labour Party's concerns, however, in this area as in others, are these days inevitably shaped by factors peculiar to the Party's own immediate past: particularly by a need to distance itself from the policies which failed between 1974 and 1979, and from those (much more radical ones) which proved electorally so unpopular in 1983. In the process of finding that middle way, the Labour Party has recently reproduced a whole series of pamphlets under a general campaign heading of 'Jobs and Industry': pamphlets with titles such as 'Investing in Britain', 'A New Partnership for Britain', and 'Working Together for Britain'. The Labour Party has a credibility problem to overcome as well as a policy to find, and for that reason its campaign has emphasised that 'Labour has practical policies to tackle unemployment and to rebuild the economy'. The Party claims that local councils under their control are already 'creating new jobs, reviving industry and training workers', prefiguring as they do so the impact of a future Labour government. The problems (apart from the Conservatives in power) which are singled out by Labour for particular attention are low investment, poor training, the export of capital, and the persistence of inequality in the context of mass unemployment and a dwindling manufacturing base. Labour's answer is a new industrial strategy based on an active partnership between government, industry and the unions (meeting in some national planning council), able to deploy new institutions of industrial intervention (a revamped National Enterprise Board, to take firms into public ownership, and a new National Investment Bank, to finance private capital investment with loans offered, if appropriate, at less than the going market rate), and drawing on new policies of increased government spending and income redistribution.

The pamphlet from which extracts are reproduced here (*Planning for Full Employment*) calls for a new government department of economic and industrial planning, a reduction in the power of multinational corporations, the spread of industrial democracy, a carefully planned expansion of public expenditure (targeted on sectors in which it can best increase productivity and competitiveness, create jobs and reduce regional inequalities) a new training policy, and quick action on low pay and equal opportunities. The attack on unemployment proposed here involves the quick spending of money to create jobs in essential services, to put capital expenditure into housing, roads and urban renewal, and to direct funds into investment in manufacturing plant and equipment.

The Labour Party continues, therefore, to put its emphasis on national planning, government intervention, public accountability and the more equal distribution of industrial power and social wealth. It also continues, however, to leave areas of ambiguity and uncertainty in its proposals. For it makes its claims now with a 'new realism' which raises doubts about how much of what the pamphlet proposes would actually materialise. In particular, doubts have been expressed about the content and quantity of the 'planning' which a future Labour government would actually undertake. As far as we can tell, Roy Hattersley's emphasis within the programme is less on *controls over* capital than on new *incentives to* them—with the National Investment Bank as the key agency rather than any new Department of Economic and Industrial Planning. As we saw in Part I, the Shadow Chancellor is an enthusiastic advocate of Labour's new realism, endeavouring to formulate policy in advance of the threats to the strategy which previously threw Labour governments off course. Roy Hattersley has mentioned in particular the threats of inflation and a collapse of sterling. He will apparently handle price rises caused by speculative hoarding through the use of selective price controls. He again wants to handle price rises caused by wage pressure by incomes policy; and price rises caused by the collapse of Sterling will be met by a 'Buy British' policy and by the use of selective and temporary import controls. Controls too can be anticipated on the export of capital, as can tax changes to give firms incentives to repatriate capital already abroad. As two of his critics put it, 'the centrepiece of Roy's approach then, are "realistic" reflation, backed up by a voluntary incomes policy and a new tax regime to encourage institutions to repatriate funds, the funds will be channelled into a National Investment Bank which will provide subsidised loans for investment.' (John Harrison and Bob Morgan, 'Hattersley's economics', *Capital and Class*, 26, Summer 1985, p. 36). This appears to be Labour's route to growth and employment in the late 1980s.

That route, though considerably more interventionist than the Alliance proposals, is a pale reflection of a much more radical 'Alternative Economic Strategy' canvassed in and by the Labour Party after 1979. The AES of those years involved greater degrees of public ownership and control, an even greater commitment to the redistribution of power, and a firmer determination to 'plan' the economy in ways that ran counter to the requirements of key centres of capitalist privilege. That earlier radicalism, though no longer evident in the documents and speeches of Labour leaders, remains publicly available in at least two places. One is the policy stance of the now tiny Communist Party, the other is in the policies advocated by the 'hard Left' inside the Labour Party itself. For both of them, the long-term solution to the weakening of manufacturing investment and to large-scale unemployment is not a managed capitalism, but the creation of a democratic socialist Britain. That perspective both gives them a different way of 'packaging' their immediate proposals and brings a greater radicalism to the proposals themselves. For what is sought here is qualitative change—not just a collection of specific amendments to policies which are still geared to lubricating and encouraging private enterprise, but a real shift in class power and the generalisation of criteria other than corporate profit to guide investment, production, and the distribution of social wealth. Tony Benn spoke for this point of view in his introduction to the pamphlet by Andrew Glyn, extracts of which are reproduced below:

> The British economy, seriously weakened by years of decline, is now being rapidly de-industrialised and only the massive oil revenues, so criminally wasted, have obscured what has really happened. We cannot correct these deep weaknesses by bringing a little pressure to bear here, and offering a few incentives there, within a basically unchanged market economy. If we are serious about restoring full employment we shall have to be ready to make some significant changes in the structure of the economy and shift the balance of power towards working people and their families for whom useful work and good services are essential.

The Glyn pamphlet spells out those 'significant changes' in some detail: extensive and effective exchange controls, the public ownership of financial institutions, price controls to stop inflation, direct planning of foreign trade, redistribution of wealth and income, and the full involvement of the labour movement in the planning of industrial investment through the extension into key areas of manufacturing industry of compulsory planning agreements and public ownership.

However, radicalism comes in different shades: not just red but also green. The ecology approach is equally radical, but totally different. The Greens are as concerned as all the others to create jobs, to alleviate poverty, and to improve the quality of life. But in complete contradiction to traditional socialism, they do not see highly centralised planned industrial development as the way forward. They are concerned to find 'jobs that last', to find a strategy for permanent employment which operates within, and is sensitive to, the looming ecological limits on world resources. Those limits, in their view, are already escalating raw material and energy prices, and so precluding the old 'economic growth' route to jobs. Instead, jobs to last will have to be found within the limits set by natural resources and human nature: and that means jobs created from the bottom up, outside the formal economy as well as within it, in small businesses as well as in large ones, in cooperatives as well as through job-sharing, and with a much higher level of self-sufficiency in the society as a whole. The road to full employment, according to the Greens, lies through 'community-based self-reliance: local production for local needs'. Extracts from a major Ecology Party pamphlet are also reproduced here, for your consideration.

6. Conditions for Full Employment*

Sir Keith Joseph

Present attitudes to unemployment stem from the 1930s, when the conditions of the unemployed were very different.

The 1930s were improving years for most of the people, but miserable years for a large, though falling, minority—the unemployed. As a result unemployment became the nightmare of the collective conscience between the Wars.

The determination, understandable and right, never to allow the recurrence of such miseries, dominated the postwar priorities of the wartime Coalition government.

It was thought that the way to abolish unemployment was known: maintain high and stable levels of aggregate demand: iron out regional disparities, while speeding up structural change. Such policies would, simultaneously, ensure high growth and smooth out cyclical crises. What more could be wished?

The Coalition's commitment was not to 'full' employment but to a 'high and stable level of employment', and even this was made conditional upon economic sense and good management. However, the pledge was translated into one of full employment and Beveridge's Report, 'Full Employment in a Free Society', though also full of sensible caveats, reinforced expectations.

For nearly a generation there was full, indeed overfull, employment—overfull in that there was a nearly continuous shortage of labour because demand was mostly kept artificially high. These were years of declining British competitiveness and discouragement to enterprise and effort, of an expanding state sector and a shrinking, increasingly regulated private sector. We did not manage, as Germany and Japan did, to combine full employment with competitiveness and negligible inflation.

* Reproduced from *Conditions for Full Employment* (London: Centre for Policy Studies, 1978).

The instrument used since the war to achieve full employment has been demand management—i.e. maintaining total spending at a level to provide work for all, regardless of the real supply and demand for labour and of wages and output. The conviction that this was sensible is no longer so widespread.

Some economists had continually warned that neo-Keynesian demand management—not a product of Keynes himself—was inherently inflationary. And world conditions made things more difficult. Increasingly severe peaks of inflation were succeeded by increasingly higher unemployment.

In 1976–77, the Labour government belatedly recognised it could not reflate the economy when inflation was raging, and because the IMF would not have extended our credit if it had. Labour jettisoned the neo-Keynesian 'solution'. Full employment policy was quietly killed off.

Expressing the new orthodoxy in a passage reminiscent of Milton Friedman, Mr Callaghan told the TUC in 1976: 'We used to think you could just spend your way out of a recession and increase employment by cutting taxes and boosting government spending. I tell you, in all candour, that the option no longer exists, and that insofar as it ever did exist, it only worked by injecting bigger doses of inflation into the economy followed by higher levels of unemployment as the next step. That is the history of the past twenty years'. . . .

But neither Mr Callaghan nor the Labour government has any inkling of the conditions necessary to restore full employment. Mr Callaghan has frankly admitted: 'We need more jobs, but I don't know the answer'. He won't find it in socialism.

The Labour Party, born as the political wing of organised labour, claiming to protect the working man from the uncertainties of economic life, is intellectually bankrupt on employment. It has only subsidies and make-work schemes to offer and these, it frankly admits, are merely palliatives.

I am not suggesting that the high unemployment since 1974 could have been altogether avoided. To a significant extent, it is an inevitable side-effect—partly of world conditions, mainly of inflation and of restraining money supply in order to master inflation.

The increased monetary demand which leads to inflation causes unsustainable growth of most sectors of the economy. As a result, there are more jobs. But the jobs created last only as long as the monetary stimulus is maintained and accelerated, and the monetary stimulus cannot be maintained without intensifying inflation. So the monetary stimulus has to be dispersed by decelerating the growth of money supply. As this occurs, malinvestment made under the hallucination of easy money becomes apparent—branch factories, opened during booms in the regions, are particularly vulnerable—and resources are re-adjusted according to the underlying conditions of supply and demand.

This painful but unavoidable process constitutes the depression. But the process embodies a recuperative element: the labour and resources shed by some industries are reallocated to expanding industries, to infant businesses and to new economic growth—provided they are not obstructed.

But this unemployment has certainly been worse and will continue higher than need be because of widespread ignorance of, and refusal to face, the realities that lie behind jobs and growth.

Full employment and rising living standards are not isolated phenomena. They are functions of the economy and of society as a whole. Growth and full employment, like happiness, are by-products. If pursued directly as prime objectives, they elude capture. Full employment—or nearly full—and rising living standards will provide themselves, if we let them. The market economy with safety-nets has a stronger propensity towards full employment at high and rising living standards than an economy where government decisions constantly replace market decisions.

But a market economy means complexity of human relationships, adapting to change: it is flexibility, spontaneous, endless adaptation and innovation that reconcile the two great forces, demand and supply, to yield constantly rising living standards. Repress the adaptation and you diminish the degree to which demand calls forth supply, and supply generates demand—restricting in the process the fullness of employment and the standard of living alike. Full employment and rising living standards are by-products of adaptability.

And it is futile to suppose that change can be resisted in a Britain which trades with the world. If change is not allowed to take place by degrees, it will force itself by convulsion.

Every human being is a consumer: most are also producers, of services as well as goods—or potential or former producers. The consumers vary in number, tastes and effective demand. There are more consumers than producers. As the capacity to produce increases, so does the scope for consumption. Since God sends with every pair of hands a mouth and a whole range of actual and potential appetites, including voluntary leisure, the population as consumers will keep occupied the population as producers provided, of course, that the financial system is so managed as to allow this to happen.

The reverse is *not* true; producers will not satisfy consumers by producing the same pattern of goods and services. Consumers change their demands because of changing income, fashion, awareness, taste, invention, innovation, advertising, and cannot be prevented from changing except by the coercion practised in socialist societies.

The trading sector of our economy has a double function. It has to trade effectively enough at home and abroad to buy the raw materials, as well as the goods and services that we need and want from abroad.

But it is also the profit-making part of the trading sector which provides the source of most of the taxes for government services. So jobs in the government sector, as well as jobs in the private, depend on the profitability and competitiveness of private enterprise. Overload the private sector by placing a top-heavy government sector on its back and the long-term job prospects in both will dwindle. We shall not have better hospital services, for instance, if we ignore this relationship.

Conversely, the more profitably competitive the trading sector, the more jobs it will provide in a growing number of firms—and the more government sector jobs we can afford.

The danger lies in treating either sector as if its function was to employ rather than to satisfy customers at home and abroad. Paradoxically, in so far as we focus on people as workers rather than as consumers, we shall destroy jobs, because consumers, here and abroad, will buy from more competitive sources overseas. If we focus on consumers—both at home and abroad—then jobs will multiply.

Profits are essential to jobs and prosperity. Profit means that costs are covered, including replacing capital, with something over to reward the risk-takers, the investors. The risk-takers, the investors, now are increasingly the wage and salary-earners who, between them, own the pension funds.

Without profit, firms and jobs either vanish or are kept going by subsidies from more efficient firms—subsidies that could have been used to reduce taxes or to provide government services.

Against this background we can consider employment and unemployment. The more profitably competitive is our trading base, the better-paid our people will be, the more desired government services we can afford and the nearer to full employment we shall get.

Profitable competitiveness depends on what is provided, how it is provided, and price.

The market creates the framework: but it is people who act within it. The endless adaptation of production to consumption, of supply to demand, is not achieved automatically. Resources do not allocate themselves: they have to be organised by people, above all by the entrepreneur—the individual, self-employed or in small, medium or large business, who perceives wants and organises to meet them—

labour, land, machinery, money, materials, etc. Without the entrepreneur demand and supply remain unrelated.

Entrepreneurship is a skill, a talent—and a great leveller. Not
everyone has it. Some managers are entrepreneurial. Some business
heads are not. Entrepreneurs are not heroes. They are no better than
anyone else. But they are indispensable.

In socialist countries it has to be exercised by politicians or bureau-
crats who are usually inefficient or corrupt or both.

Yet there is in Britain hostility to enterprise and the entrepreneur. His
role and function are scarcely understood. He is viciously taxed on
earnings and capital: discouraged by regulations and controls: hampered
by legislation and bureaucracy: may be obstructed by union Luddism:
and is crowded out by government spending, which uses the money that
the private sector needs for expansion.

Some of the damage has been by a deliberate attack upon the making
of wealth: some by well-meant but naive efforts to eliminate imperfections. The combination of government overspending, overtaxing, over-
borrowing and over-regulating destroys jobs. Socialists, dedicated to full
employment, have been busily discouraging the enterprise and adaptability on which it rests.

The results are stark. Medium-sized and small firms have, in some
cases, been discouraged from expanding. What is left after severe
inflation on top of heavy income and capital taxation is not enough to
reward the risk. Some entrepreneurs carry on: some refuse opportunities: some opt out: some emigrate to where the role of the wealth-
creator is still understood and rewarded.

The entrepreneur's motivation matters. So does the motivation of
people in the labour market which brings together the supply of and
demand for skills.

We must try to understand how it works; and remove obstacles in a
way that will cause least disruption and hardship. But in Britain it has
become customary to look to government and to its agencies as a source
and guarantor of employment. And politicians do not often confess how
limited are their powers.

The labour market is preferable to the alternative—clumsy, coercive
state direction.

Yet that is the trend with endless series of pay policies, norms and
'guidelines', with government encouraging the unions to coerce the
workforce, with government directly employing a third of the labour
force, with ministers brandishing planning agreements and industrial
'strategies'. We are moving away from a spontaneous self-adjusting
market and towards a corporate state in which people are allocated jobs
by political, bureaucratic or trade union elites.

And when things go wrong as a result of interventions, the failures are used as the pretext for yet further intervention.

That way does not lead to full employment in a free society: but a labour market, given favourable conditions—including an adequate, but not excessive growth in money supply—inclines naturally towards equilibrium between the supply of and the demand for labour, via the balancing factor of flexible wage rates, while maximising choice for employer and employee. The process *tends*—though there will always be some rigidities and distortions to mar the ideal—to provide about as many jobs as there are people wanting jobs. It is a process of endless change and adaptation, an integral part of a wider process which we call the market economy, involving a web of human relations more complex, more sophisticated and more sensitive than anything achieved by the most conscientious economic planners.

We have seen how the market adjusts itself to a jump in the supply of labour. Since the war, several million working wives—as well as many immigrants—were absorbed into jobs without action by government, without most people even being aware.

The buoyancy and effectiveness of the labour market depend crucially on human adaptability to change. Economic problems cannot be solved by politicians without adaptability by individuals. In a competitive world changes in the pattern of our industry and services are bound to come. What counts is the quality of our response: the responses of workers, of managers, and entrepreneurs. Preparedness to meet change—by new skills, different hours, moving house, new responsibilities, new jobs, revising plans and ambitions, perhaps starting a business—is essential if we are to reach higher employment and raise living standards.

If a labour market is to maximise jobs, wage negotiators must be free to determine pay on the twin bases of the supply of and the demand for skills and effort on the one hand, and of the demand for and profitability of the goods and services they produce on the other.

Serious discussion of employment and unemployment is meaningless without considering profitability and unit labour costs and the gap between the net rewards for working and for not working. These factors dominate the decisions of the employer considering whether to recruit and the employee whether to be recruited.

Flexibility in wage negotiations enables realistic and responsible negotiators to establish a wage rate for a particular skill or contribution.

Wage flexibility is the ally of full employment. If unions push wages too high, demand for labour will be reduced because customers won't buy. Similarly, wages which are too low—perhaps as a result of incomes policy or taxes—will fail to attract sufficient labour.

In those parts of the economy where there is labour shortage, wages are too low or the gap between net wages and net benefits is too low. In other parts, wages relative to output per man are remorselessly pricing people out of jobs.

It is in the interests of everyone to allow the supply of and demand for skills or effort to be reflected in the price of labour. Workers can price themselves—or be priced by their negotiators—into as well as out of work. . . . Some shopfloor negotiators implicitly recognise this truth by not pushing to implement large national wage settlements in full because they know that the consequences would be unemployment for some of their members.

Some economists say wages are not flexible because unions won't allow downward adjustments. This argument is specious. Unions can prevent a downward adjustment in *money* terms—at a cost in jobs—but cannot prevent a downward adjustment in real terms, caused by taxation and/or inflation.

The key factor for employers is unit labour cost, a compound of pay and productivity. Productivity is as important as pay: both enter into unit labour costs. We must, therefore, encourage enterprise and adaptability if we are to approach full employment. Alas, we are far from doing so.

Inflation, high government spending and borrowing; high personal taxation on income and capital; price, pay, dividend, rent controls; untaxed benefits; non-productive jobs with attractive perks: over-regulations: Luddism; all cumulatively suppress enterprise and adaptability.

Council housing policy and government destruction of private rented housing discourage mobility. Effective minimum wage norms under the Equal Opportunities and Employment Protection Acts price some least skilled and least qualified workers—the very workers meant to benefit—out of work. Price controls squeeze out jobs and add a further hazard to investment and expansion. Regulations and their bureaucracies constantly harass and divert management.

These impediments to an efficient labour market help determine the rate of unemployment, which reflects the balance of the factors encouraging and discouraging the creation and the filling of jobs. Taken together, they raise unemployment far beyond what it would otherwise be. . . .

There is damage to living standards and jobs not only from our tendency to scorn entrepreneurs and discourage adaptability, enterprise and effort but also by lack of cooperation between some managements and the shopfloor.

Economic progress has come by using profit to increase investment, thus raising the output of labour, reducing costs and raising earnings. This beneficent process, opening up markets and creating more jobs than it eliminates, depends upon cooperation between management and workforce.

It is management's task to win cooperation from the workforce by convincing them of the facts of economic life. The larger the unit, the stiffer the task of management. Management's task has been made hard by socialist and trade union mythology . . . it is made harder every time militancy has won and/or governments have rescued economic suicides. Some managements have succeeded. Some have, perhaps, not tried or tried ineffectively. Much management has been shell-shocked by the shift of power—without responsibility—to the shopfloor and their own deteriorating economic condition.

While some trade unions and some shop stewards cooperate admirably with management, others do not. Some, particularly in the nationalised industries, have challenged, as with Sunday post, the prerogative of management to manage. Most firms contain no dramas but manifest a pervasive low level of productivity.

Management quality may vary from the outstanding to the bad, but it is still true that the shopfloor can, and often does, block efforts to increase productivity.

Some unions have used their strength to squeeze profits and to impose overmanning via restrictive labour practices, thus both reducing the investment that would otherwise have taken place and keeping real pay lower, costs higher and, therefore, markets smaller and jobs fewer than they would otherwise have been.

Overmanning is not always or only on the shopfloor. It permeates much clerical and administrative work. Overmanning and restrictive labour practices are neither capitalist nor socialist. They are especially widespread and bad in Britain. They *appear* to be in the interests of those in employment, yet by raising unit labour costs, thus blunting our competitiveness, and reducing profit, they reduce both the number of jobs and their pay. Overmanning is wrongly perceived as a net augmenter of jobs when it is, in fact, a net destroyer of jobs.

The charge is not that some trades unions and shop stewards seek the interest of their members: that is their function. Some unions and some shop stewards—perhaps, in some cases, where management has not tried to convince them of the consequences but also in some cases where they have—seek their members' interests in so unenlightened a way as to damage the interest of their members and the whole country.

Trade unions can improve the lot of limited groups or individuals for limited periods, but the general effect of what I have described is to depress living standards and to reduce employment, compared to what they could otherwise be. Can trades union officials and shop stewards—or managements—be happy that we are now almost the least productive and the lowest paid of industrial nations—and that by being less competitive, we generate fewer jobs? . . .

In this vacuum five evasions of the right policies are canvassed in the Labour Party: the industrial strategy, job creation, work-sharing, protection, socialism.

The industrial strategy depends upon the government identifying 'winners' and backing them with the public's money. It is flawed because group pressures force government to back losers rather than winners. Moreover, government cannot identify winners in advance. Anyway, winners do not need taxpayers' money—and losers waste it.

The second evasion, job-creation, is based on a fundamental misunderstanding. Work is the creation of value by service to the consumer. Once the concept of a job is divorced from its social function of creating value by satisfying wants, a job is transformed from a factor of production into an article of consumption—something to be given for the recipient's benefit and given at the expense of others. In consequence, the whole economic nexus on which full employment and rising living standards depend is distorted and disrupted.

The use of emotive terms clouds the issue. Those who shout most about the 'right to work' are silent over the concomitant duty to work productively and cooperatively.

Productivity in the service of the customer—measured by the customer's readiness to buy the product at a profit—is the basis of employment; those who undermine it, destroy employment.

This truth is not always understood, so government spending on job-rescue and job-creation may sound plausible. Some jobs not justified in the service of the customer can be sustained for a time by subsidies. But subsidies do not come out of thin air! They can be created only by yet more taxing, borrowing and/or printing money at the expense of others, reducing buying power and, therefore, jobs elsewhere.

The whole process of make-work, job-rescue, job-creation destroys jobs. Whitehall admits one job destroyed for every two jobs created: I argue that it is at least one for one. You cannot save the job of Peter without sacking Paul. True, Peter is visible and identified—and has a vote. Paul is invisible and unidentified because no one knows which job will be destroyed by the extra taxing, borrowing, printing or which orders lost in unsubsidised competitors. But Paul is real. His job is destroyed so that Peter's job can be saved. We need a statue to the 'unknown unemployed' whose job is destroyed by government job-creation.

Job-saving and job-creation are described . . . as 'palliatives'. But they are worse than that. They not only destroy as many jobs as they claim to rescue. They teach the wrong lesson—that jobs come from government and not from consumers. They worsen our bane—overmanning—they back losers at the expense of winners.

The third fashionable evasion is work-sharing. If wages were to be reduced proportionately, unit labour costs would remain unchanged, and some extra workers could be employed. But those who propose shorter hours do not intend wages to be cut proportionately. They insist on raising unit labour costs. Yet to increase unit labour costs would not only not lead to more people being employed but price some workers elsewhere out of jobs and add to the number of unemployed.

The fourth evasion increasingly paraded is protection. We must build up our competitiveness, it is said, behind a tariff wall. But who will become more competitive if protected from fair competition? And will other countries permit us to protect without retaliation? (Dumping is not fair competition.)

No, attempts to preserve overmanned British business with government subsidies behind a tariff wall will produce a sluggish and ossified economy with bleak prospects for jobs, and a less and less free society, since that is how a siege society is.

A small minority hanker after full-blooded socialism. The assertion is that there is no unemployment in socialist societies. Nor is there unemployment in a prison. The Russians pay their unemployment benefit on the job: and they have police control of movement. Any society that adopts these techniques can control its visible unemployment. But you cannot achieve the Russian answer without the Russian methods.

Another small minority hanker after half-blooded socialism, with yet more nationalisation plus planning agreements with any large firms left in the private sector. There would then be even less notice taken of the customer—domestic or overseas. Poverty and unemployment would grow rapidly as we became less and less competitive.

One panacea and one fear we can dismiss. The panacea is that more investment is *all* we need. Investment is a by-product of serving the consumer. If profitable competitiveness can be expected from it, investment will occur. If, because of overmanning, restrictive labour practices, inadequate market, price control, inflation, disincentive taxation or any other combination of reasons, no reward commensurate with the risk is likely, investment will not occur.

We have invested not much less a proportion of our national income as have on average our rivals but we have much less benefit from it, partly because the shopfloor has too often insisted on overmanning.

The fear is that technical advance, which saves labour, necessarily increases unemployment. The history of the last 200 years, packed with labour-saving inventions, demonstrates the error. There is not a fixed amount of work to be done. There is a limitless demand for varying combinations of goods, services and voluntary leisure. Productivity growth increases not decreases jobs by increasing the number of people who can afford the product and by sparing resources to provide other individual wants, including voluntary leisure.

Even the imminent pervasiveness of the microprocessor should, if we adapt ourselves, enable us to reach higher living standards with less work. We may reach the four-day week or the forty-week year at rising standards of living and choice, but only if we improve our productivity enough.

How will everyone agree to what is needed to allow jobs to increase? I shall tell you how. When enough people start putting the relevant questions and making the relevant comments.

Politicians, academics, commentators, trade union officials and shop stewards who talk about unemployment should be cross-examined on the degrees to which they are ready first, to encourage job-creation by cutting marginal rates of tax at *all* levels of income and, secondly, to seek profitable competitiveness by cooperation.

Those who demand high direct taxes on potential job creators, and protect overmanning and restrictive labour practices that price existing jobs out and stop new jobs being created, should be exposed to ridicule if they complain about unemployment.

It is informed public opinion that will change attitudes so that the ignorance, shallowness and occasional humbug that sometimes parade today as compassion are replaced by understanding and constructive action.

It has become widely realised that people can price themselves, or be priced by their negotiators, out of jobs. This understanding is an advance. What is now needed is the recognition that people can price themselves, or be priced by their negotiators, into jobs too—both by moderating pay claims and by increasing productivity.

In so many ways we have encouraged a passive attitude to jobs. There is a pervasive hostility in schools, in universities and even in polytechnics, taught by some academics, and the media, to the enterprise and adaptability from which jobs and prosperity flow. Jobs are seen as flowing from the government, not from individual initiatives and effort.

This is totally to misunderstand the truth. Of course, government has a role and so do unions.

Governments can help hold the ring, provide infrastructure, maintain a stable currency, a framework of laws, implementation of law and order, provision of a safety-net, defence of property rights and all other rights involved in the economic process. Unions can help by reconciling the narrower interests of their members with the broader interests of the economy on which, in the last analysis, their members' interests depend. As we know, things have not been quite like this.

Let us not call the intentions of anyone into question, but seek the causes in failures of understanding and in the clash between particular and general interests.

Perhaps current paradoxes will stimulate greater understanding. I seek today to contribute towards it. Understanding and cooperation will produce more jobs and better jobs. Ignorance and conflict, no matter how powerful the rhetoric, will produce more unemployment and decline.

It is mad to recognise that we have high unemployment plus much concealed unemployment in overmanning and yet to discourage the job-creators who are the entrepreneurs. It is mad to allow in public debate politicians, commentators and trades union officials and shop stewards to get away with ignoring the real sources both of jobs and of rising living standards.

In no other western country, I believe, would a politician need to explain the realities set out in this talk. They would be too widely understood to need articulating. But here Labour and trade union mythology, with their emphasis on class struggle, have so indoctrinated their followers against profit, earned in competition, against cooperation with management in the service of the customer, indeed against recognition of the supremacy of the customer, against the link between productivity of earnings, against the making of wealth by the successful entrepreneurship that creates jobs, that it is hard even for those Labour politicians who would agree with all that I have said to carry through the necessary policies.

Full employment is not in the gift of governments. It should not be promised and it cannot be provided. The way to it can be explained and facilitated. Governments have their part to play in enabling it to happen. But for full employment to happen involves adaptability and cooperation by people. The first essential is understanding.

7. Employment: The Challenge for the Nation*

The Conservative Government

The great shifts in the structure of employment—the changing balance between manufacturing and other sectors, the move into non-manual jobs, the higher skills needed, the new patterns—reflect the biggest economic transformation since the first industrial revolution began two centuries ago. And the transformation is world-wide. Britain cannot opt out of it, nor stop or reverse it.

Adaptation to change is inevitable, and we are all involved. Every part of our society has its contribution to make; we cannot afford to have any group sitting back and expecting to leave the job to others—and certainly not just to government. Government cannot direct and control change, or shoulder all its burdens. The government's role, though crucial, is inescapably limited.

The government's strategy for guiding and supporting the national effort for jobs has three interlocking parts:

- First and most important is a sound and stable framework of economic and industrial policy. Sustained employment growth needs an economic setting in which enterprise can flourish and industry and commerce can compete successfully and raise output. The first priority has to be the control of inflation.
- Secondly, within the economic framework, the government is encouraging jobs in particular ways, for example by removing obstacles which hamper employers taking on workers or prevent individuals using their potential, and by helping to modernise training so that jobseekers can acquire the right skills.
- Thirdly, the government is taking direct action, as with its Community Programme, to tackle severe and deep-seated problems of unemployment for groups particularly hit by the changes in industry.

*Cmnd 9474, 1985.

... Since 1979 clear government leadership and a steady course have laid a firm foundation for lasting recovery:

in *financial and economic policy*:

- by bringing inflation under sustained control and maintaining a sound financial framework on which business planning can rely;
- by restraining public expenditure, and so not weighing down the businesses on which all jobs ultimately depend;
- by removing distortions in the tax system which weakened the incentive to work and wealth-creation, and hindered jobs;
- by lifting bureaucratic controls on pay, prices, dividends, credit and foreign exchange;

in *industrial policy*:

- by giving help and incentives to enterprise, especially in small firms;
- by supporting innovation and the exploitation of new technology;
- by reshaping regional policy, so that help to the most disadvantaged parts of Britain will give far better value for the taxpayer's money in creating jobs;
- by easing the burden of regulation and simplifying the planning system;
- by breaking up monopolies and fostering competition;
- by releasing as much business as possible out of public-sector constraints into the challenge and opportunity of a free commercial setting;

in *labour market policy*:

- by providing a surer and better balanced framework of law for responsible and constructive industrial relations;
- by removing the National Insurance Surcharge tax on jobs;
- by removing or easing impediments to taking on workers or taking up work;
- by stimulating the reform of our education and training systems to meet the needs of a competitive modern economy;
- by financing major new efforts in training for young people and adults;
- by programmes which give unemployed people not just short-term help but better chances of getting jobs afterwards;
- by modernising the information and support services for those seeking work.

New national attitudes and efforts, helped and stimulated by these policies, have begun to bring about the economic transformation we need. Despite world recession the British people have stopped the economic slide. Inflation is at its lowest levels since the 1960s. Investment is now at its highest-ever peak in real terms, and so are exports. Productivity in manufacturing has gone up by an average of $3\frac{1}{2}$ per cent a year since 1979. There was an estimated net increase in jobs of 340,000 in the year to September 1984. Self-employment—the main launch-pad of the entrepreneur—is expanding particularly fast. Our gross domestic product has grown by over 9 per cent in the past four years. And the growth can last, if together we hold firmly to the course that has made it possible.

8. Jobs—Bringing Hope*

Tory Reform Group

We back proposals from the CBI and others for increased spending on roads, housing, urban renewal, new energy sources and other crucial capital projects.

There is much worthwhile investment both public and private already being made in mines, railways, roads and industry, and more to be made. The deterioration of much of our basic infrastructure goes on apace. Reconstruction costs increase the longer it is delayed. In 1984, a NEDO Report revealed that the maintenance backlog alone would cost £2 billion for hospitals and £5 billion for public housing.

The Department of Environment's recent survey of council housing revealed that nearly £20 billion needs to be spent to bring this stock up to standard.

Economies in public as in private investment can be false. Industrial efficiency inevitably suffers. Firms raise productivity only to lose competitiveness through poor communications and infrastructure.

What kind of public housekeeping is it to spend millions on bed and breakfast accommodation for homeless families in preference to employing unemployed building workers to rescue from dereliction empty premises that can house them?

Large sums were found for the Thames barrage. Other areas also are at great risk to life and property from unsafe sea defences. Our leaking waterpipes and crumbling sewers have become legendary, but the waste and the threat to public health they represent are all too real.

This public expenditure will directly benefit industry and the argument that it risks crowding out private investment are today minimal. UK expenditure grew 5 per cent last year against 1½ per cent increase in production. Risks of public expenditure crowding out private investment no longer apply.

*Reproduced from Jim Lester and David Grayson, *Jobs—Bringing Hope* London, Tory Reform Group, 1986).

79

INFLATIONARY RISKS MINIMAL

Previous recoveries have been cut short by wage inflation: higher costs and prices, not higher output, have followed attempts to stimulate growth. Much has been learnt during the recession. There is greater realism from managers and workers. The government has had considerable success in restraining pay in the public sector—success that we believe opens a way to a new approach to job-creation. We believe it would be possible to negotiate, in advance, reasonable and binding wage agreements for specific essential and job creating public investment projects, and that this would carry far less risk of wage inflation than would follow from expansion of consumer demand in the private sector, where wage increases are already running well ahead of inflation.

The inflationary dangers would be even less with the type of strategy we are proposing. Extra spending on our cities, more emphasis on health care, on jobs for the long-term unemployed, imply additional demand just where there is currently greatest slack. With high unemployment in the construction industry, higher demand there would lead to higher output and higher employment, not faster inflation.

There are risks in the stimulation of demand, particularly when the economy starts approaching full employment. But we are a long way from that position at the moment. With a large amount of slack in the economy—capital as well as labour—the chances of an upsurge in inflation generated on the fiscal side are remote.

Public sector borrowing on a limited scale and for specific investment purposes is, we believe, entirely justified. No successful company finances investment out of current income for very long.

Most comparable countries have far higher public borrowing than we have—without high inflation and without interest rates at our levels. The pressure on rates from, say, an additional £2 billion of public borrowing would in any case be small in comparison to the pressures from oil prices and the attraction of the dollar.

Nor need we worry that borrowing more will increase inflation through its effect on public sector debt. The national debt is already down to half of the level of 20 years ago, and is still set to fall relative to national income. Even keeping it constant at today's levels would allow an increase in public borrowing; and in a recession it is right that the ratio should rise as tax receipts fall and benefit payments to the unemployed increase.

The PSBR can be increased without prejudicing confidence in the government's economic strategy.

SPENDING VERSUS TAX CUTS

A £1 billion increase in capital investment is estimated to create 165,000 new jobs, whereas the same amount of money spent on tax cuts would result in the creation of only 30,000 new jobs in the same financial year. Investment in public expenditure for the benefit of the community as a whole—for example, on construction and other public works—provides jobs for those who are now unemployed. Those people will tend to spend their new income on goods produced in this country, whereas people already on higher wages will tend to spend more on imports: i.e. the import content of extra capital investment is much smaller than that resulting from tax cuts. It makes no sense to tell the unemployed that they need the incentive of tax reductions for those in work. These people want jobs.

Opinion surveys suggest that even those who stand to gain from tax cuts would prefer that money to be devoted to job creation.

Specifically, therefore, in order of priority, the Chancellor should first increase spending on infrastructure, training and employment initiatives: then concentrate any tax cuts on the lowest paid and on employers' contributions. These should be higher priorities than over-indexation of thresholds or reductions in the standard rate of income tax.

EUROPEAN COOPERATION TO TACKLE UNEMPLOYMENT

Neither the causes nor the solutions to Britain's unemployment are to be found just in Britain. Across the European Community, unemployment in the twelve member states is more than 14 million. In addition to its own national initiatives, the government has to cooperate with our European partners for a coordinated economic recovery programme.

The Conservative Members of the European Parliament have already taken the lead in the Parliament in developing the elements of such a recovery programme. The Herman Report, adopted by the Parliament in April 1984, sets out the key elements of such a programme. It is based on a major economic report by two leading European economists, Michael Albert and James Ball.

The Report points to the squeeze in the market sector in Europe during the 1970s as economic growth and business investment fell behind public and private consumption and sharply reduced Europe's ability to market new products and to create employment. The two economists commend those governments who restrained public and private consumption and emphasise that no single European government, not even the West Germans, could get their economies going alone. However it is not only possible but vitally necessary to avoid further falls in investment and employment and a progressive deterioration of the welfare sector.

This requires coordinated European action along the lines recommended by the Herman Report namely:

- *Consolidation of the internal market*
  Harmonising technical standards, abolishing intra-community frontier controls, removing restrictions on the provision of services, opening of public markets, strengthening controls over state aids.
- *Integrated capital markets*
  Abolishing restrictions on capital movements, promoting the creation of a European stock exchange through the fiscal harmonisation of transactions in transferable securities, developing new Community instruments for mobilising private savings.
- *Development of a single currency market*
  Improve economic cooperation by moving to the next stage of the EMS, developing the ECU to be a convertible currency backed by its own reserves.
- *Targeting Community financial resources to certain priority areas*
  Community priorities to include energy, transport, communications and research into the new technologies with particular reference to the needs of small and medium sized enterprises and the old industrial regions.
- *Coordination of national economic policies*
  Development of a medium term financial strategy for Europe with the following goals: cut back growth of money supply to a target compatible with inflation rates of less than 4 per cent, reduction of public sector deficits, restructuring public expenditure to favour investment over consumption, hold real wages to a level which will enable companies to increase their profits substantially, reduction of indirect wage component and increased selectivity in allocating social benefits.
- *Adaptation of labour to new working conditions*
  Encouragement at Community level of flexitime systems so that any reduction in working time does not damage company profitability and competitiveness. Increased support through the

Social Fund for vocational training so as to produce a work force whose skills are geared to the needs of modern industries.
- *Internal cooperation*
The Community to speak with a single voice in exchanges with the United States and Japan with a view to combating protectionism, securing stable exchange rates and an improved system of managing international debt. Improving relations with the developing countries through increased trade, assistance in making them self sufficient in food production.

Europe does not need a new Messina Conference as some have suggested. What is needed is the political will and dynamism to take the necessary action. . . .

TOWARDS A NATIONAL INDUSTRIAL POLICY

A more aggressive competition policy does not reduce the need for government to have a clear industrial strategy.

Since 1979, this government has actually spent more on BL, BSC and the other nationalised industries than any previous government. It appears embarrassed to have done so. Worse, it has allowed the impression to gain ground that it is not particularly concerned by the problems of British manufacturing industry. Britain's manufacturing trade has gone from a surplus of £2.5 billion in 1982 to a deficit of £3.8 billion in 1984. It is likely to deteriorate further and shows no sign of reversing.

In the decade to 1984 British manufacturing output fell by 4.3 per cent while Japan's rose by 61 per cent; America's by 42 per cent; West Germany's by 16 per cent and Italy's by 22 per cent. Uniquely among the main industrial nations, Britain has not regained its pre-recession level of manufacturing output. Between 1978 and last year, the number of manufacturing jobs in Britain fell by over 1.7 million, import penetration rose by a fifth and as much as a sixth of manufacturing capacity was scrapped and not replaced. In the past 20 years, the UK's share of world trade has been halved.

The future looks even more disturbing.

Britain is an inventive nation—according to the Japanese MITI we have produced 55 per cent of new successful inventions since the war—but continues to find itself at a competitive and technological disadvantage: invented in Britain, developed in America, made in Japan; is an all too frequent occurrence.

Why? Research and Development is under-funded.

The OECD and various academic and official organisations in Britain have produced a number of well-researched studies over the past few years on the state of R&D in the UK, Europe, Japan and the USA. According to an OECD study published in February 1983, British companies spent only half as much per employee on R&D as their major European competitors in the second half of the 1970s: we were, in fact, second from the bottom of the OECD league for R&D spending relative to output.

In consequence, many British scientists, researchers and industrialists are very concerned that intensifying competition, lack of investment and continuing skill shortages are leading to a widening of the technological gap between Britain and its international competitors. Despite the (ongoing) improvements in the field of training, there is now a real fear that Britain will enter the 1990s with many sectors of her industry based on obsolescent technology and with a largely unskilled workforce, just at the time when declining revenues from North Sea oil expose our industry to the full force of international competition.

Services will become a more important source of jobs and wealth but services alone will not fill the gap. As the Association of British Chambers of Commerce has argued:

- most service sector output is not exportable;
- to compensate for the loss of foreign earnings of a 1 per cent fall in manufacturing exports, service exports would need to increase by almost 3 per cent;
- there is a correlation between manufactured and service exports—a fifth of the service sector's output depends on custom from the manufacturing sector—so a fall in one is unlikely to be matched by a rise in the other;
- foreign competition in financial and other services is increasing. Whereas Britain's invisible trade as a percentage of world invisible trade fell from 2.3 per cent in 1979–80 to 2 per cent in 1982, America's rose from 4.7 per cent to 5.1 per cent, Japan's from 1.2 per cent to 1.4 per cent; and France's in 1980–82, from 2.3 per cent to 2.8 per cent.

The latest Bank of England quarterly survey confirms that, since 1981, the trade surplus on invisibles has fallen. And while exports of services (excluding earnings from sea transport) have grown faster than exports of manufactures, imports of services have also grown faster than imports of manufactures. 'Trade in services', the Bank warns, 'is subject to the same influences as trade in goods', and there is no reason to think that a surplus on services is an 'intrinsic feature of the UK economy'.

- Yet the Chancellor states: 'I cannot agree that there is any special cause for concern in a deficit in trade in manufactures.'
- Reluctantly we share the conclusion of the Association of British Chambers of Commerce that 'the government has very little idea of where job and wealth-creating production might arise.'

Government needs a more coherent and proactive industrial strategy recognising that:

- even though the proportion of total jobs in manufacturing will continue to decline, Britain still needs a healthy, manufacturing centre;
- the dream of a high-tech nirvana cannot be allowed to permit our manufacturing base to shrink not just in relative but in absolute terms. Hi-tech is important but balanced economic development is essential. There is no British sun belt to run to;
- profits can still be made in mature industries provided that there is investment and precise marketing segmentation;
- government can contribute to the health of industry both through creating the right economic climate and through direct catalytic action;
- Britain must become competitive internationally.

ELEMENTS OF INDUSTRIAL STRATEGY

- Cut through the restrictive bureaucracy: for example, COCOM rules forbid the sale of home computers to the Soviet Union—so Japan is about to clean up the market!
- Encourage innovation through academic entrepreneurs; entrepreneurship within large firms and by new business.
- Stimulate greater R&D through government funds directed to specific product areas. The government is to be congratulated that 29 per cent of the DTI budget now goes on R&D and technical assistance in growth sectors compared with 6 per cent in 1979. This percentage needs to be further increased: for example, why not an experiment matching public and private funds to exploit some of Britain's more interesting inventions;
- Back EC Commission plans to double EC spending on R&D for industry in cooperative, European, public/private partnerships.

- Develop management training; encourage younger company directors and more non-executive directors.
- Encourage venture capital funds for new technology products by offering government loans on easy terms to lever out private funds.
- Learn from Japanese-style trading houses around the world which are able to collect valuable market data and business intelligence and ensure this is made available to and used by British firms.
- Apply the lessons of successful market segmentation and differentiation of products by e.g. German firms in mature industries and Japanese firms' 'laser approach' to new markets.
- At least match the political support given to foreign firms bidding for international contracts. British failures to gain the Bosphorous Bridge contract, and the Thailand bus contract fiasco for British Leyland, demonstrate the need for a more positive trade and industrial policy.
- Play to our strengths—manufacturing skills, energy independence, financial services, small firms. . . .

CONCLUSION

Further action to reduce unemployment must be taken for economic, social and political considerations.

On cost grounds alone, further action is justified. Every 190,000 on the dole represents at least 1 per cent of central government expenditure in direct payments and lost revenue—leaving aside increased administration costs. Three million unemployed represents 17 per cent of government spending. This is more than any other single area. To give some perspective: it is more than housing, transport, agriculture, and law and order put together. This is before any calculation is made of the indirect costs caused by the increase in delinquency and crime and the greater pressure on health and welfare budgets.

Social justice demands action. Those in work are getting richer year by year. Those out of work are getting relatively poorer. Two nations are emerging: the employed and the unemployed; the new industrial elite and the old industrial discards. As Francis Pym wrote in his book *The Politics of Consent*, 'we are in danger of creating a large section of the population that is permanently unemployed, living in communities of terminal decay. Computers may brighten innumerable classrooms, but they do not prevent many children from regarding school as a waste of time, life as a meaningless prospect, and delinquency as the only tolerable pastime. This is not the sort of future that we want, or that they need have, but that future will become the reality unless we take action now.'

As Archbishop William Temple wrote some 50 years ago:

The worst evil of long-term unemployment . . . is that it is creating in the unemployed a sense that they have fallen out of the common life. However much of their fiscal needs may be supplied, the gravest part of the trouble remains; they are not wanted! . . . It has not been sufficiently appreciated that this moral isolation is the heaviest burden and most corrosive poison associated with unemployment: not bodily hunger but social futility . . .

To date this social futility has largely been reflected in quiescence and resigned apathy. We do not believe, however, that people will indefinitely go quietly to the wall. They will be inevitably starting to pull that wall down and use the bricks. National cohesion requires unemployment to be reduced.

Finally, there is the political dimension. As regular canvassers we have seen the marked change in voter attitudes over the past years. In the 1983 General Election, our message that unemployment was an inevitable result of changes in the world economy was broadly accepted. This is no longer so. The mood has changed. Now we are being blamed—not so much for unemployment, but for not doing enough to tackle it and for not caring about its consequences. In contrast, the good doctor claims to be tough and tender.

Bedwelty Man claims to have discovered on the road to Sparkbrook that Britain needs a high-profit economy. The superficial appeal of the Alliance to worried southern voters coupled with Labour's temporary rediscovery of moderation makes it all the more important for Conservatives to address the political dimensions of unemployment.

These feelings will intensify and put a third term for the government at risk. That would be disastrous for the country—it would jeopardise the positive achievements of the Thatcher administration to date—and it would leave the job started in 1979 only partially completed. For all these reasons, we urge the Prime Minister and the government to adopt the practical proposals in this pamphlet, which are designed for the next election and well beyond. By doing so they will be bringing hope and new jobs and above all hope to the unemployed.

SUMMARY OF MAIN RECOMMENDATIONS

1. The government must lead a national debate on the causes, numbers, trends and solutions to unemployment, and on the future patterns of work.

2. A coordinated series of measures to fight unemployment is essential.

3. A special Cabinet committee should be established to coordinate the initiatives of different government departments to generate jobs.

4. A modest increase in the Public Sector Borrowing Requirement is justified since the inflationary risks would be minimal.

5. Any funds available to the Chancellor in the Budget should be targeted on public spending and raising tax thresholds for the lowest paid rather than for cuts in the standard rate of income tax.

6. CBI proposals to increase spending on infrastructure should be backed.

7. In total we propose initial government spending of £2 billion per annum.

8. Further funds for housing improvements and urban renewal generally should be targeted in the areas of high unemployment and for those on the lowest incomes. Tax incentives should be used to encourage public and private partnerships in infrastructure projects.

9. European cooperation is essential to tackle unemployment in particular.

10. The European internal market must be completed urgently.

11. Further European cooperation is needed on major transport infrastructure projects and in research and development of high technology projects.

12. Britain should join the European Monetary System.

13. Competition within Britain should be encouraged through further deregulation of areas such as transport, electronic and telecommunications industries. More public sector services should be opened up to private tender.

14. A national industrial strategy is needed, with specific goals to encourage innovation, develop management training and improve the marketing of British products.

15. All the separate adult training schemes should be presented as one major skills improvement programme (SKIP).

16. The current review 'Lifting the burdens' should be used to exempt more small firms from VAT, wage and employment legislation.

17. Pilot schemes to increase marketing assistance and venture capital funds for small firms are required.

18. Benefits should be made more flexible to reflect the greater variety of work patterns in the future.

19. Job-splitting and part-time retirement schemes should be extended.

20. Further government funding is needed for the Community Programme and for local employment initiatives, combined with more flexible rules for the operation of these schemes, to help those worst hit from the changes taking place in the economy.

9. Jobs and Competitiveness*

The SDP/Liberal Alliance

Our short-term boost to the economy would include four main measures:

1. We would double the size of the Community Programme for the long-term unemployed by increasing it to 460,000 places, as a move towards a jobs guarantee for the long-term unemployed. We would give priority to helping the long-term jobless in our training programme and in our plans to expand capital spending.

2. The cost of employing labour would be cut by a 10 per cent reduction in all levels of employers' National Insurance contributions. Unlike last year's Budget changes which greatly increased the cost of employing skilled staff by abolishing the upper earnings limit, this would help companies to compete. It would also assist exports and encourage firms to take on more labour.

3. Special help would be given to those worst hit by mass unemployment and to working families in poverty. This would include extending the long-term rate of supplementary benefit to the adult unemployed under 60 and continuing this under the income support provisions of the Social Security Bill. This would help single people by an extra £8.10 per week and married couples by an extra £12.25 per week. To help working families in poverty, there would be an immediate increase in the Family Income Supplement programme, and additional family support as a step towards an integrated tax and benefit system. We would increase the real value of child benefit and restore the deplorable cut in the heating allowance for pensioners.

4. An urgent programme to expand education and training would be designed to tackle skill shortages in engineering and electronics, and to move towards a full vocational education and training programme for 16–19 year olds.

*Reproduced from *SDP/Liberal Alliance Budget Priorities*, 1986.

Table 9.1: Summary of measures to increase employment

	Gross cost (£ billion) full year
1. Doubling Community Programme to 460,000 places	1.0
2. 10% cut in all rates of NICs	1.2
3. Special help to those in need	
Long-term supplementary benefit to long-term unemployed	0.5
Family support	0.2
Child benefit up-rate	0.2
Help for pensioners	0.1
4. Programme for skills	0.3
5. Capital spending on infrastructure	2.0
Total Gross Cost (first full year)	5.5
PSBR cost (first full year)	3.5

EUROPEAN MONETARY SYSTEM

Our expansion plans can only work if we are determined to control inflation. Full membership of the EMS would make this clear. The Alliance believes that Britain should enter the exchange rate mechanism now, at a competitive exchange rate. This will give the stability which our exporters need. Entry to the EMS is not a soft option. It is a clear signal to the international markets that we intend to pursue a firm monetary policy.

With the pound at a record low against the Deutschmark, we can negotiate a rate at which we can join, and hold sterling within the narrow divergence limits of the EMS. We need not fear pricing our exports out of European markets.

Only Mrs Thatcher's antipathy to Europe now stands in the way of our participation in the EMS. The CBI, the Governor of the Bank of England, the European Commission, the Chairman of the Bundesbank and even, we are told, the Chancellor of the Exchequer and the Foreign Secretary, support our entry.

Full membership would help to develop the ecu, the unit of currency used by the European reserve mechanism of the EMS, as a major trading and reserve asset. It could be part of a tripod of greater international monetary stability, including the dollar and the yen, leading to the establishment of 'target zones' for leading currencies. Membership of the EMS would be vital in achieving policies of co-ordinated expansion with our European and international partners.

JOBS AND PAY

A successful incomes strategy is critical to a sustained increase in employment. The prospects for higher employment would be undermined by earnings growing faster than productivity.

There is no crude trade-off between low pay and new jobs. Cutting the pay of those already on low incomes is unlikely to have more than a marginal benefit for employment. It would result in the substitution of some employees for others while doing nothing to upgrade the skills or productivity of the workforce.

But the benefits which could be achieved by moderating earnings growth and relating it much more to productivity, in order to channel expansion into higher employment, would be considerable. Even now, with unemployment well above 3 million, pay pressures in the private sector are still outstripping gains in productivity. As a result, unit costs are rising much faster than among our major competitors.

Nor can the blame for high settlements be laid exclusively at the door of trade union pay demands. Firms where there is no trade union representation are paying increases which are just as high. There is plenty of evidence that employers are ignoring the CBI campaign and rewarding their existing employees without regard to competitive pressures.

A new policy of expanding economic activity and employment would help companies exploit new markets and develop new products. Our incomes strategy would seek to prevent pay pressures seeping through into inflation. But it would also be aimed at giving firms an incentive to reduce labour costs and maintain competitiveness. It would ensure real improvements in pay from greater economic activity, rather than at the expense of the unemployed.

Our incomes strategy would seek first to change the climate of voluntary pay bargaining to achieve greater market realism. If this can be achieved and settlements brought down, then statutory powers would be unnecessary. It would, however, be wrong to count on such an outcome.

INCOMES STRATEGY

In present circumstances, our strategy would be as follows. We would seek to change the climate of voluntary pay bargaining.

First, a *payroll incentive*—through a rebate on employers' National Insurance contributions—could be given to companies which awarded pay increases below the inflation limit. This would be linked to longer-term pay settlements, over a period of at least two years, which would bring about greater bargaining stability and reduced inflationary expectations. As part of this incentive, companies would be able to offer their employees benefits in the form of share options which, if they retained them, would attract tax concessions.

The payroll incentive would, therefore, help companies which sought to contain unit costs. It would also encourage them to achieve a better balance between improved earnings and higher employment. This would be a transitional measure to encourage firms to move towards longer-term reforms in their pay bargaining, involving new forms of arbitration and a higher profit-sharing element within total earnings. It would help widen employee share ownership in a way which would promote much greater awareness among employees of the potential of improving competitiveness and expanding markets.

Second, if companies failed to take advantage of these new incentives and continued to award inflationary increases, the stand-by mechanism of an *inflation tax* would be used. The tax penalty would only cover increases in average earnings in excess of the declared inflation limit. But it would not seek to penalise success. Companies who genuinely sought to share profits with their employees through registered profit-sharing schemes or approved share ownership schemes would be exempt from the tax. This would apply only to companies with over 100 employees, just under 20,000 companies encompassing three-quarters of the total workforce. Since small businesses and new firms would be outside the scope of the tax, most of the fastest growing high technology and service firms would not be affected.

THE PUBLIC SECTOR

Moderating pay pressure in the private sector will help to lower claims among groups in the public sector. The gap between them has steadily widened in the last five years. This is increasingly likely to cause discontent and disputes. A quarter of the workforce and half the trade unionists in the country still work in the public sector. Some groups like the police, the armed forces and the nurses are covered by one-off pay reviews or review bodies. This had nurtured the feelings of resentment among those who have been excluded from such arrangements. They deserve greater justice.

We therefore propose a new system of comparability for the public services as a whole. A single and independent Pay Information Unit covering the whole of the public services would develop comparisons with jobs outside. This material would be made available to negotiators, but would not be binding on unions or government. A yearly efficiency audit of the public services would be undertaken by the new body, to secure accurate comparisons between productivity in public and private industry. Greater synchronisation of pay dates would help to prevent pace-setting settlements and allow for a more rational determination of comparisons. A system of pendulum arbitration linked to no-strike agreements could be established in key public services.

In the longer term, we would introduce more widespread arbitration in pay determination in the context of more decentralised pay negotiations. This would avoid the rigidity which characterised previous pay policies. Building on our payroll incentive proposal, much greater support would be given to profit-sharing schemes for the whole workforce.

JOBS AND INVESTMENT

This government has substituted narrow housekeeping economics for investing in the future. The fabric of our buildings and infrastructure has been rapidly run down. Higher living standards for those in work have been bought in a short-term consumer boom at the cost of a flood of manufactured imports. The Department of Trade's own survey has predicted a fall in industrial investment in 1986.

Public sector investment has been especially hard hit. The government's spending plans show that it will fall in real terms by a further $12\frac{1}{2}$ per cent or £$2\frac{1}{2}$ billion, over the next three years.

But this trend was established before the present government came to power. In 1970 when Roy Jenkins was Chancellor of the Exchequer, we spent 7 per cent of our national product on public investment. Today the figure has slumped to 2 per cent.

In every year from 1970 to 1983, the UK has spent less of its resources on construction than our major industrial competitors. In 1980, UK expenditure per head on construction was only 33 per cent of

Japan's, 33 per cent of West Germany's, 37 per cent of France's and 51 per cent of that of Italy.

The toll in poor housing, crumbling sewers, run-down hospitals and school buildings, deteriorating roads and dirty and out-dated railway rolling stock and stations, is now immense. There are many areas where new capital spending is urgent and would create thousands of new jobs.

CAPITAL SPENDING

The Alliance would take early action to restore the share of capital spending to the level when this government came to power. This would require a boost of around £2 billion. This initial increase would be concentrated on housebuilding, house renovation, insulation, road building, maintenance and lighting.

In the medium term, we propose a steady build-up of spending on these programmes. This would include tackling the major backlog of housing repairs and maintenance, and building and renovating homes to meet the substantial requirement for accommodation; renewing out-dated NHS hospitals; rebuilding dilapidated sewers and undertaking essential road construction schemes. Extending the planning horizon for capital spending plans to at least three years would avoid the damaging stop–go which has characterised this government's policies.

Our plans would bring the private and the public sectors together in partnership, through local enterprise trusts and agencies. As the Alliance Worksearch campaign has demonstrated, it is crucial to link new capital spending to micro-employment initiatives, locally and regionally.

Industrial competitiveness, labour mobility and more flexible patterns of work all depend critically on providing a modern housing and capital infrastructure. But on its own, such an expansion of capital spending cannot restore Britain's competitive position. Our future depends upon the goods we sell in world markets.

JOBS AND COMPETITIVENESS

The central question here is how we can stimulate industry to become more competitive. Industry has paid a heavy price for the absence of a coherent industrial strategy. The first and overriding goal must be to achieve strong and sustained growth for industrial exports. Greater industrial competitiveness too, is the only reliable foundation for sustained growth and increased employment. This can be achieved most effectively with greater European industrial cooperation.

The increasing deterioration in our international competitive position is the fundamental cause of our relative economic decline. The House of Lords Select Committee's Report on Overseas Trade makes it clear that this decline is extremely serious. The UK's share of world manufactured exports fell from 9.7 per cent in 1980 to 7.9 per cent in 1985.

The Lords' Report shows that there was a massive collapse of £12 billion between 1978 and 1984 in our balance of trade in manufactures. This was especially acute in the automotive industry, electronics, textiles, and food and drink. Last year's deficit of £3.2 billion is only just below the level of 1984, at £3.9 billion, itself the worst since the Industrial Revolution.

THE MANUFACTURING DEFICIT

The government has often claimed that we should not worry about the manufacturing trade deficit because, as North Sea oil gradually declines, the real exchange rate will fall to wipe out the deficit. The Chancellor envisaged this taking place over several years. The government's complacency has been shattered by the 40 per cent fall in the price of oil, which has halved the surplus in oil trade. This has exposed the underlying deficit in the current account much earlier than had been forecast. The deficit will be increased further by the expected decline in oil output from 1986. Government figures in the 1985 Energy Brown Book project a decline of up to £5 billion in oil export revenues, over the next four years, even before the recent oil price slump.

The harsh reality is that this rising balance of payments deficit will force the government into yet more defensive measures—such as expenditure cuts and interest rate increases—to keep the pound up and inflation down. The government has boxed itself in. Expanding the economy in these circumstances would merely worsen the current account by producing a surge in imports and a sliding exchange rate. This would set off the inflationary spiral once again, with even higher unemployment in the long term.

The UK urgently needs a higher volume of manufactured exports and services to help replace oil revenues in the trade balance. Since only 27 per cent of services can be traded, manufacturing's contribution will be vital. Our task is to improve its competitiveness. We must expand our share of export markets to win the battle against imports. This is the way to stabilise the trade balance and create jobs.

INDUSTRIAL STRATEGY

Our industrial strategy has been outlined in previous policy statements. The Cambridge econometrics model has simulated the effect of a 1 per cent improvement in competitiveness brought about by our industrial strategy. It shows that a substantial improvement in the current account could be achieved by 1988.

To meet the present challenges, the Alliance has five key priorities:

Expansion of Company Skill Training

At a time of record unemployment, there is also a widespread shortage of skilled labour. Low skill levels may well explain why, in many of our industries, there is lower productivity even in factories using the same capital equipment as our competitors. We will introduce a remissable tax system which would encourage companies to increase the level and quality of training undertaken. In addition, we would transform YTS into a comprehensive vocational and education programme for 16–19 year olds. This would bring our provision for this age group into line with standard European practice.

Increased Research and Development

The size of R&D expenditure in manufacturing financed by government and industry has fallen in real terms since 1978. Our priority would be to increase the funds allocated to industrial R&D, and to direct them at the commerical exploitation of new technology and the development of prototypes. As a target, we aim to increase our share of industrial R&D to 10 per cent of the European total by 1990, compared to 7.5 per cent in 1985. Rebuilding basic scientific research is crucial to industrial innovation and design. We propose an immediate increase of £85 million in the science budget.

Support for Exports

The government must give firm backing to UK companies competing for key projects throughout the world. They have no plans to increase the current inadequate Department of Trade and Industry allocation of £42 million. More must be spent on export services overseas trade promotion. We must give our exporters a comprehensive back-up service to assist their overseas marketing.

Finance for Investment

Industry must have the financial resources to underpin sustained growth. A well targeted industrial credit scheme—operating through the market and the banking and venture capital system—would reduce the burden of interest rates on new investment. For instance, at a cost of £100 million per annum over five years, it would be possible to release £2 billion for loans at 5 per cent below market rates. That would be of real help to companies currently paying above 12½ per cent—an all time high in real terms—on such loans. This scheme would work most effectively through new Regional Development Agencies and regional banks.

For small companies, we would expand the loan guarantee scheme by raising the maximum loan to £250,000; develop Small Firm Investment Companies (SFICs) supported by financial institutions and industrial companies; and raise the VAT threshold to £50,000. We will press for a statutory right to interest payments on unpaid commercial debts, similar to that in other European countries, which would greatly assist the cash flow position of small enterprises.

Support for Technology and Innovation

To increase the rate of new innovation, we would extend the Business Expansion Scheme to include companies, and thus encourage them to invest in new technology. First year capital depreciation allowances should be introduced for all start-up firms, including all expenditure on scientific equipment. A restructured British Technology Group would launch major new innovation programmes.

10. Planning for Full Employment*
The Labour Party

The scale of the economic problems we face is so great that reflation alone—manipulating interest rates, exchange rates and government borrowing—will not be enough. A new industrial policy is needed which will have a direct impact on investment and jobs in all parts of the country and create economic growth.

Although industries cannot be fully planned in a world market economy, it is possible to plan for the development of individual sectors and firms. We need a programme to plan key industries, sector by sector, and sometimes firm by firm, which draws on the strength of collective bargaining with trade union organisation. Cooperation between industry, unions and government at national, regional and local levels is crucial.

The Public Sector

The public sector is an important part of Britain's economy. Twenty-seven per cent of the labour force work in the public sector, producing 27 per cent of national income. Its size and influence has been under attack by the government's privatisation programme which has allowed investors to make enormous gains at the taxpayers' expense.

The main inroads into the state sector were made in the telecommunications, oil, transport and manufacturing industries. That the resources realised were given back in tax handouts is a further indictment of the government's economic and industrial policies and added proof of its concern for the finance sector at the expense of manufacturing and production.

---

* Reproduced from Labour Party, Report, chaired by John Prescott, MP (1985), pp. 15–29.

We need to rethink the role of the public sector, particularly the way we have penalised public sector industries in the past, through stringent Treasury rules on borrowing and investment which were immediately removed on privatisation.

This may require us to consider other forms of social ownership, including co-operatives which will extend accountability to the workers and to the community. . . .

Expansion of the public sector and its ownership is crucial in making industry more accountable. It has the capacity to develop good working conditions, proper rates of pay, be an innovator in industrial democracy, investment and training policies. It can use its revenue and capital base to expand in particular industries where the private sector is presently pulling out in its dash to get better returns in the financial markets. The public sector must be seen as an active engine of growth for a Labour government. Expansion of the public sector remains very much a part of Labour's programme.

How it is to be achieved, and in what order of priority is a matter for continuing debate. The sale of state assets raised over £5 billion, estimated to be £1.5 billion under priced. Well over £5 billion will be needed in compensation to purchase back privatised industries. We are committed to public spending to create jobs; our approach to renationalisation must be in the light of this priority. A greater argument could be advanced for British Telecom to be taken back into public ownership, than, say, for example, securing British Transport Hotels.

The National Strategy

The strategy for investment and production planning must be set at the national level. It will need to identify 'target' sectors and firms, the scale of public sector resources available for investment, and the broad objectives of policy. The Department of Economic and Industrial Planning and the National Planning Council would have the role of providing the planning framework, which would be implemented by the national enterprise agency and the National Investment Bank. There is also a clear need for the Party to consider a public stake in the banking sector to supplement the National Investment Bank. A Labour government, together with the trade unions also needs to tackle the power of the multinational corporations and make them more accountable to their own workers and society.

Local and regional enterprise boards can take the lead in encouraging sound investment packages and provide the vehicle for direct intervention in major industrial sectors.

REGIONAL AND LOCAL AUTHORITY ROLE

A major role will be played by local authorities and other public bodies in ensuring that the benefits of Labour's new economic policies get to those people and areas most in need. In the last few years, Labour councils have shown that in spite of formidable odds, it has been possible to preserve and create jobs, to achieve greater accountability in the decisions of individual companies, to extend industrial democracy and to improve the quality of work through better training and conditions of employment.

We must build on this experience. It is not enough to get people into jobs at any price. Industrial democracy, accountability and equal opportunities must be key elements of economic strategy.

For local authorities to play their full part, legal constraints need to be lifted. Local authorities should be able to undertake any activity not directly prohibited by statute. The present provisions of Section 137 of the Local Government Act 1972 which enable councils to spend up to a 2p rate on matters considered of general benefit to their areas, have been useful. They do not go far enough.

Evidence from councils which have been involved in job creation programmes shows that the average cost of jobs created or saved is in the range of £4000 to £6000—much lower than the cost per job through government schemes. The Greater London Enterprise Board has created or saved 3500 jobs at a cost of £3600 a job. The West Midlands Enterprise Board has created 4000 jobs at approximately £2500 a job. This is much less than the estimated £35,000 a job from the government's industrial assistance programmes, or the £6000–£7000 government cost per person on the dole. Lancashire Enterprises actually made a profit in creating jobs, as have one or two other authorities.

These figures are impressive but Labour cannot adopt a 'cheapest is best' policy; clearly some jobs subsidy schemes, particularly in high technological developments or involving a high proportion of capital, will produce jobs at a higher cost per job. These may be crucial to the rebuilding of our industrial base and the retraining of our people.

These local authority economic developments have increased accountability in tackling the economic development within their areas. Labour's *Charter for Local Enterprise* details more evidence of these exciting developments.

A NEW ROLE FOR THE TRADE UNIONS

Since 1979, the government has undermined trade unions and collective bargaining, seeing them as obstacles to their aims, and treating unions as the 'enemy within'. It is no accident that it is in the traditionally non-unionised service sector and in small firms that the government sees future jobs being created.

For planning to work, we must build on one of our collective industrial strengths—the organisation of workers in the workplace. This means repealing anti-trade union legislation introduced by this government. It also means new rights for trade unionists to have a say in company decisions, and to receive information about company policy and plans.

PLANNING PUBLIC EXPENDITURE

Public expenditure planning is a principle tool of economic generation. It ensures the direction of investment into the reconstruction of Britain's economic base.

Public expenditure of £120 billion a year, 48 per cent of the Gross Domestic Product, will play a crucial part in Labour's economic programme:

- to plan investment and production to ensure that public funds are effectively targeted at sectors and firms to increase competitiveness and productivity;
- to ensure that existing unmet economic and social needs are provided for with local authorities playing a central role;
- to make the maximum contribution to job-creation in the public and private sectors;
- to give a greater regional and local emphasis to public spending in order to reduce the growing disparities in jobs and wealth between the different parts of the United Kingdom.

It is essential that we open up the public expenditure planning process (PESC) to more democratic and public scrutiny. New accounting procedures, looking at the wider economic and spending consequences of decisions, must be subject to an open process of social audit. . . .

AN INTEGRATED TRAINING POLICY

Training is an integral part of an alternative programme. Report after report has decried British industry's appalling record on training. . . . A new training policy must be linked to the industrial planning process. Youth training and adult retraining must equip people with the skills they need to handle the new technologies, new production methods and new modes of work organisation. Groups traditionally disadvantaged in the labour market must receive special attention, particularly the long-term unemployed and ethnic minority groups.

The role of the MSC must revert to its original function; developing a national training policy and labour plan in line with national economic and industrial strategy. It will need a broader representation of views than at present. Proposals on training from sector working parties in key industries would be fed into a national training plan. Implementation of these plans at local level would be through reconstituted area MSC boards.

The TUC–Labour Party *Plan for Training*, spells out many of the policies necessary to implement a proper training programme. Accountability and the role of the agencies administering the education and training programmes require more work. . . .

The Training Strategy

Britain needs a skilled and motivated workforce in a world of technological change. We need training which can help men and women fulfill their potential as individuals. We need a training policy seen in the context of overall economic policy and an integrated strategy between industrial development and the extension of public services.

All young people should have the right to high-quality initial education and training which is assessed as a contribution to a recognised qualification.

There should be a minimum allowance for trainees linked to the cost of living and 'topped up' by collective bargaining alongside action to promote equal opportunities for young women and disadvantaged minorities.

Spending on adult training in the public and private sector should be at least equal to 2 per cent of the annual wages bill, like our competitors, with all adults having the right to participate.

There needs to be a fivefold increase in MSC work preparation and training programmes for unemployed adults, linked to industrial sector planning.

TACKLING WEALTH AND INCOME

We reject the notion that the only way to reduce unemployment is through reductions in wages in Britain's low-wage economy. The reverse is the case. Changes in personal and company taxation and a redistribution of pay of those in work by means of a statutory minimum wage policy would assist demand led growth. Labour Party Conference was right to demand an effective minimum wage policy. In the past, we have relied on collective bargaining and wages councils, but these have failed to prevent the growth in the numbers of low paid, now estimated at over eight million.

A New Partnership: A New Britain has now called for a discussion on the minimum wage.

We believe that collective bargaining should be strengthened. Trade union recognition should be a condition of contracts from the public sector. The Fair Wages Resolution, Schedule 11 of the Employment Protection Act, a strengthened Wages Inspectorate should all be given a high priority by a Labour government. However, we have to recognise that just as collective bargaining, on its own, did little to achieve equal pay for women, collective bargaining has failed, on its own, to improve the position of the low paid. Nor does collective bargaining at present deal with the problems posed by the growth of part-time and contract labour and home-working.

The Party has decided that tackling low pay should be a priority for the next Labour government and a statutory minimum wage should be introduced. We now need discussions with the trade union movement on how it will be phased in and enforced. We believe that given the recent work done in this field by Labour local authorities, there is a strong case for placing a strengthened Wages Inspectorate under local authority control, to underpin trade union bargaining and enforcement in much the same way as trading standards is a statutory duty of the county councils. The recent OECD study of the French economy pointed out that in spite of a significant increase in the national minimum wage, no increase in inflation could be attributed to this improvement of the conditions of the lowest paid.

ACTION ON EQUAL OPPORTUNITIES

Positive action programmes to assist groups traditionally disadvantaged in the labour market—women, young people, ethnic minorities, people with disabilities—are needed throughout the planning process and at every stage of public intervention.

Experience shows that general improvements in economic performance do not necessarily 'filter down' and meet the needs of these groups. Women continue to suffer discrimination in spite of much of the legislation passed by previous Labour governments. For a time following the passage of Labour's equal pay legislation, the differentials between women's and men's pay narrowed. But since 1979, the relaxation of those laws, together with a hostile employment environment, has seen those differentials widen once again.

Women earn 25 per cent less than men and are still largely segregated into a narrow range of unskilled and semi-skilled occupations. They have fewer opportunities than men for higher levels of education and training.

Women receive inadequate support for dependants—be they children, disabled or elderly people. They are further denied equal rights with men in many areas including taxation, social security, pensions, and superannuation.

It is clearly established that black people suffer particular disadvantages in the labour market. In the inner cities, black unemployment levels are scandalously high.

Special initiatives to promote equal employment opportunities levels and to assist ethnic minority businesses, launched by local authorities, are proving effective but must be greatly expanded.

The next Labour government must tackle the particular needs of women and other disadvantaged groups. We need:

- employment and recruitment monitoring;
- special schemes for women's and ethnic minority business development;
- to enforce equal opportunities policies in the civil service, nationalised industries and other public agencies;
- to open up recruitment processes, changing job advertising methods;
- to place a statutory duty on government, local authorities and public sector contractors to pursue equal opportunities policies;
- to monitor training opportunities offered by government sponsored or funded training organisations to ensure equal access to facilities;
- better childcare facilities, job sharing, and flexible working hours.

As well as being a powerful weapon in relation to equal opportunities, contracts compliance and enterprise planning can also play an important part in promoting proper pay and conditions, trade union recognition and health and safety standards amongst private firms supplying the public sector.

PROGRAMME FOR JOBS

Given the difficulties a Labour government will face, we must begin now to make our plans; to think through the amount and mix of public expenditure needed to create a million jobs within two years. Equally important, we must map out the steps which will begin the longer term process of industrial restructuring and rebuilding our manufacturing base.

An expanded public expenditure programme will require the active cooperation of local and regional tiers, government departments and nationalised industries. So there is no reason why the planning process could not begin now. Labour local authorities should be encouraged to start planning their contribution to our jobs target of a reduction in unemployment by one million in two years. They should be given a clear indication of the resources that will be available to them.

The Churches, national newspapers, political and trade union groups, all believe more jobs can be created. They have produced various plans which involve extra public expenditure and differing orders and amounts and mixes. The plan published in the *Daily Mirror* by Metcalf and Currie showed that by an increased net cost of £3.8 billion on public expenditure, one could reduce unemployment by 1.4 million. It also spelt out the areas where such expenditure could take place, which would produce 520,000 jobs by measures that increased labour demand, 540,000 jobs by cutting labour supply, by extra places in education, youth and adult training, and early retirement and a further estimated 340,000 jobs by expanding investment in social facilities such as roads, sewers and hospitals.

The recent TUC Economic Review builds upon its 1984 statement, *The Reconstruction of Britain*, which states that an extra £30 billion of public expenditure over a five year period could put right the huge backlog of housing maintenance work, and the transport, energy and communications industries. In their view, 600,000 jobs could be created in this way.

However, we need to plan expenditure in a more strategic way than has been discussed in any of these documents. We need to consider the order of priority of expenditure not only to meet the needs of people, creating new jobs and setting higher community standards, but also in its contribution to the rebuilding of our industrial base. Expenditure in transport is a good example.

If we wish to expand the electrification of the railway system, we would have to give sufficient resources to British Rail to carry out that programme and sustain our domestic engineering base. We reject the government's view that electrification should be paid for by increasing the redundancy rate, and reductions in government support, although British Railways is already the least financed European rail system.

A further example of the strategic approach to public spending is in our commitment to cheap fares, successfully pursued by Labour authorities such as South Yorkshire and the GLC. Increased public financial support for cheap fares, similar to that pursued in most other European countries, has the effect of encouraging more people to use public transport, more people to be employed, and more buses ordered to meet the new demand.

Tory policy of reducing public subsidies and deregulating the industry has had a disastrous effect on orders in the bus industry. Orders for new buses have collapsed from almost 26,000 in 1979 to 9,255, further undermining our industrial base. Public sector expenditure has substantial effects on private sector demand.

An expanded transport system must not encourage the purchase of buses from abroad simply because they are not available domestically. Money should be used to encourage not only a better transport system creating jobs and meeting needs, but as a contribution to the rebuilding of our industrial base with continuity of long term orders.

While we give £500 million support for cheap revenue fare systems, we also provide subsidies of £2000 million tax relief for company cars. A successful public transport policy will have an effect on the demand for cars and on the rate of deterioration of the road system. This gives important leverage for negotiation with the car industry, particularly multinationals and their trade policy and the use of British components. The government has a powerful weapon through the tax and subsidy policies it pursues as well as through measures such as party policy contract compliance.

These arguments apply in all areas of public spending. Considerable thought needs to be given to how public expenditure will assist in developing the manufacturing sector to create the wealth and the jobs essential for British economic recovery.

The Battle for Jobs

Full employment requires a firm commitment to rebuilding British manufacturing industry after the devastation of six years of Tory government.

It won't be easy. The government, the City and some industrialists have thrown in the towel as far as manufacturing industry is concerned. They are content to see Britain as little more than an offshore tax haven. Labour has to become the party of production.

Labour's programme for jobs will have three integral parts. First, Labour will need a programme of revenue schemes through central and local government to boost essential services such as education, health, social services and leisure. This means, crudely, to increase public spending to create a large number of useful jobs in the shortest possible time at a relatively low cost.

The second part is to begin a major expansion of capital infrastructure works through the public sector with substantial spin-offs for private sector demand. In this programme, we should aim to create 400,000 jobs through a £1½ billion construction programme in housing, roads and urban renewal. A further 600,000 jobs could be created—at a lower cost per job—through other measures which boost the demand for labour, including the possibility of an extra jobs subsidy. Both these stages will produce a million jobs in two years, and with a public sector borrowing requirement not greatly larger than the present government's, but reflecting a different order of expenditure priorities with greater emphasis on job creation.

Third is the longer term programme of industrial restructuring to rebuild manufacturing industries. It must begin on day one of a Labour government. We aim to overcome one of the major failings of past Labour governments—an incoherence between short-term macro-economic objectives and long-term industrial policy.

The framework of industrial policy must be in place by the time Labour comes to office. It must form the permanent context and guide for fiscal and monetary policy. This will restrict the ability of the Treasury to blow our industrial strategy off course.

INDUSTRIAL PLANNING

Britain's traditional industries, and the communities which grew up around them, have contracted, with the run down, relocation or complete closure of many workplaces, large-scale losses of jobs and the dislocation of whole communities. The new microelectronic-based technologies pose further threats to existing jobs and skills, as well as opportunities for new products, new industries and new employment. These changes may prove to be the death throes of the second industrial revolution and the birth pangs of the third. They are being left to take place within the 'logic' of international capitalism.

Far from challenging deindustrialisation, in some cases, the EEC and the UK government, with their free market beliefs, have actively assisted, at the expense of workers in those industries and the communities which support them.

Current economic and industrial policies have failed to handle these changes constructively. . . . In sharp contrast, some Labour local authorities have developed new economic and employment initiatives. These show that it is possible to plan a more efficient and effective use of industrial and human resources to meet the needs of the local community and the national economy.

Enterprise Boards in Greater London, West Midlands, Lancashire and West Yorkshire together with local authorities in several major cities have shown over the last five years that it is possible for public sector bodies:

- to analyse their local economy, to assess the needs of industry and of the local community, and to develop integrated plans for particular sectors, firms and groups;
- to use their position as elected bodies, to challenge the closure, rundown or relocation of major local employers, and to put forward alternative proposals to prevent the collapse of local firms;
- to stimulate new investment, products, technologies and enterprises, drawing on the expertise of universities, polytechnics and research and trade associations, as well as local firms;
- to make selective investments in particular firms as part of a strategy for the sector as a whole;
- to relate financial assistance to an integrated business plan, including proposals for the development and marketing of new products, reorganisation of the production process, organisational or managerial change, tailor-made training and equal opportunities programmes;
- to extend marketing strategies of the firms or sectors through commissioned market surveys, participation in trade exhibitions and fairs, and through public sector purchasing;
- to be active in both the formulation and funding of such plans, and in their implementation and monitoring through equity shareholdings, seats on the Board, planning and employment agreements, participation by shop stewards;
- to influence and improve the quality and continuity of employment (e.g. health and safety, equal opportunities, training, wages and conditions) as part of the assistance and advice package negotiated with firms;
- to explore new forms of social ownership, industrial democracy and greater accountability, extending workers' and co-operative control over their enterprises and their work;
- to create new permanent jobs at proper rates of pay and at a cost

per job far less than most of the government's own job-creation schemes. . . .

Experience suggests the need for direct hands-on involvement and intervention in the production process of assisted firms or projects, including buying in appropriate skills from abroad where necessary, not just indirect, arm's length help through industrial sites, factory units, business promotion or grants and subsidies. We shall also need tighter coordination of the main forms of government assistance to industry (finance, product development, training, trade) so that they can be combined more effectively as part of an integrated plan for key sectors and firms.

We must have closer involvement of people with local community and shopfloor knowledge and experience, not only with the process of formulating economic and industrial policy, but also with the implementation and monitoring of those policies. This involves strengthening the input of workers, shop stewards, trade union officials, local councillors, MPs and others with detailed knowledge, into the development of plans for particular sectors and firms.

NEW NATIONAL INSTITUTIONS

We shall need new processes and structures at a national level to support sectoral and regional planning—just as local authorities have had to develop new processes and structures at local level. . . .

A number of mechanisms were developed under previous Labour governments which accelerated, by thousands of millions of pounds, urgently needed new manufacturing investment. For example, during the investment recession of 1976/77 companies were encouraged to increase their investment programmes by an inducement of £72 million. This produced £600 million of extra investment. Financial assistance of £250 million towards specific industrial and sector schemes led to extra investment spending of over £1200 million in 3000 companies creating many thousands of jobs.

The Prices Commission, set up by the Heath government, was given a radically different role by the last Labour government. It helped the Labour government to reduce an inherited 20 per cent inflation rate to 10 per cent, while increasing the numbers in work by over a quarter of a million. It developed an effective investigatory role into business pricing and other aspects of corporate policy. These policies lifted manufacturing investment to a higher level. Labour must consolidate the role of a prices commission to tackle inflationary pricing policies and to develop the government's counterveiling powers against multinationals, reinforced by planning and development agreements.

Planning cannot ignore the real world in which it seeks to secure a better economic and employment performance. High rates of interest have caused the loss of many jobs, particularly in manufacturing. The mobility of capital from pension funds, and multinational corporations has led to a record flow of capital abroad for investment. Proposals for repatriating this money, together with plans for a National Investment Bank are detailed in *Investing in Britain* presented to the 1985 Party Conference.

Tackling the Multinationals

Traditional policy concentrated on providing an attractive environment for multinationals, rather than seeking to curtail or control them. Policies have included grants, tax concessions, exemptions from rates and other financial support, based on the premise that such incentive packages will encourage multinationals to set up, or retain plants in specific regions.

Past attempts by governments to control and direct multinational investment and job creation activities have been ineffective. Companies have tended to accept the best offer and to move again when a better package is offered. In 1975, Chrysler threatened to wind down its operations in the UK unless the government gave it a multi-million pound injection and underwrote its losses for four years. The eventual rescue package did not prevent Chrysler later selling out to Peugeot-Citröen, or the closure of major plants at Linwood and Whitley, Coventry.

Bids and counter-bids made for the Nissan plant are a recent example. Regional and local authorities vied with each other to offer the most advantageous package. The company seeks the best package with the least strings.

All this leads to substantial payments from public funds to multinational companies. For example, it has been estimated that Ford UK received £143 million from the British government between 1979 and 1982.

In the long run, the process is self-defeating. The main criterion becomes: how much can you offer a corporation to set up in your region, or country, and how cheap and malleable a workforce can you offer? It is an unholy auction across national and continental boundaries, with Third World and Metropolitan countries in desperate competition.

Yet governments have not been prepared to use the strongest cards they hold.

Multinational corporations need markets. The bargain that a government can offer is that if the company wishes to sell in their market, they must produce, research, develop products and source components within that market. Such a policy is now viable only on a continental basis. Policy must be based on inter-governmental cooperation over controls on multinationals and close links between government and trade union campaigns.

For example, Kodak workers in Britain have combined with their European counterparts to protest against European and American management decisions to limit research and development in Europe.

Whilst a national policy for multinationals is essential, only effective international cooperation can confront the scale of power the companies represent. Components have become more interchangeable, products more standardised, and sourcing policy more flexible, and companies have standardised on a world basis.

Nationalisation is not a straightforward solution. European subsidiaries of motor industry multinationals are not independent companies. Decisions on manufacturing, new products, new technologies and lines of research and development are taken at the headquarters of the parent company in the United States or Japan. They are also implemented there: almost all long term research and development of Ford and General Motors is undertaken by the parent company. The parent company controls decisions about raw materials, components and processes. A nationalised subsidiary in the UK would be faced with buying at prices dictated by the parent company.

Multinational companies are now substantially insulated against the traditional instruments of economic policy as they affect international trade—exchange rates, and monetary and fiscal policy. Internal funding of investment means that variations in external market interest rates between companies need not affect investment decisions. Similarly, transfers within corporations enable them to declare profits only under the most favourable tax regimes and to avoid taxation in other circumstances. The EEC Commission ruling that the practice of transfer pricing—whereby different parts of the same transnational corporation charge each other false prices for transfers within the firm to evade taxation and excise or to justify that a particular British plant is unprofitable—is not illegal under the Treaty, nor even a subject for examination, explodes the myth that the EEC is an effective counterveiling power to the growth of multinationals.

But it would not be satisfactory to replace competition in incentives with competition in control: effective international cooperation must be achieved by the widest possible international agreement.

Fundamental to this is cooperation with trade union organisations. For years, the state locally, regionally and nationally has assisted the organisation of capital and provided funds for multinational companies. It needs also to support organisation of labour to provide a counterveiling power. GLC experience suggests that the provision of facilities—conference facilities, translation and educational materials—is important.

We must be prepared to work with sympathetic governments in other countries in their relations with UK-based multinationals. Here, planning and development agreements will be of considerable importance, and there is scope for extensions of public ownership.

In summary, although transnational corporations expose the limitations of any national economic strategy, sector planning does provide important sources of leverage:

- refusal of access to sell in UK markets unless the company agrees to produce, assemble, research and source components in the UK;
- no financial or other industrial assistance to firms without a detailed planning and employment agreement signed between the company, the trade unions and management;
- public sector purchasing (e.g. of vehicles by local authorities, health authorities, fire, police, highways and transport undertakings) can be made dependent upon similar contractual agreements by the firms tendering for the business, committing them in exchange to manufacture, assembly and source within the UK, plus compliance with conditions about the quality and conditions of employment offered;
- support for new forms of international trade union cooperation and organisational linkage between worker representatives;
- information disclosure legislation;
- negotiation with sympathetic governments in other countries to coordinate approaches.

Investment, Intervention and Implementation

From past experiences, we conclude that planning must be linked to investment, intervention and implementation. NEDO sector plans would have been more effective if they had been used to harness and target financial assistance via the DTI and NEB, and employment and training via the Department of Employment and the MSC. Conversely, DTI and NEB financial assistance and Department of Employment and

MSC employment and training programmes would have been less piecemeal if they had been based on industrial/sectoral plans generated through NEDO and linked with regional plans.

New macroeconomic strategies cannot alone tackle the needs of different industrial sectors and regions. Centralised planning methods are insensitive to sectoral and local needs and opportunities. The planning process must strengthen the dialogue between the centre and the periphery. The National Planning Council will have its broad parameters set by macroeconomic assessment, but it must also have strong and lively input from sub-groups, tackling problems at the micro level (e.g. shop stewards, trade union officers, managers, local councillors and community groups and others concerned with the needs of particular industries, firms, regions and cities). Equally, the structures for *implementing* sectoral and regional plans must include strong lines of accountability to those at the base. Not simply to increase industrial democracy but also to monitor the quality and effectiveness of implementation.

Objectives of a New Recovery Policy

- Restructuring industrial sectors according to both commercial and social criteria
- Fair distribution of resources and opportunities (geographically and between groups of people)
- Involvement of both sides of industry in drawing up and implementing strategies
- Effective influence on the investment and restructuring plans of multinational corporations
- Raising the finance necessary for industrial restructuring at national, regional and local level, and making its allocation conditional upon agreed business plans, negotiated within the framework of sectoral and regional planning
- Planning Britain's training policy to meet the needs of changing modes of production and of particular sectors

There are three essential and interlinked functions—planning, implementation and resourcing—at all levels of the economy, local, regional and national. The planning framework must be democratically accountable, and decentralised in contrast to past bureaucratic, corporatist and centralised models of intervention.

The proposed framework has four levels:

Political Accountability and Overall Strategy

The Department of Economic and Industrial Planning is responsible for developing the overall strategy and providing political accountability at national level to government and Parliament. This accountability must be complemented at regional level by regional planning boards or regionally elected assemblies and at local level by local authorities, as advocated in our *Alternative Regional Strategy*.

Planning

Planning has three overlapping elements: the planning of public spending, regional and local planning, and industry sector planning.

Development

We need a variety of investment, training and trade agencies at national and regional level. The key agency, the re-cast NEB which we have called the *British Enterprise Board*, would coordinate perhaps 20 to 25 sector and regional enterprise boards.

Resources

Traditional forms of finance must be augmented through a National Investment Bank and regional banking initiatives to channel pension funds and other investment cash into industry. These financing initiatives will need to be developed at regional as well as national levels.

Department of Economic and Industrial Planning (DEIP)

The new DEIP should be the centrepiece of the strategy, the focus and coordinator of economic, industrial, sectoral, regional, and labour planning. It should be the central economic department of the government working within the policy framework set down by the Cabinet Economic Committee. Responsible for the development activities of the British Enterprise Board and the National Investment Bank, it should also be responsible for the jobs audit, priorities in public expenditure planning, and the annual Public Expenditure Survey Committee (PESC) exercise.

DEIP will work in close liaison with the National Planning Council, Sector Planning Committees and the Regional Planning Council. The Department will leave the administration of individual investments to the British Enterprise Board, or to the sectoral or regional boards.

INDUSTRIAL SECTOR PLANNING

We have to identify those industrial sectors where strategic intervention is essential. Sector Planning Committees must be established for these key industries. The Committees would be coordinated through the National Planning Council, but they would not be exclusively tripartite. They must include: investment expertise (British Enterprise Board); financial expertise (National Investment Bank); policy priorities (DEIP); regional dimension (relevant enterprise and planning boards); industry expertise (secondment, appointment or co-option); trade union knowledge (nomination by shop stewards combine committees and/or relevant unions). Other interests would be included as appropriate.

Sector Planning Committees would be the focus for work done elsewhere in trade unions, companies, research institutions, and local communities. The role of the Committees will be as much to stimulate and enable action to be taken elsewhere, as to execute policy themselves. In this context, industrial democracy and extending rights of workers to information and consultation are crucial.

These Committees will require new statutory powers to negotiate with firms and to compel essential information to be disclosed (within acceptable limitations of commercial confidentiality). This is a sharp break with the existing, consultative role of the NEDC.

The sector plans and their associated investment proposals would thus provide a framework into which smaller industries could fit their longer term plans. For example it would be important to stimulate local planning work in the main car assembly regions and to build links between them (as well as in Europe and world wide). This planning would link more closely to the components industry and other key suppliers—glass, carpets, rubber—as part of a coordinated strategy for the auto complex as a whole.

Initial plans and proposals must be seen as consultative, open to wide debate and comment. There may be no final plan. More a series of objectives, each stage attracting contributions from a range of interests. The plans would seek also to balance social and commercial objectives, job creation, the quality and distribution of jobs, as well as industrial and production organisation.

This approach could be initiated immediately in 15 to 20 industries where the organisation of the industry is predominantly national or international and where it occupies a central role in the economy. Within such industries there are always extensive sub-sectors with more local organisation and markets. For example, ethnic food production in the multinational dominated food sector. There is thus substantial scope for action by regional and local agencies.

In some industries, such as the printing industry, where much of the industry and its problems are concentrated in a few localities, a more federal planning approach would be necessary. There might be a national framework but most of the detailed work would be at local level.

The two central elements are:

National Planning Council

To coordinate the work of the regional planning bodies through the Regional Planning Council and the Sector Planning Committees, into interrelated plans for investment and intervention.

To be the industrial planning feed into the Department of Economic and Industrial Planning, drawing on the views and work from both sides of industry and elsewhere.

To work closely with the British Enterprise Board and the National Investment Bank, and regional and industry boards in developing effective sectoral intervention.

Sector Planning Committees

To bring together trade union officials, industrialists, researchers, local councillors, MPs, community representatives, and others, developing plans for particular industries.

To draw on the knowledge, experience and creativity of workers at plant level about the problems and opportunities faced in their particular firm, and to provide a forum for them to link up with colleagues in other firms in other parts of the country, or overseas.

IMPLEMENTATION OF INDUSTRIAL POLICY

Sector plans and investment are the basis of the industrial recovery programme. Implementation will depend on a variety of agencies.

In many cases, firms will not require external resources or support. But necessary changes, such as a boost to investment, or research and development, may only come about through economic pressure or collective bargaining. That is why we stress the right to information and consultation both for joint union committees in the firm and for union representatives on the Sector Planning Committees. Industrial democracy must have new structures and rights to support workers' own plans and priorities.

In some cases, there will be a need for further measures. A national industry for example will demand concerted action by a number of agencies.

Action	Agency
Trade policy	Government departments, British Overseas Trade Board
Investment in key firms	British/Regional Enterprise Boards
Finance	National and Regional Investment Banks/Pension Fund/Banks
Training	DoE/Manpower Services Commission

The sector planning process must therefore have sufficient power and authority to ensure that strategies are implemented. Otherwise, we return to indicative rather than interventionist planning. Equally, it is important that intervention is based on a philosophy which sees local and national resources as part of a planning agreement in which companies must fulfil both strategic and social objectives in exchange for public resources.

The Sector Enterprise Boards would carry out investment plans of the sector planning committees and would need specialist skills and experience. The Sector Boards would establish industry wide schemes (e.g. supporting innovation at research and production stages) as well as making direct investments in selected firms. The British Enterprise Board would be the central instrument for implementing industrial investment and intervention plans. It would also coordinate and integrate the work of the sector and Regional Enterprise Boards.

FINANCE FOR INDUSTRIAL INTERVENTION

When comparing investment per capita, Britain is almost at the bottom of the 27 OECD countries. While the problems of British industry do not revolve around finance alone, British financial institutions have hampered and frustrated industrial and technological development by their short term horizons and their notorious caution in providing long-term risk capital or equity finance.

Funds available to the NEB and the ICFC have been too small to allow them to initiate major rescue deals or restructuring plans. The proposed National Investment Bank must therefore have substantial funds to back investment plans. It must be committed to long term capital growth rather than short term, high rates of return. It will draw these funds from the City and Pension funds.

The National Investment Bank should have the function of providing resources; it should not be involved in development activities.

It would aim:

To act as a channel for the funds required by the British Enterprise Board (and the sectoral and regional boards) to be obtained via the financial institutions of the City, the Pension funds, Banks and other financial institutions;
To attract other sources of finance for particular sectors and regions (eg: the European Regional Development Fund).

The Treasury

The experience of past Labour governments with the Treasury has not been happy. The Department of Economic Affairs, and the Wilson government's attempts to introduce indicative planning foundered largely as a result of Treasury power and influence. Its strategic position, the relationship to the Prime Minister, the control over not only the macroeconomic levers but of the whole public expenditure planning process gives it the pivotal role in the management of the economy.

The scale of the task facing the next Labour government and the need for longer-term industrial planning, means that the role of the Treasury will have to change. The new Department of Economic and Industrial Planning, which will take over the functions of the Department of Trade and Industry, must become the main planning ministry for economic and industrial development.

This will be more than a name change. DEIP should take over the strategic economic planning functions of the Treasury, and responsibility for jobs-related public expenditure planning. Together with the National Planning Council, it will be responsible for planning the economy as a whole. DEIP must have a planning, development and financial function to meet its objectives.

The Treasury would have responsibilities in areas such as exchange rates, interest rates and public sector borrowing, as well as revenue gathering, but the overall macroeconomic stance and the short- and long-term growth strategy must be opened up to wider scrutiny in Cabinet and in the National Planning Council. The Treasury would have an important part to play in marshalling the resources necessary for a National Investment Bank. . . .

BASIC PRINCIPLES

Collective bargaining and trade union organisation are central to Labour's vision of democratic socialism. They express the capacity of working people to shape the future of their economy and their society. In the Party's joint statement with the TUC, *A New Partnership. A New Britain*, those principles are reflected in twin themes of involvement and fairness. The task for the Party between now and the general election is to develop these themes into detailed policies for the next Labour government.

The so-called trade union problem has to be redefined. The present government has made unions the scapegoat for its own failures. In most industries and services, workers are excluded from the decisions that affect them. In spite of a professed commitment to employee involvement, this government has fostered authoritarian management and a climate of insecurity. Government policies, as the recent Employment White Paper made clear, aim to bring down the wage levels of the majority of Britain's workforce in a shift to a low-tech, service economy. This is presented as a modern and sophisticated cure for unemployment. In reality, it is an admission of defeat. Doctrinaire reliance on the market has failed to generate the investment required to put Britain's manufacturing sector into the high productivity, high wage league of West Germany and Japan.

We want to extend workers' rights in a positive industrial relations framework, bringing democratic accountability into the workplace itself. Lasting jobs and growth depend on the injection of a new force into British industrial management. We need to encourage vitally needed management skills and practice, together with the creativity of the workforce.

WORKING TOGETHER

Labour's new partnership with the trade union movement will only be credible if it goes beyond the social contract. We must show that the

Party has learned the lessons of the attempt at 'industrial strategy' and the breakdown of wages policy. While the government's confrontationist approach may be increasingly unpopular, the electorate will not turn to us unless they are convinced that our partnership alternative has a good chance of working.

One distinguishing feature of our proposed new partnership is its emphasis on involvement. Instead of placing workers in a legal straitjacket—like the Tory government—the aim is to widen the bargaining agenda beyond wages to include the whole range of company decisions. Here we can build on the last Labour government's reform of industrial relations legislation. This took account of the shift over the previous decade to plant- and company-level bargaining.

The next Labour government must introduce legislation which enables working people to play a constructive and responsible role in economic management. At present, decisions on investment, research and development, and training are controlled almost exclusively by the employers, with no accountability to workers or society. New rights which allow workers to influence crucial investment decisions can simultaneously establish a firm foundation for industrial policy and ensure that the balance between investment and consumption is struck within the collective bargaining process itself. This will require the development of industrial plant and place of work joint planning committees to support the collective and representative strength of workers at their place of work. This needs legislation for the provision of information and consultative rights.

When this happens it will be less necessary to concentrate almost exclusively on general pay norms, the central element of previous incomes policies. General pay norms have always proved to be unworkable—in the long run because they impose a straitjacket on collective bargaining. Their only result has been to build up tensions, cause more industrial conflict and produce an inflationary pay explosion when they collapse. They never can be more than short term emergency measures.

Imposed pay norms tend to restrain wages and increase profits. In the past these resources were not channelled into increased investment. Consequently, workers' short-term sacrifices did not bring sustained economic expansion, though the last Labour government's incomes policy did help reduce inflation by half while increasing the numbers in work by a quarter of a million. Only by extending workers' influence over economic management will it be possible to ensure that wage bargaining is conducted within a framework of agreed economic and industrial strategy.

A FAIRER SOCIETY

A civilised society would reject the notion that wage rates are determined solely by a 'free' market which justifies massive increases in top pay, and cuts in real wages for the low paid. It is more accurate to describe the problem of low pay as one of unfair pay. Millions of workers are paid poverty wages, well below the official TUC rate of two thirds of the national average, currently £104 per week. Teachers legitimately claim that they are not paid a rate in accordance with the work they perform and, therefore, are low paid.

Any strategy for the elimination of low pay must be sufficiently flexible to distinguish between unfair differentials (such as those based on sex discrimination) which can and must be squeezed, and differentials which are seen as fair because they reflect legitimate notions of skill and responsibility.

It is now widely accepted that collective bargaining will not be sufficient to deal with low pay without statutory support. The main drawback of purely voluntary bargaining is that it is fragmented and uneven across occupations and sectors; further, many workers are not even organised in unions.

The fragmented nature of bargaining has been offset in the past by various types of legal support, which have evolved haphazardly over the years. Examples are the Fair Wages Resolution, and Schedule 11 of the Employment Protection Act. Since these provisions have been abolished by the present government, we have an opportunity to review statutory support for collective bargaining and how it might be developed by a Labour government.

The first step has already been taken with the statement in *A New Partnership. A New Britain* calling for a fair wages strategy. This would require extensive rights to comparability and arbitration and involve the whole scope of statutory support necessary to end low pay and reduce employment insecurity. We must aim to develop a more coherent approach to the value of people's jobs which does not substitute for bargaining and organisation but assists trade unions to overcome problems arising from weaknesses in the position of some groups.

11. A Million Jobs a Year*

Campaign Group of Labour MPs

To argue that there are no physical bars to full employment does not of course imply that severe economic problems will not have to be overcome. Their precise quantitative extent, let alone the form they will take, cannot be predicted without much detailed work, matching available capacities and skills with priorities for expenditure, identifying key sectors for modernisation and so forth. Yet the broad nature of the problems to be faced are clear enough—flights of capital, problems of financing increased government expenditure, inflation, controlling trade, ensuring adequate investment. If the exercise of constructing a Plan for Full Employment is to be more than empty rhetoric, then convincing general solutions have to be given to these problems. In what follows each of these issues is discussed, not in order of importance but in the order they would be faced by a Labour government committed to restoring full employment. In each case a contrast is drawn between what seems clearly to be necessary and the ideas currently being proposed. After looking at each problem in turn we are brought face to face with the key issue of how a Labour government could make effective the various measures necessary to overcome these problems. The crucial question, then, is whether the solutions advocated below are consistent with private ownership of the major financial and industrial companies which dominate the economy.

FLIGHT OF CAPITAL

With monotonous regularity Labour governments have been compelled to abandon their plans in the face of capital flights and runs on the

* Reproduced from A. Glyn, *A Million Jobs a Year* (London, Verso, 1985), pp. 18–37, with the caveat that its contents, though not necessarily representing the views of the whole of the Campaign Group, deserve urgent consideration throughout the labour movement. The pamphlet was published alongside the names of the Group's membership.

123

pound. Harold Wilson recorded how this pressure was exercised in late 1964:

> That night we had our most desperate meeting with the Governor of the Bank. Claiming that our failure to act in accordance with his advice had precipitated the crisis, he was now demanding all-round cuts in expenditure, regardless of social or even economic priorities. . . . Not for the first time, I said that we had now reached the situation where a newly-elected Government with a mandate from the people was being told, not so much by the Governor of the Bank of England but by international speculators, that the policies on which we had fought the election could not be implemented; that the Government was to be forced into the adoption of Tory policies to which it was fundamentally opposed. The Governor . . . had to admit that that was what his argument meant, because of the sheer compulsion of the economic dictation of those who exercised decisive economic power.

A serious flight of capital from the UK would push the value of the pound through the floor (making imports more expensive and cutting living standards) and interest rates through the ceiling (as banks struggled to keep depositors from shunting their money abroad). It does not require any kind of conspiracy for a capital flight to get going, simply fears that Labour's policies would in one way or another reduce the returns from keeping cash in the UK. The sums of money involved are gigantic.

Overseas investors in the UK own around £20 billion of shares and government bonds and £24 billion of bank deposits in sterling. These could be withdrawn very rapidly and further pressure would come from overseas owners of UK factories (worth some £35 billion) covering themselves for exchange risk. In addition British banks might find that overseas holders who had deposited their dollars in the UK (the so-called Eurodollar market) wanted to move their money from London to avoid controls. Within a period of three months the banks could find themselves short of some $30 billion. Moreover UK residents are just as likely to try and pull their money out and invest in banks or securities overseas (they already own nearly £70 billion worth). In the face of these enormous potential outflows the UK government has reserves of £13 billion. Without assistance from overseas central banks, which would be available on terms that required the abandonment of Labour's programme, the reserves would stand up to barely a few minutes outflow.

Labour is therefore faced with a stark choice. Either it tones down all its policies to such an extent that they are acceptable to those who control international capital. This would certainly rule out implementing a plan for full employment. Alternatively Labour has to put into effect whatever measures are actually necessary to prevent the free flow of capital from wrecking its plans. Extensive exchange controls would be necessary. 'Commercial' transactions associated with trade would have to be separated out from 'investment accounts'. Transfers of capital overseas would have to cease and procedures drawn up to ensure repatriation by financial institutions and trusts of their enormous overseas holdings of securities (overseas subsidiaries of UK companies would require separate measures). Each year the government might supply (from repatriated UK overseas investments) a certain amount of dollars to a separate free market confined to those overseas holders wishing to withdraw their investments from the UK, who would therefore be obliged to pay a very heavy premium to get out.

The cutting off of the UK from international capital markets would have its costs. The ending of dealing in these Eurodollar and other transactions would cost the UK balance of payments some £2 billion per year, but at 2 per cent of exports this is trivial as compared with the benefits of being able to control exchange and interest rates. The running-down of UK assets overseas would have little real cost, since even the Bank of England was forced to admit that the real return on them, after allowing for inflation, was only 'slightly positive'.

Devising a really comprehensive set of capital controls would involve plenty of technical difficulties. Analysis of the experience of the UK up to 1979 and of most countries in the world at present will provide many of the answers as to how they should be implemented. It is even said that the electronic transmission of money makes exchange control impossible. This is about as convincing as claiming that the telephone makes it impossible to prevent spying. Who could doubt that if the UK was involved in a major non-nuclear war effective controls would be slapped on overnight? Present proposals for introducing tax changes that would make worthwhile the repatriation of the bulk of the UK financial institutions' overseas investment (£20 billion is the figure) do not address the question of capital flight at all. They would not impinge on foreign investors in the UK, or on UK companies and they would not even prevent UK financial institutions from indulging in massive short-term movements of capital abroad. They are directed to an entirely different issue (encouraging UK financial institutions to lend to UK industry) and would do nothing whatsoever to reduce the UK's vulnerability to pressure from international capital.

Many people who sympathise with the objective of comprehensive exchange controls feel that they would be impossible to implement because the threat of their imposition would cause speculation against sterling and the ruination of Labour's electoral chances. This is to take a very defensive approach. For on the contrary such speculation should be used in an election campaign to demonstrate that financial interests (at home as well as abroad) were bitterly hostile to, and intent on wrecking, Labour's 'Plan for Full Employment'. Even Wilson recognised this in his conversation with the Governor of the Bank of England: 'I warned him that if I went to the country on the issue of dictation by overseas financiers I would have a landslide. He said ruefully that he believed I would.' A decline of the exchange rate in the weeks before the election would involve temporary disruption of trade and perhaps big price increases. But the rate could be pegged at the desired rate as soon as the exchange controls were put in place. Those who had got out of sterling would have done so at heavy cost to themselves. Nothing could more clearly establish the case for exchange controls than pre-election speculation, and Labour would have to go on the offensive on the issue.

FINANCING PUBLIC BORROWING

The precise implications of a Plan for Full Employment for government borrowing depend on a thousand details—the size of the various public spending increases and decreases (dole payments and defence, for example), the extent to which taxes are raised on higher incomes, the degree to which profits are 'socialised' by nationalisation, the amount of compensation paid for assets taken over, etc. Pending the detailed work which should be set in train on the various possibilities it is worth looking at the rough orders of magnitude involved and the problems that would arise.

It seems likely that a public sector based expansion to full employment might increase the public sector deficit, over 4–5 years, by the order of £10–15 billion, that is reaching a figure of £20–25 billion. Total public sector borrowing would rise substantially more than this when account is taken of compensation for assets taken over, though capital taxes should be able to offset a good deal of this. Given that GDP would be increasing, the rise in the public deficit (to around 7 per cent of GDP) would not be huge by historical standards.

That is hardly the point, however. A substantial rise in the PSBR is feared not for itself, but for what it would stand for—a determination to control the economy on the basis of social need rather than financial orthodoxy. The City, which has fought strenuously to drive down public expenditure and borrowing, would be bitterly opposed to any such expansion. Inflation, rising interest rates, a falling value of the pound would be predicted and the predictions could be self-fulfilling if not prevented, as investors piled out of UK government securities and attempted to take their capital overseas. Obviously exchange controls would be a necessary part of the armoury, as already discussed. But they would not be sufficient to ensure that the government could find lenders. The financial institutions, trusts and individuals who hold government securities would try and get out before the prices of them fell, thus provoking the very fall they feared and forecast. Were that to be allowed to happen any government might find it impossible to pay for extra spending other than by pumping up the money supply much more rapidly than was desirable, leading to self-fulfilling fears of inflation as people scrambled to hold real commodities to protect their savings.

The only solution would be for the government to *oblige* the financial institutions to hold more government debt in some proportion to their assets. They already hold more than half the debt of around £140 billion, and it would be necessary to draw up precise requirements for each type of institution (banks, building societies, pension funds, insurance companies). It is important to emphasise that the problem is not that there would be no extra savings available which the government could borrow. On the contrary the expansion of the economy would of itself generate the required level of savings (providing taxation was adjusted appropriately). This in large part happens automatically as workers taken on save part of their incomes (for example when they contribute to public sector pension schemes). The question is whether those institutions and individuals which control savings would be prepared to lend them to the government. In fact they would have to be required to do so.

The money raised in this way would have to be properly used. If it was squandered on additional weapons for example, there would be no contribution to the productive potential of the economy. As more and more debt piled up year after year, the interest on it would become a burden and taxes would have to be raised. To look at the matter in real terms, the government would be piling up obligations to pay people better pensions (reflected in the holdings of government securities by pension funds) but there would be no extra wealth generated to pay them. Either the promise to pay better pensions would not be honoured, or those at work would find the burden of taxation on them growing.

The solution must be to ensure a growing economy, and of course most of the additional government expenditure would contribute directly or indirectly to this end—better education and training improves the productivity of labour, better infrastructure improves the productive system (and spending a certain amount now may save many times the sum later), providing communal child care facilities releases labour time for use in other sectors, investment in new factories improves labour productivity and so forth. To spend, as we are now doing, vast sums on the dole, the ultimate in unproductive spending, in order to save a little more in expenditure which would contribute to productive capacity, spells future impoverishment, not the guarantee of prosperity.

Various changes have been suggested in the way public spending and borrowing is presented, notably focusing on the fact that the ratio of the national debt to production is at low levels, and emphasising its 'underlying long-term trend'. This is all designed to 'reassure the markets that they would not be expected to absorb an unacceptably high amount of debt'. But 'unacceptable' to whom? The markets presumably. In the past they have judged as 'unacceptable' increases in public spending and borrowing which were entirely justified from the point of view of the needs of the people and the productive capacity of the economy. Conversely they found 'acceptable' much greater increases in spending in wartime. To start from the position that what Labour does must be 'acceptable' to the financial markets necessarily limits what can be done. If this is the position, it is not then a question of 'marginally' adjusting Labour's targets to keep the markets happy: the whole programme would have to be designed with the markets' criteria in view, and Labour would end up being limited to 'marginal' adjustments to Tory policies. The question is immediately raised, as it was with exchange controls, of how effective controls could be put on the financial system to ensure adequate government financing. In principle the Bank of England could be instructed to instruct the banks and financial institutions as to what was required. Would the banks obey these instructions, or use every device possible to evade them? For the government to have sufficient control over the financial system those who work in those institutions must be persuaded of the necessity of the measures proposed, and mobilised to put them into effect.

INFLATION

The fear that full employment is beyond reach, because a determined expansion would collapse under accelerating inflation, is perhaps the biggest obstacle that Labour has to overcome in building support for a Plan for Full Employment. Whilst these fears have been built up by Tory monetarist propaganda, the experience of the last twenty years shows that they are far from groundless.

In one important way, however, a major expansion is in fact anti-inflationary. Inflation is a phenomenon of shortage, too much money chasing too few goods according to the monetarists, too many people chasing too few goods according to the 'competing claims' explanation. A major expansion means more goods, not less. If sufficient controls are taken to deal with the problem of financing the government's deficit, then the expansion of money and credit can be tailored to the achievement of a non-inflationary expansion. Maintenance of the exchange rate, by adequate controls over trade and capital movements, is also required to prevent a declining pound pushing up import prices. The pattern of the expansion must also be planned to reduce the importance of temporary shortages and bottlenecks.

Price controls would have to be put in place to prevent firms taking advantage of the expanding markets to boost profits by banging up prices. With the expansion being planned to ensure that shortages did not occur there would be no reason for price controls to lead to queues in the shops and black markets. The controls would have to apply to nationalised industries as well as firms left in the private sector. The boards of nationalised industries might feel justified in increasing their share of investment funds by raising their prices and their surpluses, yet the allocation of these funds has to be subject to the overall availability of resources and the planning of priorities. Price controls, which set a ceiling on price increases, would also be absolutely necessary to ensure that the wage increases freely bargained by trade unions were not wiped out by rising inflation.

Support for a 'Plan for Full Employment' would depend on it being recognised as fair, something which is patently impossible with the present unequal distribution of income and wealth. The outcry against top salary increases in the public sector, in contrast to teachers' struggling to make ends meet, illustrates the importance of these feelings. As the *Financial Times* pointed out, what was being handed out in the public sector was merely aping the City where 'the market' delivers 'rewards in inverse proportion to the apparent productive contribution'. Higher rates of taxation on high incomes, on capital gains, on transfers of wealth and on items of luxury consumption would be essential. Action by trade unions and a Labour government together must ensure adequate incomes for those in work and those relying on state benefits below which no one can fall, including a minimum wage.

Labour's present ideas for controlling inflation, appear to offer the trade union movement a modified version of monetarism. The suggestion is to use taxation, public spending and monetary policy to increase the demand for goods by a certain money percentage. If wages and prices rise slowly, then this will be translated into a rapid rise in real demand and production. If wages and prices rise rapidly then most of the extra monetary demand will be dissipated and employment and production will hardly grow. This is still to use the threat of unemployment as a weapon against wage increases.

The infamous wage norms introduced as part of incomes policies in the past have been aimed at reducing real wages to the level which would make producing, investing and exporting profitable for private business. It is one of the absurdities of the capitalist system that workers are enjoined to show restraint even while the barrage of advertising identifies self-respect with the ownership of consumer durables and the media regale us with the extravagant life styles of speculators and aristocrats. A 'Plan for Full Employment' has an entirely different basis. The whole thrust of economic policy would be to eliminate unemployment, build up the public services and restore industry so that productivity and living standards could continue to grow steadily.

Nobody can pretend that inflation is a technical question, dealt with by technical devices like control of the money supply. It reflects the whole social organisation of the economy. A democratically planned expansion of the economy would require full access to information about the enterprise or institution for all those who work in it, as a basis from which they can play their part in running it. If changing the way the economy operates seems to imply a high price in effort, argument and struggle, it has to be set against the waste of resources, disruption and misery of mass unemployment which is the way in which the present economic system attempts to suppress conflict.

TRADE

A planned expansion to full employment would tend to pull in more imports as demand for consumer goods and capital goods rose. If nothing was done the deficit on the balance of payments could rise to £20 billion or more. Even a very effective industrial policy and a huge investment programme to modernise industry would be most unlikely to solve the problem quickly. Continued stagnation in the advanced countries making up most of the UK's markets, and their own attempts to rationalise and modernise makes it most improbable that exports could be increased enough to pay for all the additional imports.

The classical solution would be to engineer a devaluation of the pound to increase sales of exports and to improve the competitiveness of home substitutes for imports. The problem is that the cost of imports is increased by a devaluation, boosting inflation and representing a permanent cut in living standards. Competitiveness means either higher productivity or lower real wages; if productivity cannot be boosted sufficiently and swiftly enough real wages have to be cut. If this was just a small effect, easily absorbed within the expansion of total production, then it could be readily contemplated. But unfortunately this is not the case. Exports and imports are not very sensitive to devaluation; this means that the devaluation has to be large, with a consequently large effect on living standards. The cost could well be of the same order of magnitude as the size of the potential balance of payments deficit being avoided. A large chunk of the extra production generated by the expansion would have to be channelled into exports to pay this cost, seriously reducing the benefits from, and thus the viability of, the expansion.

Planning the pattern of imports and exports, in order to maintain a balance in total trade would thus be a necessity. Some progress could be made on the export front by negotiating trade deals. It would be economically justifiable to sell exports below the domestic cost of production, if the foreign exchange was thereby generated which allowed the economy to expand, and production and employment to increase. It is likely, however, that the main weight, at least in the short term, would fall on restriction of imports. Since extra materials, and some specialised capital goods, would have to be imported, the biggest reductions would have to be in imports of consumer goods. How could this be achieved? Much the most direct method would be to identify the main importers, including the subsidiaries of multinationals like Ford and the major retailing chains, and fix limits on their imports. Again the active involvement of the workforce to ensure compliance seems absolutely essential.

Initially trade policy would be focused on defensive measures to ensure that expansion was not overwhelmed by a flood of imports. In the longer run, however, the objective would be to develop new patterns of trade based on the mutual benefit of the economies concerned, rather than the private profit of multinational companies. Far from proceeding towards a siege economy the aim would be to end the present situation, in which the British economy is besieged by world market forces wholly outside its control, and replace it by the conscious planning of international economic relations.

Of course retaliation and opposition should be anticipated. But there is no benefit in pretending that all that is being done is to tinker with the free market, as supporters of a general tariff have tended to suggest. Planning of trade would be proclaimed to be the objective, and this would require the activities of the major importers to be planned too. The benefits of a blunt approach were, rather surprisingly, spelled out by a former US Under-Secretary of Agriculture who said that centralised buying agencies have no need to 'violate GATT because GATT rules are irrelevant. Who needs tariffs and import quotas when a central buying agency can say "sorry we are not importing this year"'. An example in the UK has been the CEGB's traditional policy of buying virtually no imported coal. Such an approach, even if it evaded the wrath of GATT, would not satisfy the EEC. Trade restrictions and capital controls are contrary to the principles of the EEC; Britain's withdrawal from the EEC would be inevitable. Although there would be costs involved as tariffs on UK exports to the EEC would be increased, trade would still continue as it does between the EEC and other non-members. It would be ridiculous, however, to pretend that the interlocking of the world economy does not pose real problems for independent socialist development in the UK. The GATT, the EEC and the IMF are the reflections of the internationalisation of the capitalist system, the implications of which cannot be avoided simply by ending the UK's participation in these institutions. Breaking the UK's subservience to world markets will obviously impose losses on overseas interests. Labour's potential allies overseas are the labour movements and it would have to be to them that Labour would appeal to minimise the disruptive action of foreign governments and employers. The rather tentative measures for import controls in certain sectors, which the Labour leadership is now proposing, would be neither mild enough to avoid overseas fury, nor strong enough to allow a rapid expansion.

Some people may feel that the real costs of restricted access to imported consumer goods are too high; that having to wait longer for a Toyota or a Sony Hi-Fi is too big a sacrifice. But there will be UK substitutes available, hopefully of comparable performance and price. If the choice is presented honestly, to be what it really is, *either* ready availability of Toyotas rather than a substitute *or* reduced unemployment plus reduced queues for hip operations plus decent housing plus modernised industry plus extended training for young people plus readily available BL cars, is it really any choice?

INVESTMENT AND EMPLOYMENT

A major programme of investment is universally acknowledged as necessary to modernise UK industry. To allow the manufacturing capital stock to grow by 5 per cent a year (rapid by historical UK standards, but not in relation to what has been achieved in Germany or Japan), would require the present level of investment to be trebled. As much as one quarter of the resources generated by the expansion to full employment would have to be devoted to such a task. Effective modernisation would require investment to be balanced between sectors, concentrated where import substitution was the priority and generally targeted to meet Labour's objectives. It is literally inconceivable that private industry would willingly undertake such a programme, let alone passively allow itself to be steered in the necessary direction. Even though the expansion itself would encourage investment, all the fears and uncertainties with which private business views a Labour government, let alone one committed to radical policies, would act in the other direction. Funds channelled to industry through strong controls on the banking system, only find takers if the climate of confidence (not to mention profitability) is right. The National Investment Bank, currently proposed by Labour to be funded from repatriated overseas investments and directed towards small and medium firms, could make a contribution, but in no way would it guarantee a major expansion of investment. The recent emphasis on local enterprise boards and local initiatives is a welcome new component: co-ops and small local companies have a part to play. But they are the foothills of the economy. We cannot retreat from the ideas of planning and controlling investment, towards attempting to encourage it by reassuring the private sector.

Would private firms even be prepared to take on additional labour as the expansion proceeded? If it was profitable for them to do so then this seems straightforward enough. Expanding production on existing plants requires very little commitment of additional capital (only buying stocks of materials etc). If it was profitable, private capitalists would do it, even if they were too lacking in 'confidence' to commit large amounts of new capital to putting up new factories. But even so employers might hold back from adding to their labour force in circumstances where it would be expensive or difficult to sack workers should demand falter. Moreover some employment which is required for the economy as a whole would not be profitable for the employer concerned. The decrepit state of much of industry means that some capacity would have to be brought back into operation which was not profitable *for the firm* because labour productivity did not cover wage and material costs. Using this capacity would still be beneficial *for the country* because it would yield extra production which would find a market in meeting the additional purchasing power. This revenue would pay the extra costs of employing the workers rather than keeping them on the dole so that the rest of the economy would actually benefit economically for their being employed.

How could firms be obliged to produce this extra output? In principle they could be directed to do so, covering their losses on this part of what they produced by cutting their dividends. But as with longer-term investments deemed unprofitable to the company, the difficulties of forcing private companies to do this, let alone of devising a set of subsidies which would cajole them in the same direction, pose formidable problems.

SOCIAL CONTROL AND PUBLIC OWNERSHIP

The previous sections have argued that a 'Plan for Full Employment' would only be feasible on the basis of extensive controls over foreign exchange transactions, over the financial system, over prices, over trade and over investment and employment in the private sector. It has also been argued that to devise and implement effectively such controls would require greater powers for the workforce. For the proper functioning of the planning system it is essential that all those affected in the various sectors and enterprises, as workers and consumers, are involved in both long-range planning and day-to-day operating decisions. The proper working out of such measures of control and democratic systems of planning is an urgent task, for which the resources of the labour movement, and the experience and expertise of Labour supporters, should be mobilised.

The domination of the economy by giant firms means that planning and control would have to be focussed on them. The thousands of small and medium-sized firms are in general so dependent on the giants, either as customers or suppliers, that controlling the giants gives control over the rest. The list of companies, whose activities would have to be immediately and extensively controlled, if a Labour government were to be able to plan the economy as a whole, requires detailed examination, sector by sector. The last comprehensive survey we have available is for 1975, when the biggest 250 industrial and commercial companies owned 50 per cent of the UK assets of all UK companies (and virtually all their overseas assets). These firms controlled half or more of the assets of most major sectors of the economy. Since that time further takeovers, which were at a record level in 1984, must have further increased the degree of concentration. A dozen or more of the top 250 have themselves been swallowed up. Concentration is just as strong in the financial sector, the biggest six banks plus the biggest six building societies plus the biggest six insurance companies plus the biggest six finance houses, merchant banks and discount houses together control over £350 billion of assets. These, then, are the commanding heights.

A crucial question remains however. Could a 'Plan for Full Employment' along the lines sketched out be implemented on the basis of the present economic structure where private ownership occupies most of these commanding heights? All the measures already discussed, which would be required to make the expansion durable, involve constraints on free market forces: movement of capital (controlled by exchanged controls, credit controls, investment plans imposed on firms), movement of goods (trade controls), freedom to exploit market opportunities (price controls), freedom to organise work (workers' control). Could the banks and financial institutions be relied on to implement stringent exchange controls and to finance whatever public deficit was required? Would industrial companies be ready to expand investment and employment, to limit imports to specified levels and to fix prices? Would all enterprises agree to revolutionise their system of management by the full involvement of their employees in all relevant decisions?

It is true, of course, that during the Second World War, finance and industry accepted a very comprehensive set of controls. Being committed to the objective of winning the war, they were bound to abide more or less by them. The controls were imposed by a government to which they were broadly sympathetic (since Labour's participation in the coalition brought obvious benefits). The controls were often implemented by the employers themselves. Whilst taxation was high, profit levels were guaranteed. Joint committees set up with unions did not challenge managerial prerogatives.

The position could hardly be more different now. The City and big business are frightened of the implications of full employment and would be bitterly hostile to a Labour government committed to imposing such controls as were necessary to achieve it. The whole basis of the plan would be that production should take place where it was beneficial to society, not where it was profitable for employers, and these two guidance systems differ radically in what they imply. The right to deploy capital wherever appears most immediately profitable would be checked by exchange, financing and investment controls. The other pillar of capitalism, the absolute right of management to manage, would be superseded by the democratisation of industry.

The Labour government of 1974–79 faced a storm of opposition to its plans for steering industry. The *Financial Times* reported that 'the CBI told Mr Wilson that there was absolutely no room for manoeuvre or negotiation about further state intervention in industry and further nationalisation.' The head of the CBI told him that 'price control, profit limitations and socialist threats . . . could bring the country down within a year'. After the autumn election in 1974 Pilkington's, the giant glass producer, announced that their investment programme would be shelved 'until such time as essential changes are made in taxation and price control'. These attitudes were echoed in the civil service. The Permanent Secretary of the Department of Trade and Industry reportedly greeted Tony Benn with the words: 'I presume, Secretary of State, that you don't intend to implement the industrial strategy in the Labour Party's programme.' It does not require much imagination to foresee the degree of opposition from business and the City which would greet a 'Plan for Full Employment' which included the range of essential controls outlined above.

What are the steps necessary to carry the policy through? The major financial institutions are capitalism's nerve centre, with a dense web of links to industry, and capable of causing financial chaos in a matter of minutes by moving out of sterling or away from lending to the government. Taking them into immediate public ownership seems absolutely indispensable if a Labour government is to prevent financial crisis and be enabled to use the credit system as part of planning for full employment. An extensive campaign will be necessary to convince those who work in the financial sector that this is an essential step. Indeed, their wholehearted involvement in planning and running the financial institutions will be absolutely necessary if they are to operate satisfactorily. Depositors in, and contributors to, these institutions will also have to be convinced that nationalisation will not jeopardise their interests. The fact that the government, in the guise of the Bank of England, has repeatedly organised rescue operations to protect the clients of financial institutions in difficulties can be used to show that taking the financial sector into public ownership, and operating them as part of a growing economy, offers much more security than the present situation where cut-throat competition and speculation prevails.

The capacity of the major industrial firms to frustrate a Labour government's 'Plan for Full Employment' is less immediate than the threat posed by the financial sector. Factories cannot be removed overseas overnight; production would in general be maintained. The problems arise, rather, in securing the implementation of plans for expansion, including controls over imports, investment and so forth. Any board of directors would argue that its responsibilities were to its shareholders, and would try to resist pressure from government and workforce to carry out policies which they felt were contrary to shareholders' interests. Such non-compliance, and resulting economic failures, would have the very serious political effect of generating popular disillusionment with the government.

There are a number of approaches to this problem which have been canvassed in recent years in the labour movement. Since the early 1970s the idea of planning agreements between major firms and the government has been proposed. These would cover the various fields of activity of the firm—employment, investment, prices, imports and exports—and would be designed to ensure that they meshed in with the overall objectives of the government. It has never seemed very plausible that such planning agreements, if they were voluntary, would be of much use in steering the economy. In a negotiation about an investment programme, which is essential for the Plan, but which the directors regard as unprofitable, there is little room for meaningful compromise. Or rather the pressure to compromise would always be on the government since they would be attempting to persuade those who ultimately take the decisions.

This is exactly what happened when the last Labour government abandoned its policy of making planning agreements compulsory. It did sign one with Chrysler UK which was given more than £100 million of government support; in return the government was not even informed in advance when the company was sold to Peugeot. A senior manager in another company explained the attitude of big business rather clearly: 'we would sign a planning agreement tomorrow if we could do it our way ... we are not reassured by the way in which the government sees planning agreements and so we will not sign one'.

It is clear, therefore, that to have real effect planning agreements would have to be compulsory, and backed by powers of enforcement. For example, large companies could be required to produce, within a specified period, a plan covering all their activities in order that they could be integrated with the 'Plan for Full Employment'. Workers in the firm and government planners would have to have rights to access to all the company's books and records in order that independent assessments could be made of the various factors involved. They would be able to propose modifications and adjustments which, after discussion, the company would be obliged to accept. Strict monitoring of progress with fulfilment of the plan would be necessary, with both planners and workers involved.

Failure by management to produce an adequate plan, or failure to implement it effectively, would require a decisive response. One possibility, suggested by Labour's 1973 Programme, would be to devise a procedure paralleling that now used for bankruptcy. If a company is technically bankrupt a Receiver is appointed by the court to take over the affairs of the company and to run it in the interest of the company's creditors. Similarly if a company was not living up to its obligations as defined by its specified role in the plan, this would justify the government having the power to appoint a new management structure, involving workers and planners, to run the firm in the interests of society.

A second approach to the problem of planning and controlling industry would be to build on the ideas of 'industrial democracy' which have been widely canvassed in the labour movement in recent years. We cannot be satisfied with the election of a minority of workers' representatives on to Boards of Directors, which would leave them in a position of taking responsibility for majority decisions made by the rest of the Board. Even if a group of mutually acceptable 'independents' held the balance of power between shareholders' and workers' representatives, as proposed by the Bullock Report, they would tend to support management's commercial judgements. To ensure that companies made their contribution to the plan it would be necessary to 'socialise' them in a much more thorough-going manner. To be certain that shareholder interests, as interpreted by existing boards, no longer dominated it would be necessary that the new boards should contain a majority of members who worked in the industry, or who used its products or were appointed by the government. Such boards would themselves be responsible for drawing up plans for the company, ensuring that they were in line with the overall plan (this being the particular responsibility of government appointees) and that they were implemented after negotiation and agreement with the trade unions.

The first approach, via compulsory planning agreements, allows existing managements to come up with plans which would then have to be accepted by government and workforce. The second approach, socialisation of boards of management, directly recognises the broad social interest in the direction of enterprises, without removing ownership of shares from the existing shareholders and without incorporating all major firms directly into the public sector. Taking over the financial sector, including some system for consolidating control over the disposition of pension funds, would in any case put majority control of most major companies' shares directly in public hands. This is because the financial institutions own half of these companies' shares at present. This would give the government another channel of control over most industrial companies, additional to that provided by compulsory planning agreements or socialisation of management boards. It can be argued that such approaches to the control of industry would have the advantage of demonstrating, through the process of struggling to shape the development of the economy, the justification and eventual necessity for the full implementation of Clause IV.

But the real difficulties in attempting to control industry without explicitly taking it over became clear in post-war discussions about control of the steel industry. A recent authoritative account summarised what happened as follows: 'From start to finish the issue was never whether there should be public control of the industry but was essentially whether any realistic and effective scheme of control could be devised that fell short of outright nationalisation. The conclusion to which the government was driven was that it was very difficult to reconcile thoroughgoing public control with private ownership or to find a half-way house that made provision for private participation or left some part of the industry in private hands.' Nationalisation of all the commanding heights of the economy is the most direct way of asserting society's control over its resources. The legitimacy of management's rights to manage firms in the interests of shareholders would be explicitly denied and their power to do so removed.

Discussion and evaluation of these various approaches to controlling industry, in order to hammer out proposals that will guarantee real control, is an absolute priority if a convincing 'Plan for Full Employment' is to be constructed.

What of compensation for those companies which would be taken over? Over half the shares of UK companies (including holdings in other financial companies) are owned by financial institutions, mainly pension funds and insurance companies. The pensions of their contributors must be protected, and in exchange for shares in these companies the funds could be given non marketable government securities which would yield a comparable income. The actual level of pensions which an economy can afford depends on its productiveness, not on the wizardry of overpaid investment analysts trying to second guess one another in the City. The crisis over SERPS simply reflects the continued appalling performance of the economy. The answer to guaranteeing decent pensions to all is to secure the economic growth which finances them.

For individual shareholders the basis of compensation could be similar to that for institutions, bearing in mind that the real cost to the government of compensating the wealthy would be extremely small because they would be paying almost all of the interest they received back as tax. Some device such as this would be essential to preserve fairness between people whose savings were in companies taken over or in other assets.

Our conclusion is that the immediate subordination of the investment, employment, financing, pricing and trade strategies of the major firms to the achievement of a 'Plan for Full Employment' requires a decisive and fundamental shift in the way they are controlled and operated. It would be irresponsible to suggest that such a shift would be achieved as soon as a parliamentary majority had been elected to carry it out. Active support would be required at every step to ensure that the main economic levers were both removed from their present controllers and were operated in society's interest. Those who currently exercise economic power have non-economic weapons as well, through their influence on the state machine. The history of all previous attempts to transfer control of the economy indicate that the highest degree of active support and commitment would be required from Labour's supporters to overcome the threat of such extra-parliamentary opposition. To accept the existing domination of market forces, and the economic structures which enshrine them, is to accept the inevitability of mass unemployment for the foreseeable future, unless that is you believe that a new capitalist boom is just around the corner. Is there *anybody* who believes that now?

Above we have urged a radical extension of public ownership and control as a necessary means for achieving full employment. Planning and social ownership of the sort advocated will also be necessary if we are to build a fundamentally more equal and responsible society, based on the release of the initiative and creativity of working people, the guarantee of genuine equal employment opportunities to women and ethnic minorities, the implementation of effective measures to ensure a safe and attractive environment, the making of proper provision for health, education and welfare needs, and the inauguration of a meaningful and democratic debate on social priorities, both nationally and internationally.

SUMMARY

This pamphlet has argued that:

1. The elimination of mass unemployment is as essential if those currently in work are to have improved social services and living standards as it is for the unemployed. A million jobs a year should be Labour's basic demand.
2. Full employment is not ruled out by 'physical' problems of technology or availability of capacity but by problems of economic organisation.
3. Previous periods of very rapid increases in employment, at the beginning and after the end of the war, took place under conditions where sufficient controls were introduced to ensure that maximum utilisation of resources was not blocked.

4. Under present economic conditions, in the UK and world economy, a successful 'Plan for Full Employment' requires effective controls over all foreign exchange transactions, trade, prices, credit, and investment. It is impossible to see how these can be imposed without public ownership of the credit system and subjection of all major companies, by one means or another, to thoroughgoing democratic control and planning. This must include statutory rights for workers in the planning of priorities for the economy, in the management of enterprises and in the running of their workplaces.

5. The problem of reaching full employment is fundamentally one of political determination. People must be convinced of the need for the necessary policies in the light of the lack of real alternatives. Their active role in framing these policies and implementing them is essential. This, then, is the case for giving top priority to formulating a 'Plan for Full Employment'. The various types of controls and planning mechanisms require working out and refining in great detail. Projections for the economy as a whole, for each sector and indeed region are necessary if a consistent and coherent Plan is to be evolved. And of course an enormous campaign must be mounted to convince first the labour movement and then wider layers of the population that such a plan is feasible. War on unemployment must be declared, the demobilisation of the reserve army made the central objective, and the necessary measures set in train.

To deny that they are feasible is to accept that market forces *must* dominate and that all that Labour can do is to massage the market and share out the misery rather more equally. The degree to which these proposals represent a radical break with the recent past shows how far we have become reconciled to mass unemployment. If a less radical road to full employment was on offer most people would prefer to give it a chance. But no alternative *is* being offered. And another period in office during which Labour failed to deal with the social disaster of mass unemployment could well bring even worse problems for the Labour movement than those represented by Thatcher's term of office.

12. Jobs for Keeps*

The Ecology Party

UNEMPLOYMENT—THE CHALLENGE

Unemployment is the greatest social problem which we face in Britain today. It is not simply a question of the numbers involved—although these are higher than would have been believed possible only a few years ago. Nor is it just a matter of the distress behind the figures, grievous thought that is.

Most disturbing of all, given the length of time the problem has been growing, is the helpless impotence of our politicians to do anything about it. Something is deeply wrong with our society when this can happen. For there is so much that cries out to be done, all around us. There ought to be more than enough work today for anyone who wants it. Yet our system goes on condemning us to the gigantic wastefulness of mass unemployment—the waste of human talents and energies. These are the most precious resources of all in our human world. They are being squandered, along with our material resources, as if there were no tomorrow.

Such a system cannot long keep the respect of its people. It does not deserve their respect. There are real dangers of instability and breakdown in that situation, and the politicians know it. Their promises of quick solutions become more dogmatic as their nervousness grows; but it is quite evident that none of the analyses and programmes proposed, right across the spectrum of conventional politics from so-called 'radical' Toryism to the so-called 'radical' Left, begin to approach the true *roots* of the problem.

In this pamphlet we explain that failure. We also set out our own, genuinely radical proposals for a solution which will last—a programme of jobs for keeps. These are practical proposals, designed to start

* Reproduced from *Jobs for Keeps* (Ecology Party, 1982).

making a difference right away.

What distinguishes them from those of others is that they also try to strike the balance between real work, real needs and real resources which political thinking has so long neglected, and without which no permanent solution can be achieved.

We believe these ideas deserve the serious attention of anyone concerned to have in Britain a stable, just and democratic society employing the energies of all its people.

THE SCALE OF THE PROBLEM

2,500,000 people were registered as unemployed in the Spring of 1981—the highest number recorded since the 1930s. Many more are without work but do not even bother to register.

Unemployment has risen under each successive government since 1966, and numbers are now increasing more rapidly than ever. Some have predicted 5 million out of work by 1990. The cost of even the present level is enormous—around £8500 million a year in benefits paid, revenue lost and allied costs.

The cost to the individuals concerned is also high. Those who lose their jobs can suffer not only loss of income (in many cases bringing real hardship with it) but also loss of status in the community, in the eyes of their families and even in their own eyes. Most people rely on their jobs for comradeship and a sense of purpose in life as well as for money; to be robbed of all these can breed deep resentment. The young especially, many of whom see little prospect of ever gaining proper work, are becoming dangerously alienated.

Worst of all, while the unemployed are told that there is no work for them to do, they need only look around them to see plainly that this is nonsense. Children leave our schools unable to read or write properly while teachers cannot find posts. Tenants live in damp or poorly insulated homes next door to building workers without jobs. Consumer goods get shoddier and repair and maintenance services harder to find, while young craftsmen are first trained and then returned to the dole queues. Huge quantities of scarce materials are wasted because we do not organise the work of saving and recycling them. The prices of food and energy climb dramatically, and hungry old people die of hypothermia, while those who could be producing these necessities cheaply, stand idle. Our economic system is thoroughly out of balance when it produces this vast and bitter absurdity.

THE FAILURE OF CONVENTIONAL REMEDIES

All You Need is Growth

Since before the last war, politicians of both Left and Right have had only one answer to the question of how to create and preserve full employment. That answer has been *economic growth*—to encourage manufacturing industry to produce more and people to consume more, so that expanding production generates jobs both within industry and as a consequence throughout the economy.

By growth they have always meant expansion within the existing economic framework. Methods and emphases have differed, but the basic mixture has always been a blend of incentives, directed public expenditure, prices and incomes policy and State intervention in key sectors. Only the proportions of these ingredients have changed as Labour and Tory governments have swapped around. The general consensus has never been in any doubt about fundamentals: if the managed mixed economy is to grow it has to be 'rationalised' and 'centralised' to achieve 'economies of scale' so that production can be kept on the rise.

The trouble is that this approach just has not worked. For at least twenty years it has been in difficulties, and over the last decade its failure has become harshly obvious. Governments simply have not been able to overcome the built-in defect that their attempts to achieve higher economic growth have always resulted in rising inflation. If allowed to continue unchecked, this destroys jobs; but attempts to cope with the danger by dampening down demand have produced still worse unemployment. Expansionist strategies have been paralysed again and again by this contradiction.

Recent Political Developments

Three different reactions to this continuing failure may be observed in conventional politics.

The *Liberal and Social Democratic* approach is the most topical and in many ways the least appealing. It offers the same mixture as before, but with the label on the bottle changed. Once again we are promised the thriving mixed economy, plenty of government intervention and invest-ment, and a gimmick or two like profit-sharing to temper the bracing winds of competition. All that is new and radical about this is the cheek of calling it new and radical. The whole affair is nothing more than a confidence trick played on a worried electorate with the connivance of much of the media. That it should be swallowed so eagerly by so many thoughtful people shows what a state we are in.

Thatcherism was at least honest by its own lights. It aimed to reduce inflation by severe restrictions on the money supply and on government spending, to stimulate demand by cutting taxes and thus create new jobs in revitalised industries. It departed from the postwar consensus in its bold acceptance that this would mean—'at the outset'—not only very much higher unemployment, but also a sharp reduction in public services. This was held to be a necessary discipline; meanwhile the government would see us through to the sunlit uplands beyond, by firmness in pursuit of its monetary targets.

It was never likely to work. Now . . . it is in ruins. Taxation is higher than ever, the money supply is out of control, government resolution over public sector pay deals is crumbling, firms collapse daily (including many of the smaller firms which the policy was supposed to revitalise), and unemployment climbs . . . with not the remotest prospect of a reduction in sight.

The Left claim that their alternative has not yet been tried in full. It involves massive public expenditure to reflate the economy centrally. The whole of our revenues from North Sea oil are to be staked in this giant gamble to boost production—and, in addition, quite clearly, a lot of money will just have to be printed. There will be unprecedented state intervention in industry to ensure that the benefits of this bonanza go where the government wants.

A degree of state control and direction is proposed here which will hardly be accepted in Britain. People will not readily pawn their freedom, even to pursue the illusion of conventional full employment.

But in any case, the odds are overwhelmingly against the success of any such strategy. The reason for this is fundamental. It underlies the failure of all the other approaches too. *It is quite simply that economic growth cannot any longer generate lasting employment*.

Why Economic Growth Must Fail the Jobless

Economic growth—expansion of the centralised capital- and energy-intensive formal economy—cannot any longer be relied upon to generate an overall increase in employment. Indeed growth on this pattern has *declining* employment built into it for the future. From the ecological perspective this statement can be seen for the plain truth it is.

From such a perspective it is evident that the real costs of the whole industrial system are rising rapidly. They are doing so because we are approaching limits imposed by the Earth's resources. As these *costs*, which cannot be evaded, continue to rise they must work their way through to higher *prices*—and this is what causes the inflation that affects industrial economies, the creeping inflation which destroys jobs as fast as they can be artificially created.

What are these real costs?

Rising Energy Costs: Our economy depends on massive inputs of fossil fuel energy. The clear trend is for oil and other fuel costs to rise steadily, and as resources are depleted and extraction and development costs correspondingly increase, the trend is bound to continue. Nor can North Sea oil rescue us from this situation for long.

Raw Materials Costs: Industrialism feeds greedily on raw materials—but reserves are finite. As supplies diminish so world prices increase; this is already occurring for many essential metals such as aluminium, lead and tin. Once the cost of a raw material increases, it is inevitable that the price of finished products will increase too.

Spin-off Costs: The scale of these is enormous, far greater than traditional economics has ever admitted. They are now increasing exponentially. There are distribution costs, in a society which scorns local production; the cost of our vast wasteful bureaucracies; the costs of coping with the pollution and rubbish which industrial society produces in such huge quantities. And then there are the spiralling medical, welfare and crime prevention costs which must be included because our society damages people's health and breaks up their communities.

Personal Costs: Most people want to work at producing good, useful things in which they can take pride. Too often the way we organise work reduces them to button-pushers, or forces them to help produce rubbish. Human beings can only take so much of this, even to earn a living. Beyond a certain point their natural resentment emerges as tension in industrial relations, absenteeism, indifference and the drive to push up wages and salaries in sheer compensation for their sacrificed humanity.

All of these factors keep the costs of production constantly on the rise. These costs passed on to the consumer as price rises of course provoke further pay demands—and so the whole inflationary spiral continues, destroying jobs as it goes.

The New Technology

As if all this were not enough, we must also reckon with the totally unprecedented impact of the new microelectronic technology on employment patterns in the economy.

This technology can be applied to improve efficiency and productivity across all manufacturing, service and distributive industries. Its whole point is to do this by *reducing* employment. And given the logic of industrialism, the emphasis on production and consumption, there can be no doubt that it will be applied in that way.

Authoritative estimates have predicted that 60 per cent of all occupations could be at risk. 1.8 million jobs could be lost in the manufacturing sector alone over the next fifteen years, many of them in areas of traditionally skilled work. The service sector and all kinds of office work are even more vulnerable—here over 4 million jobs may well be lost in the same period. Compared with this broad swathe cut through conventional employment, the job-creating potential of micro-technology is tiny—a few new products, a few electronic toys, a few thousand jobs at most.

It must be emphasised very strongly that those who argue for growth and expansion of the economy are inescapably arguing for this job-destructive development, as well as all the others outlined.

So one thing should now be abundantly clear. Attempts to solve the problem of unemployment through expansion of the industrial economy are doomed to failure.

It is in fact a classic case of filling the bath with the plug out. The difference between the policies of the conventional parties in this respect amounts to the difference between trying to do this by running the hot tap, by running the cold tap or by running both together.

SUSTAINABLE EMPLOYMENT

It can now be seen just how radical—in the true sense of attacking the *roots* of the problem—must be any serious solution to unemployment.

The first and fundamental principle of any such solution must be that new jobs made to last can only be generated through economic activity which is *not* vulnerable to the inflationary and technological pressures described. We must look for the jobs which will always need doing, and for ways of doing them which can always be sustained. That means always working within the limits imposed by the Earth's resources and by human nature.

In the *primary* sector of the economy there is enormous scope for employment. We shall always need energy and food, and Britain could be far more self-sufficient in these than it is. Indeed it will shortly have to be. At present we obtain most of our primaries from abroad in exchange for the manufactured goods which we export. But our manufacturing base is declining, the prices of our goods must go on rising, and their competitiveness in world markets will continue to fall. As energy and resource constraints on industrial production start to bite fiercely, it will increasingly be primaries which will form the 'hard currency' of the world economy.

But production, even of food and energy, requires an input of energy—and this must increasingly be *human* energy, or we are just going in a circle. We cannot hope to increase our food production by employing more oil-burning machinery and oil-based fertilisers—the oil won't be there. The same argument applies to the huge energy investment needed to build nuclear power stations, even were these not unacceptable on other grounds. Sustainable primary production has to be much more *labour-intensive* than we have been used to for many years. And so does the necessary accompaniment, conservation: a national home insulation scheme, for instance, would have to employ building trades workers up and down the country.

We must also look for ways of producing as many as possible of our *goods and services* independently of the declining conventional economy. We must look for small-scale, localised production, cooperative in its organisation and therefore responsive to changing local needs. We must look for production to last, not to throw away—and this means making things as human beings ought to make them, with care and love. We must redevelop the highly labour-intensive repair and maintenance trades. We must look for the supply of many services by communities for themselves, drawing flexibly and creatively on the talents of local people.

Clearly a society in which the economic balance had shifted in this direction would be a rather different society from the one we have at present—though the charge that it would be 'a return to the Dark Ages' is just hysterical. There are many who would argue that it would in fact be a better society simply in itself: more responsible and more humane. There are many more who are now ready to acknowledge that some such alternative will *have* to be developed, as the limits of our planet's capacity to support full-blooded industrialism draw ever nearer. We contend that in any event it is the only sort of society which can *now* guarantee lasting work for all who want it.

Such a society is no mere ideal goal. The transition towards it could be started in Britain tomorrow. And we could make that start with measures to relieve the plight of those who are today without work or hope of work.

THE TRANSITIONAL ECONOMY

Striking the Balance

When people talk about the 'economy' they generally mean what we have called in this pamphlet the *formal* economy: they mean conventional production of goods and services, providing full-time taxed employment at fixed rates—highly capital-intensive, based on towns and cities and often centrally planned.

But there is always a lot else going on, outside this framework, which should equally be recognised as economic activity—work done to provide material benefits. It includes part-time work, 'domestic' or self-service activities, community and voluntary work, and self-employment both 'official' and 'unofficial' (the 'moonlighting' of the so-called black economy). We term all this the *informal economy* to distinguish it from the formal. But this does *not* mean that it is somehow all casual or second-best. In fact, as everyone knows, such work very often calls forth far more of people's skills and creativity than do their 'real' jobs; and often, too, far more of genuine value is produced.

The crucial points about 'informal' economic activity are, first, that it is highly *flexible*: it is locally-based and responds to the changing needs of the people it serves. Unlike formal activity it does not depend on massive fixed assets, capital commitments, expensive advertising and marketing, or over-complex systems of legislation and negotiation. Secondly, it is *sustainable*: it can make careful use of scarce materials just because of the small scale of its operations, and it does not require great inputs of precious fossil-fuel energy. Most of its energy, indeed, comes from *people*.

The informal economy is at present squeezed to the margins—a kind of additional, 'poor-relation' sector of the economy, seen from the conventional viewpoint. *But as a way of working, it shows us what work for keeps must be like.*

The radical strategy which we must pursue is therefore clear. We must find 'informal' ways of meeting many needs which people now look to the formal economy to meet. In parallel, we must carefully manage the decline of that formal economy, so that those areas of it which remain will provide a leaner, healthier framework.

Sustainable Enterprise: Local Production for Real Needs

We have to revitalise the economy 'from the bottom up'. Informal activity must be encouraged to grow from the natural local roots—it would be self-defeating to try to organise it centrally. Sustainability depends on economic as well as political decentralisation.

A nationwide network of *Community Employment Agencies* should be established. These Agencies would take over the job-finding role of existing Job Centres, but they would interpret it much more imaginatively: their prime task would be to *stimulate* locally-based employment.

They would monitor all skills available and required. Working closely with schools, craft and professional bodies, they would ensure that appropriate training and retraining schemes were provided at local Skills Centres, which they would manage. They would provide free practical and financial advice to those wanting to set up new local businesses. They would help organise markets for local home production. These Agencies would be the focal points for economic regeneration in each locality.

Community Savings Banks should also be set up to work closely with the Community Employment Agencies. Their job would be to channel local finance into local enterprises. Their rates of interest could be very low—they would not be aiming for the disgracefully large profits of the big banks. The local knowledge of their associated Agencies would enable them to risk their funds very productively—they would support the kind of small businesses or home-based ventures which conventional banks would not touch.

These local banks would have to have their deposits topped up by central government funds in the early years of the scheme—they would provide a much more efficient means of applying public money for job creation than the multi-billion pound, centrally-administered transfusions to ailing industries which we see at present.

Such 'local reflation' would have an enormous advantage over the conventional approach—it would work to reduce prices. The kind of small enterprise involved would have low costs and be able to charge very competitive prices. The big concerns, which have got used to a monopoly position where they can ignore the market and pass on all their costs to the consumer, would have to cut prices to stay in business. Thus we should have a kind of reflation which would combat inflation *and* provide jobs nationwide.

Sustainable Security: the National Income Scheme

Informal economic activity depends to a large extent on people's willingness to work for variable rates of pay according to changing conditions of supply and demand. Part-time and voluntary working will also play a greater role.

People will only be prepared to accept such changes if their *basic* material security is absolutely guaranteed, and if there is a real redistribution of the national wealth to make social justice visible.

We therefore propose the phased introduction of a national income tax credit scheme. When the scheme was in full operation the vast majority of social security benefits and all tax allowances would be replaced by a single automatic payment to everyone, which could be taken in cash or used as a credit against tax liability. These payments would be made *without qualification* and would be unaffected in value whatever other income was being received. In effect there would be a permanent national minimum income below which people *could not* fall.

At levels of payment comparable to present supplementary benefit assessment rates, the scheme would cost about £20 billion annually. This figure takes into account all the savings in social security benefits, tax allowances and associated spending which would result.

Part of this cost would have to be met out of government expenditure—nuclear weapons programmes, nuclear power stations and toys like Concorde would have to go. The rest would be raised through indirect taxation and through income tax, which under this scheme would be chargeable on all earned income. Since credits would be much more generous than existing personal tax allowances, new tax rates would be set to ensure that only those on lower incomes received any net financial gain. The result would be the most progressive taxation system Britain has ever seen.

These are radical proposals. But the gains from introducing such a scheme would be out of all proportion to its costs. The poverty trap would disappear—there would be no loss of national income whatever one earned in addition, and so the incentive to work would be restored. An impossibly complex welfare benefits system would be simplified so that claimants could actually understand it.

Even more importantly, the rigid distinction between employment and unemployment which has developed in industrial society would begin to break down. In its place we should have a multitude of varying, interwoven patterns of work and leisure. We might rediscover an energy source which we have almost forgotten—the tremendous force of human creativity.

Sustainable Wealth: Working for a Future

Building up such alternatives to our present ways of working is crucial if we are to create lasting real wealth as well as providing jobs immediately.

The formal economy is also of crucial importance. It must decline, but for many years it will go on providing us with foreign exchange, home consumption and essential tax revenue. And there will always remain a 'formal' underpinning of the wealth of any sustainable economy.

Central government has an important role to play in adapting the formal economy to face the future. We must begin by creating hundreds of thousands of jobs *now*—jobs for which the conventional Parties, hooked on old-fashioned notions of expansion, simply cannot see the need.

How are these jobs to be created?

By a drive towards self-sufficiency: Finance should be provided to encourage food production at every level. The reclamation of derelict land must be a priority. There should also be an ambitious re-afforestation programme.

A massive safe-energy programme should be substituted for the spendthrift and lunatic 'nuclear economy'. Conservation of energy, including a national Home Insulation Scheme, should be funded as a matter of urgency.

Import controls should be introduced to provide selective protection for our economy (though the interests of Third World producers must be safeguarded where appropriate), tariffs on imported food and raw materials will act as a resources tax, encouraging home production and the elimination of waste.

Recycling schemes for domestic and industrial waste should be introduced in all our towns and cities.

Powerful tax incentives should be provided for all repair and maintenance work.

By adapting existing structures: Corporation tax should be replaced by a turnover tax on cashflow to encourage large firms to decentralise into more manageable units. Encouragement should also be given to workers of all kinds to set up cooperative schemes. These smaller, more democratic units are much more likely than large companies to be sensitive to the needs of the communities where the workers actually live, and therefore to produce the socially useful things for which there will always be a market.

Work-sharing arrangements should also be encouraged. The disincentive to firms employing part-time workers should be diminished by phasing out the employer's element of the national insurance levy, which now acts as a tax on jobs.

By investment where it is really needed: There should be substantial investment in British Rail to provide the cheap and fuel-efficient transport which we shall increasingly need. The repair and extension of our canal system—unmatchable as a route for certain kinds of freight—should be mounted on a national scale.

Increased investment in the coal industry should seek to improve techniques, so that as many pits as possible can go on employing men to produce vital fuel.

Let us say clearly again: we are not talking about some distant ideal. This is a programme for here and now. Our plans for formal and informal economic renewal offer the chance of employment to those who are jobless *today*.

But it is also a programme for tomorrow. It means that not only will there be work in future, but there will also be a future in which to work.

IT CAN BE DONE

Even some who are sympathetic to the case we have made out in this pamphlet may ask whether our proposals are politically realistic. We call for significant adjustments in people's ways of working, yet our strategy does not appear to further the economic interests of any particular power group in society as against the others. And economic self-interest has long been the engine of all major social change. So in whose interest *are* our proposals? Who will fight for them?

We answer quite simply that our policies are in the interest—the plainest economic interest—of *everyone*.

A realistic alternative to otherwise inevitable decline and disintegration must be in everyone's interest. The stability of our society must be in everyone's interest.

Stability does not mean rigidity. It certainly does not mean any permanent fixing or freezing-in of existing inequalities and injustices. Nor does it mean a 'strong hand on the tiller'—a dictatorial regime established in the name of 'order'. In fact, regimes of this kind, whether of Right or Left, are inherently *un*stable (though this will not stop people fleeing in desperation to such 'solutions' if they can see no other alternative to chaos).

A truly stable society is one which can adapt to changing circumstances while preserving its fundamental identity. In Britain this means a social order which offers not only jobs, but a tolerant, humane and democratic way of life—for keeps.

Given the situation which now confronts us after two centuries of industrialism, only the sustainable society offers any prospects for such stability. The programme we have outlined for moving towards it is in the clear economic interest of the *jobless*—it offers them work now and work to last. It is in the interest of *entrepreneurs*—it offers the only reliable basis for future production. It is in the interest of *organised labour*—without it there will soon be little labour left to organise. It is in the interest of all who *invest*, whether individuals or firms or families— all who depend on there being a stable future. It is in the interest of our *children* whose lives that future will be.

It is in *your* interest.

What we have described can be done; the people of Britain must decide whether it will be done. The Ecology Party exists to offer them that choice.

PART III:
Cross-Party Views

The political parties have not been the only source of ideas for industrial regeneration. Politicians, trade union leaders and industrialists have surfaced in other guises too, arguing for policy change. Three such initiatives have been particularly significant of late. The first, which emerged in April 1985, was the all-party Employment Institute in which Conservative 'wets', leading SDP and Labour moderates combined. James Callaghan, Edward Heath and Harold Wilson were all patrons of the Institute and its 120 council members included politicians such as Roy Hattersley and Shirley Williams, industrialists like Lord Ezra, and leading trade unionists, bankers, former civil servants, academics, journalists, clergymen and entertainers. Their *Charter for Jobs* argued for a reflation of the economy, particularly through greater government capital expenditure on infrastructure, a cut in National Insurance contributions to lower the cost of taking on labour, and a job guarantee for the long-term unemployed. It was with the plight of the long-term unemployed that the House of Commons All-Party Employment Committee was concerned in their report, published in January 1986. Special employment measures for those out of work over a long period were, on the committee's findings, a cheaper and more certain way of producing jobs even than investment in infrastructure, and certainly than tax cuts. The Committee suggested that in order to create one extra job a government would have to give away £47,000 in tax cuts, £26,000 if capital expenditure was its chosen job-creating strategy, £15,000 if it concentrated on current expenditure, but as little as £2,650 if special employment measures were adopted instead. Important as this report was, however, it did not address the longer-term problems of industrial regeneration. The House of Lords Select Committee on Overseas Trade did; and their report made an enormous impact when first published. From their deliberations a long list of suggested policy changes emerged: changes in education practices, wage restraint and quality improvements, and systematic government aid on investment, research

157

and development, training, infrastructure, export promotion, import substitution, stable exchange rates, low rates of interest, and tax concessions to business. Neither of these reports escaped government criticism. Kenneth Clarke, then an Employment Minister, reacted to the House of Commons call for an expansion of the Community Programme in this way:

> If we tried to speed up the new places beyond the 10,000 a month we are managing now, we would risk repeating the mistakes that occurred in the early days of job creation. We would also take jobs away from people who already have work, to give to the unemployed. The committee is proposing several billion pounds of additional public expenditure. While more special measures may be necessary, and it is right that unemployment should be our No. 1 priority, it would be ironic if the cost to the economy caused greater damage to business and the job market in other ways. (*Guardian*, 5 February 1986, p. 2)

The government response to the House of Lords report was even less enthusiastic and took the unusual form of a White Paper. Parts of that are also reproduced in this section.

13. We *Can* Cut Unemployment[*]

Charter for Jobs

Unemployment in Britain today is as high as in the 1930s. On present policies it is unlikely to fall substantially for many years. This is a terrible waste of precious economic resources. If unemployment were as low as in 1979, we would be producing £20 billion more of output per year. Large-scale unemployment also creates deep personal misery among those affected, and it is a threat to our social and political stability.

Many people are deeply sceptical about whether the government can do anything about it. Such defeatism was also prevalent in the 1930s. Yet for nearly thirty years after the war we experienced full employment. More recently there is the experience of the United States, where unemployment has fallen from nearly 11 per cent two years ago to around 7 per cent now. This was possible because the government budget helped the recovery. These examples should give us hope.

Perhaps the strongest ground for hope is the fact that only six years ago we ourselves had under 6 per cent unemployment, compared with the 13 per cent unemployment rate we have now.

CAUSES OF UNEMPLOYMENT

Fears that our troubles are inevitable are misplaced. The most common explanation is that high unemployment is due to machines replacing people. Yet machines have been replacing people for centuries without unemployment increasing. And in fact the rate at which machines have replaced people (as reflected in the rate of productivity growth) has actually been slower in the last ten years than in the full-employment 1950s and 1960s. Unemployment is up, not because productivity has grown fast, but because output has grown slowly, and was little higher in 1984 than in 1979. And output has grown slowly because of low demand. To see that productivity growth is not the problem, one has

[*] Employment Institute, 1985.

159

only to look at Japan where productivity growth is among the highest in the world and unemployment among the lowest.

Another myth is that unemployed workers are now much less suited to the available vacancies than used to be the case: they are in the wrong place or have the wrong skills. Though such mismatch has always been a problem, there is no evidence that it is any worse than in the past.

So what *has* caused the rise in unemployment from around 3 per cent in the late 1960s to 13 per cent today? Supply-side influences may have contributed to the rise. These may include a less punitive social security system, more wage pressure in the labour market, and higher taxes on jobs (i.e. employers' National Insurance contributions). But the rise in unemployment since the late 1970s must mainly reflect low demand. This has been due to:

tight fiscal policy (high tax rates and constraints on public spending),

the world recession (due largely to tight fiscal policies in so many countries), and

the high real exchange rate (especially relative to Europe), which made so much of our industry uncompetitive.

REMEDIES

So what can be done? Many of the factors we have mentioned are subject to government control, and three policy measures should be taken at once:

(i)   A substantial rise in public infrastructure investment with an emphasis on labour-intensive projects.

(ii) A cut in employers' national insurance contributions, to reduce the cost of labour.

(iii) A form of job guarantee for the one and a quarter million long-term unemployed on projects such as those provided by the Community Programme.

This would involve an increase in the budget deficit.

Such an increase is not a recipe for increased inflation, for the following reasons:

(a) The cut in employers' National Insurance contributions would cut labour costs, and lead to lower prices.

(b) When there is as much slack in the economy as there is now, extra demand will mainly affect output rather than prices. Today's position is totally different from that of the 1970s. There are now fewer labour shortages than there were even over the recession years 1975/76.

(c) Present policy is extremely deflationary and should not be considered neutral. Less deflation is not the same as irresponsible reflation. It would be possible to expand the budget and still, over a run of years, keep the national debt stable relative to the national income. Thus an expanded budget deficit now would not cause financial instability. The national debt is now lower relative to national income than at almost any time since the war. A higher deficit is in order when there is mass unemployment.

(d) This need not lead to a fall in the exchange rate (and hence a boost to inflation) provided monetary policy is suitably cautious, with interest rates as high as necessary to protect sterling, and provided the new policy is well presented. In this way Britain could avoid the mistakes the French made in 1981.

(e) Some believe that quite large falls in unemployment could be achieved without extra inflation and that an incomes and prices policy might be unnecessary. Others believe the inflation problem would emerge more rapidly. But, if it proves impossible to reduce unemployment below present levels without inflation increasing, we would all consider some comprehensive approach including incomes and prices policy to be better than doing nothing to reduce unemployment. This would only succeed if undertaken after appropriate consultation and negotiations. The central point is that we are simply not willing to accept 13 per cent unemployment into the indefinite future.

The government claimed its policy would reduce unemployment. Instead, it has raised it. We offer an alternative policy which responsible people can support. We ask the government to heed our suggestions and to restore hope to the millions without work.

WHAT HAS GONE WRONG?

Our present unemployment is totally abnormal. It is now the same as in the 1930s and quite out of line with ordinary historical experience.

The first step therefore is to understand how we got into our present position. We begin with various faulty diagnoses, before coming to our own explanation.

Not 'More Technological Unemployment'

The first faulty diagnosis is that the high level of unemployment has been caused by a sudden surge in the rate at which machines are used to replace human labour. This idea rings true to many industrialists, who are familiar with capital expenditure proposals over recent years involving sharp reductions in numbers employed. Yet the facts are that in the 1970s and 1980s output per worker-hour grew not faster but *less* fast than in the preceding decades of full employment. It was in the 1950s and 1960s that productivity was growing most rapidly. Yet unemployment was lower than ever before.

The problem in the 1970s and 1980s has been the slow growth of output, not the high growth of productivity. Output growth was slow from 1974 onwards but was most dismal in the last five years, with non-oil output in 1984 about the same as in 1979 (a triumph of 'wealth-creation').

Thus the key question is: 'Why is output so low?' One theory about output is that it is now limited by satiation. People have all they want or they need. This may be true of millionaires, but it is not true of machinists. A quarter of the households in this country have net incomes below £80 a week, and spend under £40 a year on holidays away from home. It is outrageous that people should discuss our present unemployment as though the level of output were limited by human wants.

A more plausible theory of output says it is limited by the availability of machines. But throughout the period of growing unemployment our machines have been less heavily used than ever before. So this can hardly have been a limiting factor. Looking to the future, shortages of capital cannot provide any absolute limit to output, given the scope for heavier use of plant and for variations in manning. Moreover, the majority of jobs are in services where there is a much looser relation between capital and output than in manufacturing.

The cardinal sin in thinking about unemployment is to take output as given. This is the 'lump of output fallacy'. Instead we can have more output, if we have less deflationary policies. And higher output will mean more jobs.

Since output is not given, we need not worry about productivity growth. In fact in the short-run higher productivity growth would be likely to raise rather than lower employment by increasing our ability to compete in world markets. And, looking to the past, we repeat our simple argument that the rise in unemployment cannot be due to a rise in productivity growth, since productivity growth fell.

But even if productivity growth has been low, has it caused greater problems due to its greater unevenness? Or, more generally, are we suffering from unprecedented structural problems due to technical change, higher oil prices, foreign competition and the like?

Factors such as these have always caused problems and always will. If productivity growth is more rapid in one industry than elsewhere, and the demand for the industry's output does not rise sufficiently when its relative price falls, then employment in that industry falls. The most dramatic example was in agriculture, which a century ago employed half of all workers in advanced countries. The progressive mechanisation of agriculture led to a collapse of agricultural employment. As farm-workers moved to the towns, there was inevitably transitional unemployment until they found other work.

Similar declines in employment have occurred in many industries, like the docks, in which spectacular technical changes have occurred. Moreover, even if technical change does not alter the total employment in any industry, it may transform its character, eliminating traditional craft and unskilled jobs and increasing employment for technically-qualified people. This causes transitional unemployment until people upgrade their skills.

Changes in the mix of employment are also generated by new products and by changes in the world prices of products and inputs. The motor car eliminated the occupation of horsemen, and in the 1960s cheaper oil led Britain to halve its manpower in the mines.

Such changes have gone on throughout human history. But are they now more extreme and does this account for the rise of unemployment? There is no evidence for this. The pattern of labour demand has not shifted between industries any more rapidly in recent years than earlier. Nor are the unemployed less well matched to the available job vacancies. There are of course serious problems of mismatch both across regions and across skills. But this has always been the case, and was much worse in the 1930s. Better education and training is an essential part of the strategy for attacking unemployment. But these problems are not new and, if other things had not gone wrong, we should be coping quite well with structural change.

So what has gone wrong?

The Inflation Problem and Demand-Deficiency

The problem of unemployment is closely related to the problem of inflation. A standard account runs as follows. There is a level of unemployment below which inflation will tend to increase. Actual unemployment can be above or below this. If it is below, there is excess demand, and inflation increases. If it is above, there is deficient demand. On this basis the rise in unemployment since the 1960s can be broken into two parts: (a) a rise in the level of unemployment necessary to stop inflation increasing, and (b) a rise in demand-deficient unemployment.

Factors behind the first of these rises may include a less punitive social security system, more wage pressure in the labour market, and higher taxes on jobs (employers' National Insurance contributions). These factors have led to pressure for real wages which are high relative to the level of wages justified by our underlying productivity. And productivity itself has been held down by overmanning. The resulting imbalance between desired real wages and productivity inevitably led, as it was accommodated, to increasing inflation. Then unemployment increased as part of the process of restraining real wages to stop inflation rising further.

The factors we have discussed so far are important, but they do not account for anything like the whole of the increase in unemployment, especially since 1979. The rise since 1979 is largely due to an increase in demand-deficient unemployment, undertaken mainly in order to reduce inflation rather than to hold it constant. The main factors behind this increase in demand-deficient unemployment are the budgetary cuts, the world recession and, for much of the time, the high real exchange rate. We shall devote some time to these influences in order to understand how a policy reversal would work.

The budget

Consider first the budgetary stance. There has been a major budgetary squeeze, mainly through a massive increase in tax rates. Taxes have risen from 40 per cent to 45 per cent of GDP between 1979 and 1983.

This may seem paradoxical, given the substantial budget deficit we are still running (some 3 per cent of gross national product). But to evaluate the overall effect of the budget on employment, one does not look at the crude budget deficit and say that a high deficit indicates an expansionary policy. The deficit needs adjusting in two ways. First, if there is a depression, low national income causes low tax receipts and thus a high deficit, even if policy is not expansionary. To assess the policy stance one needs to look at the deficit as it would be on present policies if output was on trend. Second, if there is inflation, the real value of the government debt is constantly being eroded. This is a capital gain to the government (and a capital loss to the holders of the debt). This magnitude therefore needs to be subtracted from the actual deficit. The most sensible way to do this is to replace the nominal interest component of the deficit by an estimate of the real interest paid. That shows the massive budgetary squeeze in 1980 and 1981. There has indeed been some relaxation since then, but we are still running a budget *surplus* (evaluated at trend output).

As can be seen, other Europeans have followed Britain's budget-cutting lead. In both Britain and the EEC as a whole the government's contribution to GDP has been slashed by at least 3 percentage points of GDP since 1979. It is not therefore surprising that output is low, especially when European governments are pledged to no relaxation in future (or even to further tightening). By contrast in the US the budgetary stance has been fairly level, with a mild expansion since 1982 and further expansion possible.

Turning to the unemployment experience of the different countries, there is a prima facie connection between this and the corresponding fiscal positions. Britain and Europe deflated, and unemployment there stayed up; the US did not deflate, and unemployment fell. The Chancellor in his Mais Lecture, argued that employment in the US has *always* increased faster than in Europe and that recent US employment growth is not therefore attributable to fiscal policy. But this is to miss the point. The US labour force has always grown faster than the European—hence the higher employment trend. It is not remarkable that employment has grown in the US but it is remarkable that, despite the rapid growth of the labour force, *unemployment has fallen* by nearly 4 percentage points in two years. This is surely connected with a confidence that the demand for output will be there—a confidence Europeans used to feel, but have lost due to constant budget-cutting.

The world recession
Jobs in Britain have also suffered from the world recession. The fall in world trade below its trend accounts for perhaps 2 percentage points of our present unemployment. But much of that is due to budget-cutting overseas.

The exchange rates
Another problem for Britain until recently has been the high exchange rate. This has had a disastrous effect on our competitiveness in world markets. Even in September 1984, with the trade-weighted exchange rate down to 77 (from 95 in 1980–81), British normal unit labour costs relative to our competitors' were still 17 per cent higher than in the average of the 1970s. This was obscured from popular view by the fact that the dollar is high against all currencies. But Britain's main trade is with Europe. The high sterling exchange rate made it impossible for whole sections of our manufacturing industry to compete in world

markets and they were simply wiped out. The exchange rate was high
partly due to North Sea oil and partly due to a monetary policy that did
nothing to offset this. Recent events make the future level of competitiveness unclear. But the central worry will remain the budgetary
position of the government. So what should be done?

WHAT TO DO

A Less Deflationary Budget, and Why it Will Work

The first thing is to adopt less deflationary budgetary policies, in order to
reduce the demand-deficient component of our unemployment. Some
people will answer that this is the old remedy, which has been tried and
failed. They will be sure to say that:

1. It will not raise output, but only prices.
2. It will increase the national debt and the money supply.
3. It will lead to a fall in the exchange rate.
4. It will lead to wage pressure.

We have answers to all these arguments.

Argument 1: It will not raise output, but only prices:
Answer: What can be achieved by a change in fiscal policy depends
crucially on the *level of existing slack* in the economy. If the economy is
operating without much slack, then extra demand will naturally affect
prices rather than output. In 1978, at the time of the Bonn Summit, the
labour market was already near to its average level of tightness. By
contrast nowadays only 12 per cent of manufacturing firms say that
shortages of skilled labour are likely to limit their output. This is lower
than in the recession years of 1975–76. Thus there is enormous slack in
the labour market, and every reason to think that a higher level of
demand for labour would mainly raise employment rather than wages
and prices. As regards physical capacity, the rate of capacity utilisation
in manufacturing is now rather higher than its historic average. But in
many industries much more could be produced before major bottlenecks appeared. And in services, where the bulk of new employment
would occur, capacity constraints are much less relevant. So we have the
resources to produce much more than we are producing.

How much extra output could be produced is difficult to quantify. It
depends above all on how quickly wage inflation emerges (which is
discussed under Argument 4). But we have no doubt that an expansion
of output is possible.

Against this view, one often hears the following misleading argument. It begins with the fact that, on average over the last 20 years, spending in money terms has risen by 12 per cent per annum, prices by 10 per cent and output by 2 per cent. It then concludes that of necessity a negligible fraction of any higher money spending 'goes into' output rather than prices. The conclusion is false. It is perfectly true that over the long haul the growth of output depends on real forces in the economy and not on the level of money spending. But a change in the growth rate of money spending can have profound short-term effects on output. For example, between 1980 and 1984 the growth rate of money spending in Britain was cut from 17 per cent a year to 6 per cent. This led to a massive contraction in output. The US recession in 1982 was also caused by a fall in money spending. But the Americans had the sense to reverse this fall. If we did the same, we too could have a big rise in output. The reason why money spending matters is that inflation has its own inertia, so that cuts in money spending cut output, and boosts to money spending raise it.

Thus we can confidently claim that, given the existing slack in the economy, a boost to demand will raise employment. How far demand rises when we boost the budget depends, of course, on how far interest rates rise to offset the budgetary boost. If the money supply targets are left unchanged, interest rates will certainly rise. But even then there is no sensible model in which the expansionary effect of the budgetary stimulus anywhere near crowds out an equivalent amount of other spending (via the interest rate effect)—so long as there are unemployed resources. One has only to look at the recent US experience to support this view: the US deficit has not harmed employment in the US, despite the rise in interest rates.

Economic analyses which suggest the government cannot stimulate output in a recession are based on faulty assumptions and contrary to the empirical evidence. The key question is whether there are genuinely unemployed resources. Since we have them in abundance, the present position is uniquely favourable for an effect of demand upon output rather than prices.

Argument 2: It will increase the national debt and the money supply:
Answer: This depends on whether the present budget is tight or not. Those who oppose a looser budgetary policy try to inhibit their opponents by talking as though the present stance is neutral. Relaxation from it is therefore reflationary and ruled out by analogy with previous attempts at reflation. But the present stance is *highly deflationary*. We are not repeating the old cry of 'more reflation'. Rather we are saying 'less deflation, please'.

So would a budgetary reflation imply a growth in money supply, or in the ratio of national debt to national income? The answer begins with a basic logical point and then proceeds to the facts of our present situation.

A budget deficit need never imply a growth in the money supply. It is always possible to cover the deficit by borrowing outside the banking system. By far the greater part of the budget deficit is always covered in this way, which is why the year-to-year relation between the budget deficit and the growth of money is practically non-existent.

The question then arises of whether, if we cover the whole deficit by borrowing, this will lead to unacceptable increases in the national debt, and hence excessive interest rates (to make people willing to hold the debt). In thinking about what level of debt is acceptable, one should note that in the prosperous 1950s the level of debt (relative to national income) was double what it is now. We would not wish to return to that level, but we could certainly accept a small rise in the debt/income ratio if it resulted from a temporary demand stimulus applied in a recession. For one would expect the debt/income ratio to grow in such circumstances, both because of low tax receipts induced by the recession and because of counter-cyclical budgetary policy. It makes sense to vary the budget from year to year, so that policy is more expansionary in a depression.

So how much room for manoeuvre is there? On present policies the debt/income ratio is intended to fall. There is therefore significant elbow-room for change. Less deflation would not be financially irresponsible.

Argument 3: It will lead to a fall in the exchange rate:
Answer: This depends on what monetary policy is pursued. If interest rates are kept high enough, this will attract money from abroad and stop the exchange rate depreciating. How high interest rates will be needed depends in part on how well the markets understand the point made in our answer to Argument 2. But, as we have said already, any induced rise in interest rates could only partly offset the job-creating effects of the expansion. In Britain, as in the US, a more expansionary fiscal position would raise employment even if interest rates rose.

So why did the French fiscal expansion of 1981 fail where the US succeeded. The French gave substantial pay rises, nationalised many firms and kept the lid on interest rates. Given all this, the exchange rate fell, inflation increased and the government was forced to put the expansion in reverse. With an appropriate monetary policy and a more sensible approach to pay, there is no reason why we should not succeed where the French failed.

Exchange rate problems would of course be much less likely if other countries were expanding at the same time. This is the main argument for having an internationally-concerted reflation in which many countries expand together. For if one country expands on its own the current account of its balance of payment deteriorates, unless it allows a fall in its exchange rate. By contrast, if all countries expand together, there need be little change in the pattern of current accounts with unchanged exchange rates. Thus from an exchange rate point of view a concerted reflation is much more attractive. However, given the current attitudes of the German and Japanese governments, we cannot be too hopeful about this and will continue to make our case that a purely British fiscal reflation can work without a major fall in the exchange rate *if* it is accompanied by a properly cautious monetary policy.

Argument 4: It will lead to wage pressure:
Answer: Apart from the exchange rate, the main source of inflationary pressure is in the labour market. As this tightens, upwards pressure on money income and prices may develop. Before going on, we should point out that the same result would follow from an export-led expansion, which many people would welcome while opposing a fiscally-driven expansion. But, either way, the problem cannot be ignored.

People differ about the speed with which upwards pressure on money income and prices would emerge. Some believe that quite large falls in unemployment could be achieved without extra inflation and that an incomes and prices policy might be unnecessary. Others believe the inflation problem would emerge more rapidly. But, if it proves impossible to reduce unemployment below present levels without inflation increasing, we would all consider some comprehensive approach including incomes and prices policy to be better than doing nothing to reduce unemployment. This would only succeed if undertaken after appropriate consultation and negotiations. The central point is that we are simply not willing to accept 13 per cent unemployment into the indefinite future.

The structure of the expansion
The success of a fiscal reflation depends also on its structure. Some forms of stimulus add at least £15,000 a year to the government deficit for every job they create. Hence a million jobs thus created might add over £15 billion a year to the budget deficit—or something like 5 per cent of the national income. The kinds of stimulus falling into this category include a typical increase in public investment or a cut in income tax. There are two problems with this type of stimulus. First, a substantial proportion of the spending leaks into imports and, second,

many of the jobs created are highly paid, reducing the total number of jobs created. One should therefore give priority to measures that stimulate demand for (a) home-produced output rather than imports and (b) less-skilled rather than more-skilled labour. But policies should also be judged by the value of the extra goods and services produced. If we use all these criteria together, good policies seem to include:

(i) infrastructure investment, especially in the renovation of our cities and the health of our people, and
(ii) cuts in taxes on jobs.

People will again differ on the detailed balance of policy, but we wish to lay special stress on one particular policy, to which we now turn.

A Job Guarantee for the Long-Term Unemployed

There are at present 1.25 million of our fellow citizens who have been out of work for over a year, and half of them have been out of work for over two years. This is a national disgrace. It is a terrible waste of resources and for many of the unemployed it is a source of deep misery and shame.

Humanitarian arguments suggest that special efforts should be made to get these people back to work. But there are also strong economic grounds for giving them priority. First, many of them have more or less given up looking for work. Their presence in the army of surplus labour thus does little to hold down inflation (or certainly less than the presence of people more recently made redundant). In fact, the evidence suggests that only the number of people unemployed for six months or less has any effect in restraining inflation. Those unemployed for over six months are performing no role in the fight against inflation. So if the extra demand for labour could be directed especially towards the long-term unemployed, there would be much less danger of its rekindling inflation than if it were spread over the whole of the labour force. Second, the longer people are away from work the more they lose their former skills and habits of work. Prudent investment, if nothing else, requires that we try our utmost to re-employ these people.

What can be done? We suggest that they should be guaranteed the offer of a job on a project such as those run by the Community Programme. These could be socially useful projects on which those employed would gain useful experience while being paid the hourly rate for the job. It would be unrealistic to expect that everyone would be offered a job as attractive as his or her last one, and many workers would use the experience as a staging-post on the way back to a better job. But it would provide a first break, which these people so desperately need.

It would cost the public a bit more than the dole. But what is the sense of the public losing £6500 a year (in taxes lost and benefits paid) when someone is unemployed, when for another £2000 the person could be employed on a useful project? For a net Exchequer cost of only £1 billion we could provide half a million jobs this way. The same money spent in more traditional ways would employ under 100,000 people.

We do not know what fraction of the unemployed would take up the offer of such a job, but meeting the demand for the jobs would require a major national effort of the same order as has been devoted to the Youth Training Scheme. The guarantee could not of course be a legal right but, as with the Youth Training Scheme, a firm statement of government intent. We believe that in a humane and sensible society this is the least we can attempt, rather than leave our fellow citizens to their quiet misery.

Other Issues

What we have outlined above is a basic programme, which could have a major effect in reversing the tide of unemployment. Those who believe that something can and must be done can unite on that. Within the programme there will be important differences of emphasis and of scale. Some will be more worried about the inflation problem. They will favour a smaller budgetary injection, with microeconomic policies to shift demand into the slacker parts of the labour market (via for example private sector job subsidies to the long-term unemployed and to the unskilled). There will be others who favour a larger programme with in some cases an increased reliance on public capital and public ownership.

In addition the long-run level of unemployment consistent with stable inflation depends on a whole range of labour market institutions. It depends on the training system—the willingness of employers and of unions to develop agreements on training to standards. It depends on the nature of bargaining arrangements and their relation to real wages and employment; and on many other factors. These are major issues and should be matters for debate up and down the land within the context of any serious campaign for jobs. But the first step is to secure the support for the immediate policies we have outlined of all who believe that something can and should be done.

THE COST OF DOING NOTHING

The reason why this matters is that the cost of doing nothing is so enormous.

First, and most obvious, is the simple loss of current output. If we had 5 per cent less unemployment, we could all be at least 5 per cent richer, in terms of output.

But, second, there is the loss of future output. The longer an experienced worker is unemployed, the more that worker loses skills and habits of work. At the same time young people simply fail to get trained—the current recession has seen a collapse of apprenticeship. Equally important, mass bankruptcies destroy the structure of business. For new businesses to replace them fully is not easy. They have to establish their credentials, which takes time, and meantime there are no jobs. Thus, though the recession may possibly yield some gains in cutting out old wood, the long-term costs enormously outweigh the gains. This campaign is as much against bankruptcy as in favour of jobs.

These are the purely economic effects. But on top of them are the less measurable psychological and social effects. Many of the unemployed are deeply depressed. Everyone needs to be needed, and for many people a job is an essential element in feeling needed. The fact that the unemployed are not out on the streets does not mean they are not suffering. Many of them are suffering, quietly.

Others are less quiet. We have already had youth riots. We do not want more. But this should not be our prime motive for action. A sober economic calculus, linked to humanitarian concern, is enough to make us act.

14. Selective Employment Measures and the Long-term Unemployed*

House of Commons Employment Committee

THE PROBLEM

We believe that unemployment is increasingly becoming the main social, moral and economic problem facing the country. At present, there are at least 3.278 million unemployed claimants. This is the official figure. We are concerned for the long-term unemployed, defined as those of all ages workless for at least a year, of whom there are now 1.352 million plus the 193,500 under-25s workless for between 6 and 12 months. These people are now about 40 per cent of total unemployed, a percentage which increases relentlessly. The longer someone has been unemployed the less likely they are to get a job. Successful job applicants tend to come from those who have recently joined the queue, while those who have been in it longest find their skills (if any) and work habits rusting as their hope dies until they may cease to look for work at all. We are, of course, concerned for all the unemployed, but more particularly with these long-term unemployed and, among them, with the 532,573 who have been unemployed for three years or more. Many of those who lost their jobs in the 1981–82 period did so at a time when alternative employment was particularly difficult to find and they now constitute a special category.

The costs of unemployment, including long-term unemployment, are not to be measured only in terms of benefit paid, taxes forgone and output lost. The associated increase of family breakdown, drug abuse, sickness, suicide and crime have a high economic and social cost.

POSSIBLE ANSWERS

The Committee heard that special employment measures are only one of the possible responses to the problem of high unemployment. Others

* Session 1985–86, published 29 January 1986.

include tax cuts and increased public expenditure. These are not necessarily exclusive, either of each other or of special employment measures, and a given sum of money can be spent on an almost infinite variety of permutations. Whatever other policy mix is adopted special employment measures would be needed to act quickly alongside. They are primarily intended to lower the number of unemployed in the *short term* in a cost effective way whilst other policies take effect, and help them eventually to get permanent jobs.

It was suggested to the Committee that tax cuts are a comparatively expensive way of creating jobs. Cost estimates vary, but Gavyn Davies estimated the net cost per person out of unemployment of income tax cuts as £47,000 in the second year. They also take much longer to create jobs than do other possibilities, but against this it can be argued that they do lead eventually to long-term market-related jobs.

Some witnesses thought that infrastructure investment would have a quicker effect in terms of jobs than would tax cuts, and the end result would be much-needed road, sewer, hospital, school and housing refurbishment. Such investment is less likely than tax cuts to generate imports. However, it is also expensive, by most estimates, though less so than tax cuts; Gavyn Davies estimated the net cost per person out of unemployment as £15,000 if this was achieved by current spending, £26,000 for capital spending, though estimates vary downwards as well as upwards. Both tax cuts and increased public investment have the disadvantage, in terms of help for the long-term unemployed, that they are likely to employ first people who have most recently been in work.

Special employment measures cost very much less per person no longer unemployed than either of the other possibilities. The annual net cost per person no longer unemployed was estimated by the DE to be from £2650 downwards. They also have the advantage that they can be targeted on particular groups such as the long-term unemployed.

Most of our witnesses agreed that some measures should be taken to help the long-term unemployed in particular. Some of these saw them as 'short-term patchwork response' (TUC) or 'palliatives' (CBI) to be applied simultaneously with and while awaiting the success of other measures designed to improve the economy. The Archbishop and Bishop of Liverpool took a longer-term view and spoke of people who may never get jobs and of 'unconventional work'. With the exception, again of the Liverpool bishops, most witnesses believed that the most valuable measures were those with the greatest element of training, though the DE and MSC stressed the value of the Community Programme (CP) even without the specific training element which has recently been added, as getting people back into the habit and pride of work.

On social as on economic grounds, and despite the problems regarding valuation of output described below, the Committee regard the special employment measures as the 'best buy' for the Chancellor of the Exchequer. . . .

CRITICISMS OF EXISTING MEASURES

A number of criticisms, practical and philosophical, can be levelled at the existing SEMs, and indeed at the whole concept of such schemes. Any expansion of the system will have to meet these.

A programme targeted on a particular group must, to be efficient, be sure of getting its message through to them. When we asked the DE witnesses how they made Community Programme schemes known to the long-term unemployed they replied: 'The schemes would be advertised in Jobcentres . . . In some cases the schemes are advertised, and advertised in Unemployment Benefit Offices where people go in week by week to sign.' However, it is no longer a requirement for unemployed people to register in the Jobcentres for work. The Department assured us that more people use Jobcentres than register for work, and referred to a survey showing that 70 per cent of long-term unemployed in Scotland and 65 per cent in the South-East visit them. They also suggested that the fact that there has so far been no shortage of applicants for CP places argues that people do get the necessary information. We believe that the present system of informing people about what is available should be improved. It is important that information should reach those who may have given up the search as well as those who are actively seeking work.

Among the criticisms of SEMs made to us was that unless they contribute to a lowering of wage expectations they are not only cosmetic in that they displace workers elsewhere rather than increasing the number of jobs, but also actually harmful because they raise public expenditure and taxation, with a consequent negative effect on employment. The fear of displacement of existing workers was also expressed by the TUC in respect particularly of the Enterprise Allowance Scheme, a programme which, the DE Memorandum accepted, carried this risk. The CBI, while recommending greater involvement of the private sector with the Community Programme, urged adequate consultation to eliminate the possibility of substitution. The Volunteer Centre told us that programmes could harm voluntary projects as well, and the DE witnesses admitted that perhaps 4 per cent of projects displaced voluntary activity. While the Committee favours a more equitable sharing of available jobs than the market provides, we accept that displacement can be disruptive.

A problem with special measures of the job-creation type is how output is to be valued if there is no market for the product, as Gavyn Davies said. Most of our witnesses stressed that the greatest value of the CP lay not so much in the value of its product as in the long-term benefit of bringing people back into the labour market. However we note that the government is now talking in terms of special employment measures creating 'real jobs'. Furthermore, of course, for the present it is a choice between some output or no output.

It is also argued that some SEMs carry 'deadweight'—that is, that a number of people helped by a particular scheme would have found work in any case. The EAS, in particular, is open to this criticism; the DE estimate, on the basis of surveys conducted, that 50 per cent of the enterprises supported would have been started anyway. The CP, the largest programme, is remarkably 'clean' in this respect; the rules have been drawn very tightly to prevent the undertaking of projects which would have been carried out under some other auspices, and the DE estimate that its impact on unemployment is 93 per cent. Deadweight increases the cost of a scheme for each additional job created.

The limited time-scale of CP projects (up to one year for each employee) was also the subject of adverse comment. The Liverpool Churches felt that the effects of becoming unemployed again after a year, in an area where there are very few jobs to be had, is so harmful to the individual that it might be better to 'spread the jam a little less thinly' by providing permanent jobs for fewer people. Neighbourhood Energy Action claimed that it would be easier to run projects if staff, and especially managerial staff, could be retained for longer than a year. The Volunteer Centre complained that the turnover of SEM staff disrupted projects run in conjunction with the voluntary sector.

Another criticism of the CP is that the rate of pay—up to an average of £63 a week—is too low to attract men with families who will receive more on benefit. The DE told us that there had so far been no difficulty in getting people to take up existing numbers of places, but that does not necessarily mean that the remuneration is not a bar to some. At present most people on the programme are aged between 18 and 25. To expand the numbers to bring in men with families would mean increasing the allowance.

The problem of long-term unemployment is so large that private sector involvement is essential, and yet Community Programme projects are run overwhelmingly by the public and voluntary sectors. The DE told us that only 2 per cent were run by the private sector; they explained that there were difficulties caused by the 'no private gain rule', but that they were investigating ways of getting the private sector to play a bigger part. They said: 'That means increasing knowledge amongst employers to get them to come into the Community Programme in a bigger way, and it could be by trying out newer approaches with the private sector to get employers to take on long-term unemployed people, maybe, in clearing derelict sites . . . These are areas where we will be carrying out experiments this year, and there could be potential for expansion if the resources were available.' The CBI, who told us that a survey at the end of 1984 showed that 40 per cent of respondent companies believed that business should play a direct part in helping the unemployed via the special employment measures, welcomed the initiatives.

One obvious way in which the private sector could be encouraged to give more help to the long-term unemployed would be by paying them to do so, perhaps to the extent of the benefit the worker would otherwise have received. One SEM which does at present subsidise employers, to the tune of £15 a week for every 17-year-old taken on at £50 a week or less, is the Young Workers Scheme, but that closed for applications in March 1986 as a result of the extension of YTS.

We asked the DE their views on an employment subsidy. They were unenthusiastic. In written evidence they told us: 'Experience with the Department of Employment's previous job subsidy schemes . . . suggests that such arrangements involve comparatively high levels of dead-weight and substitution.'

Gavyn Davies was in favour of a marginal employment subsidy: 'If you target the marginal change in employment you are likely to end up with a much lower deadweight element [and] you reduce the administrative burden of the problems we have been talking about, and administration would be reduced by a subsidy which was applied across the board to the private sector [and] it would be good for our international competitiveness. It would reduce our marginal labour costs, which would come down, which is what we are trying to achieve in countless different directions. I have not thought about any major disadvantages, except for the cost. I think it is hard to predict what the cost would be in advance, but I am sure from my knowledge of what the Department of Employment thinks they will feel that the net cost of such a subsidy will be much higher than the net cost of the Community Programme. The output will be much more useful in general than the Community Programme output.'

The existing measures are just not extensive enough. With a client group of 1.6 million, programmes which support a maximum of 344,000 not all of whom will be long-term unemployed at any one time, *before* allowing for deadweight and displacement, are inadequate, touching less than 1 in 6 of those concerned.

OUR RECOMMENDATIONS

To deal effectively with this major moral, economic and social problem, resources and actions must be targeted directly on those hardest hit— the long-term unemployed. We make recommendations whereby over a period a *job guarantee* could be given to all the long-term unemployed (beginning with those out of work for longest) who wanted one, and we set them out in the following paragraphs.

In order to meet the criticisms outlined above, the special measures necessary must create additional jobs; must create them at the lowest feasible net cost to the Exchequer, taking into account the value of the work done; must be directed to the most socially valuable tasks not presently being undertaken; must involve the private sector; must lead to regular jobs with regular employers; and must pay the rate for the job for a full week if required. The aim must be to provide all those who want work with the chance to do something constructive for society. It would obviously be preferable if those jobs were long-term since it is demoralising for someone who has been out of work for a long time to be pitched out of work again after only a short spell.

It is not possible to estimate the number of long-term unemployed who would take up the offer of a guaranteed job. Much would, of course, depend on the nature of the job on offer. Some people could be expected to wait to get a job in the traditional way or in their chosen or specialist field, and there may well be some people who have adjusted to not having a job, or have special personal problems. We think 750,000 extra places, in addition to the 230,000 on the CP, at the peak of the scheme, would probably be sufficient. We have therefore considered ways in which 750,000 extra jobs could be created.

Obviously it would not be possible to provide these jobs at once; we envisage a build-up over a period of three years. It would be important to establish pilot schemes at once in selected areas of high unemployment in order to learn what detailed proposals are most feasible. There could thereafter be an eventual gradual dismantling of the system when no longer needed. The aim of the measures would be not merely to provide temporary employment but to qualify the long-term un-employed to take up market-related jobs as and when these become available.

Where would the extra jobs be found? One obvious area is in urban rehabilitation and here we recommend a new programme, a building improvement programme similar to the suggestions of the CBI. Many of the areas of highest long-term unemployment are also the most physically derelict in Britain. There is an enormous backlog in main-tenance work and the construction industry is employing half a million fewer workers than it did a decade or so ago. Many of the skills already exist or could be learned through an expansion of on- and off-the-job training.

The involvement of the private sector is desirable, to manage the projects and supply any additional skilled labour and supervision required. Local authorities and private agencies, firms and individuals could propose schemes and the MSC would decide on which should be supported. Private contractors would then tender for the projects. The long-term unemployed should then be paid the rate for the job, with a maximum average wage cost laid down by the MSC. This would currently be around £105 a week.

Jobs provided under this scheme would be for one year, and the MSC would need to provide intensive counselling and assistance for partici-pants as the termination of employment approached.

Projects which would be supported under this part of the scheme might include redecoration and renovation of private houses, especially those belonging to those in special need, council houses where it was clear that they would not otherwise be dealt with, and privately rented houses provided the tenants were low-paid (and it is desirable that the landlords should provide a reasonable fee); the redecoration and reno-vation of schools and hospitals, minor road repairs and site clearance and environmental improvement. We suggest that local authorities and the NHS would probably not pay for work done for them, to avoid pol-itical difficulties about whether the jobs are additional (additionality).

The question of additionality might still arise, if a scheme led a council to do less of its own work and cut its rates, or a private person not to embark on a particular scheme. However, on the government's own arguments regarding tax cuts, the money saved by ratepayers or indi-viduals could be expected to be spent elsewhere, thus generating em-ployment.

This programme would cost more per job than the CP because of higher wage costs, and higher costs of supervision and the materials for the more ambitious projects. Assuming a saving on unemployment benefit of £2000 per head, we estimate the net cost per job at £5000 (perhaps £4000 if there were significant receipts). On this basis the provision of 300,000 extra jobs would cost £1.5 billion a year once the scheme was in full operation.

The second part of our programme is in the health and personal social services, which are highly labour-intensive, and offers another field for the employment of long-term unemployed. It is government policy to move wherever possible from institutional care of the mentally or physically infirm to 'community care', and this, as the recent Report of the Select Committee on Social Services makes clear, is more labour-intensive.

The Social Services at present employ some half a million people. We suggest that 50,000 long-term unemployed could be employed in the personal social services by local authorities or voluntary organisations, working for instance in short-stay units or supporting those discharged from hospital, and 50,000 in the NHS. The allocation of tasks and the screening and supervision of individuals will present some problems especially in the initial stages, but there is a wealth of experience, particularly in the voluntary sector, which shows how such problems might be overcome. Some kinds of care are a matter of aptitude as much as of extensive training, and the system would be a great deal better than discharging someone back 'into the community' to receive either no help or that of some devoted relative whose own work may be severely disrupted as a result.

We should like to see these workers employed on a normal employment contract for one year in the first instance. Their first year's wages would be paid by the MSC, at an average rate of, perhaps, £120, depending on the level of skills required and the nature of the work undertaken, and after that year we hope that given the relatively rapid turnover in these occupations they could be established and the subsidised employment given to someone else.

The total cost of this recommendation would be about £0.4 billion.

The third part of the programme we recommend would be a wage subsidy to employers in the private sector (other than in construction) who take on long-term unemployed. We suggest £40 a week (the average benefit a long-term unemployed can expect to receive), to be paid for a year providing that non-subsidised employment by the employer does not fall. This proposal differs from the government's existing scheme to pay £20 a week to people to encourage them to accept low paid jobs, as we suggest that payment should be made to the employer and should not be linked to any particular level of pay. Both schemes could operate simultaneously and complement each other.

We think that for a cost of £1.4 billion about 350,000 new jobs could be created by this means at a cost per job of £4000, even allowing for a high proportion of those provided for being employed in any case.

The total net cost of our recommendations, when operating fully, would be £3.3 billion. The cost for the 823,000 out of work for over two years or more would be about £1.5 billion and for the 533,000 out of work for over three years, £1 billion.

The scheme overall should be run by the MSC. It is they who must be responsible for placing the long-term unemployed on their books in jobs, and for counselling them and actively helping those on the temporary schemes to get further employment. We therefore suggest that the MSC decide which building, etc. projects be supported, that they pay the wages of the workers in the social services field and that private employers outside construction wishing to use the £40 a week inducement would, in the first instance, either approach or be approached by them. This MSC involvement might have cost implications for the Commission itself.

CONCLUSIONS

Some people have reservations about special measures as a way of cutting unemployment. They ask: If we are going to spend more, why not spend it through normal channels? The answer is that such expenditure would be unlikely to reach the long-term unemployed and particularly the very long-term unemployed. That is the first reason why we want to concentrate expenditure directly on those who have been out of work for a long time. The second reason is that it is a relatively cheap way of creating jobs, and the third is the obvious moral case for helping those who are most in need.

What we are recommending is not make-work. It is real work, with a socially useful output. In the social services, NHS and the non-construction private sector, these jobs would be normal jobs, although government financial support for each individual would be for twelve months. In the building improvement scheme the jobs would be temporary (one-year), and it would be important that those involved received intensive counselling and placement as the year comes to an end. A key part of our strategy is the obligation we are putting on the MSC to give priority to the placement of the long-term unemployed, and of the ex-long-term unemployed after their one-year placements. For this reason we welcome the government's new plans for intensive counselling of the long-term unemployed.

Long-term unemployment on the present scale requires the kind of response which the nation gave in wartime. Within the limits of the Chancellor's fiscal adjustment (estimated at £9.5 billion in the 1985 Red Book) the expenditure proposed in this Report is neither excessive nor unmanageable.

SUMMARY OF RECOMMENDATIONS

We recommend that a job guarantee should be given to the long-term unemployed, prefaced by immediate pilot projects concentrated in areas of high unemployment. This should be achieved by:

(a)   the establishment of a building improvement scheme to provide 300,000 extra year-long jobs for the long-term unemployed through a building improvement programme;

(b)   the employment of 100,000 long-term unemployed in the social services and NHS; and

(c)   the introduction of a subsidy to private employers to take on long-term unemployed additionally to their existing employees, to an overall total of 350,000 additional jobs.

15. Report*

House of Lords Select Committee on Overseas Trade

There has been a steady trend of deterioration in Britain's manufacturing performance taken as a whole, over many years. It has been argued before the Committee, notably by the Treasury, that the sharp deterioration apparent in the last few years will be reversed when inflation has been cured or reduced to low levels, and when the special effects of North Sea oil with large surplus earnings on the oil account have disappeared. The Committee reject the concept that it will happen automatically and in time. While healthy world trade demands imports as well as exports—in response to the law of comparative advantage— the pattern of our visible trade is unbalanced. The increase in imports and reduction in British exports' share of world trade are two sides of the same coin—lack of overall competitiveness and consequent reduction in capacity of manufacturing industry as a whole. There are, in the Committee's opinion, important long-term problems to be tackled, which will take time to cure; and there are some shorter term proposals which can produce more immediate improvements. But whether long-term or short-term all members agree that there is an urgency about the position of manufacturing industry that needs tackling by the whole nation at once. It is neither exaggeration, nor irresponsible, to say that the present situation undoubtedly contains the seeds of a major political and economic crisis in the foreseeable future. Yet the nation at large appears to be unaware of the seriousness of its predicament. The Committee have therefore shaped their Report so as to help gain recognition of the true situation.

* House of Lords, Session 1984–85 (238-I), pp. 56–77.

A CHANGE IN NATIONAL ATTITUDE

The Committee believe that a neglect of manufacturing matched by a decline in the benefits that accrue from North Sea oil will have grave consequences for Britain. The Committee think that these are symptomatic of a general lack of awareness of the importance of manufacturing and of a healthy performance in international trade, and it is reflected in the inadequate social esteem accorded to industry and trade in modern British culture.

It has not been a British attitude to treat manufacturing as an activity which merits high priority. People of the highest potential have neither been educated nor encouraged to go into industry. The diplomatic or home civil service, the City, the professions, and academia have been preferred, both in esteem and in some cases in rewards. And yet over many decades the country's ability to import the food and raw materials it needs has depended on the ability to export manufactured goods, and the standard of living improved largely because of the success of manufacturers in producing the right products for the home and overseas markets at competitive prices and quality. Expectations of improved standards of living and of improved social services have assumed that manufacturers will produce the wealth. Yet insufficient importance has been given by the nation as a whole to the needs of a competitive manufacturing industry.

The political parties have not acknowledged that there is a need for consistency and continuity of government policies, particularly fiscal policies, aimed at ensuring the health and success of manufacturing industry. This contrasts with what has generally been the case in West Germany, France and Japan. Manufacturing decisions have to anticipate conditions far beyond the term of any one Parliament and confidence depends on the certainty that government policies will be helpful and not damaging.

Nor is there sufficient unity of purpose in manufacturing industry between management and their employees. An adversarial climate in industry discourages good recruits, hinders good management, reduces productivity and puts off customers both at home and overseas.

This has to change. If it does not, the standard of living in this country will continue to improve less than in others and may indeed fall, our social services will be in jeopardy and unemployment will remain high. The Committee are convinced that British people must recognise that success in manufacturing and trade is the *sine qua non* both of their happiness and prosperity as individuals and of the collective harmony and stability of the nation and its institutions. This calls for a fundamental change of attitude from all sections of society followed by a national effort of will to apply the creed in daily life. The Committee naturally look to government, having the greatest influence and resources at its disposal, to help set the tone. But all people and all sections of society—whether they be politicians, managers or the workforce, industry or financial institutions, or the media or consumers—need to acquire a common understanding about the vital place in the life of the nation of manufacturing and trade which transcends party political ideology.

The Committee do not stand alone in this matter. Many experienced witnesses share this opinion in varying degrees. Indeed the Secretary of State for Trade and Industry told the Committee that the 'single most important factor' in achieving the extra growth which the country needs was a 'change in culture'. The Committee agree with this.

But how is the change to be achieved? The Committee believe that the role of the education system is crucial. As a recent report by another Select Committee of this house pointed out, a number of schemes exist which link industry and schools under the auspices of the Standing Conference on Schools Science and Technology, the CBI's Understanding British Industry Project, the Schools Council Industry Project and the Industrial Society. The Committee support these efforts.

But the Committee think that there is a strong case for adjustments in curriculum and syllabus wherever this may be necessary in order to guarantee that an understanding of industry and commerce and their importance is inculcated in the young. The Committee note that the government have announced their intention of issuing statements of policy in matters of curriculum. They also note that the government take the view that 'some awareness of economic matters' should feature in the secondary school curriculum. The Committee wholeheartedly endorse this view and hope that the government will issue clear policy statements to ensure that such instruction will in fact be given and that teachers will be trained and equipped accordingly and will be encouraged by Education Authorities to learn about the practical work of manufacturing industry in their area.

To achieve the quickest possible change in national attitudes, the Committee urge that publicity campaigns and promotional exercises like Industry Year (1986) and its Education Working Group be widely supported so as to achieve improved recognition by the British people of the nature of manufacturing and trade.

COMPETITIVENESS

The success of manufacturing industry both in the domestic market and overseas is dependent upon the competitiveness of the goods which are produced. The only way to expand manufacturing is to produce goods which are competitive in every sense. Competitiveness is a function of price competitiveness, including productivity, and non-price factors.

When measured against overseas wholesale prices, the prices of United Kingdom exports of manufactures have become more competitive since 1980 and 1981 when they were, relatively speaking, very uncompetitive indeed. Similar improvements have been observed when United Kingdom wholesale prices are measured against the price of foreign imports. But unit labour costs when measured in national currencies are getting worse in relation to those of our competitors.

This implies that improvements in productivity are being eroded by labour costs. A limited competitive advantage was restored by the downward movements in the value of sterling since 1981, but in 1985 the trends are being reversed. Given that productivity has improved (though partly as a consequence of the contraction of the industrial base and the closure of less efficient plants) and given that the downward drift of sterling since 1981 has also acted in favour of price competitiveness, it seems clear that unit labour costs are rising too quickly. They are eroding the advantages gained with such great effort on other fronts. Evidence received by the Committee from the ABCC showed that the deterioration in United Kingdom competitiveness between 1970 and 1980 had much to do with the fact that United Kingdom wages costs rose faster than those of competitors. In the latter period productivity gains were also much lower in the United Kingdom than elsewhere. The importance of wages as a determinant of competitiveness leads the Committee to conclude that pay settlements in manufacturing must have regard to the cost competitiveness of the manufactures which are produced. These criteria must influence the pay settlements of shopfloor and all ranks of management alike. Such agreements will be easier where firms show a willingness to invest so that the efforts of employees will not be frustrated by out of date equipment and where they involve their employees in investment decisions so that the equipment is fully used.

Some witnesses also complained of the inequalities between the United Kingdom and competitor countries in the prices of other inputs like electricity. The tarriff on high-load energy was particularly unpopular. Energy, and other government-affected costs, had risen faster than inflation and this too affected price-competitiveness adversely. The Committee were informed that on average energy costs amounted to no more than 3 per cent of total costs of British industry. But some industries like chemicals, steel, paper and board and glass, were so dependent on energy that its price determined the price-competitiveness of products. Although the CEGB gave discounts for customers who practise load management, they were prevented from offering cheaper prices because of primary energy costs. Nor were they able to offer subsidies because of statutory regulation. The Committee recommend, in the case of electricity, that steps should be taken to enable the industry to offer energy at prices which are comparable to those enjoyed by our overseas competitors.

Price competitiveness depends also on productivity. Poor productivity can put British products at a considerable price disadvantage at home and abroad. Productivity gains in the United Kingdom have consistently been lower than those of competitors and have failed to compensate for increased wages costs. Productivity has improved but there seems to be considerable scope for further gains. The gaps developed in the 1970s remain as wide as ever. The Committee were struck by the wide disparities in productivity, measured on a comparable basis, between various plants of the Ford Motor Company. In 1984 for example the Dagenham and Halewood assembly plants utilised only 60 per cent of installed capacity while the continental plants achieved 100 per cent. In Britain ten vehicles are produced per employee per year, while on the Continent they produce eighteen. Yet in some of the smaller production lines Ford United Kingdom's productivity is better than that of its Continental plants. The Committee believe that all in industry must understand that they share a common interest in improving the productivity of British industry as they will share in the disaster if they do not.

There are many non-price factors which govern competitiveness. For example quality, design, reliability, delivery times, after-sales service and any other factors which influence the relative attractiveness of the product. Market research is also vital. Non-price factors are increasingly important and the Committee think that the practice of the best companies in this field should be applied by all manufacturers. Three factors have been emphasised to the Committee as particularly important.

The first is quality. It is most important for British goods to regain their reputation for quality and reliability. Quality control—whereby workers check the quality of their own products—is being widely introduced into British industry and this is to be commended. While in Japan, the Committee became acquainted with the zero defect method. An even more rigorous check on the quality of goods can be achieved by statistical process control (SPC) whereby workers monitor statistically the precision with which their particular process produces components. SPC (which some members of the Committee saw in operation to very great effect at the latest installations in the engine plant of the Ford Motor Company) has great potential and should be applied as widely as possible in British industry. Not only does it make for improved quality but also improves worker involvement and interest in the job.

A second factor is design. In the past too many goods were produced with little regard for the precise requirements of the export markets which were expected to take them. In the Committee's view the answer lies readily to hand in the form of in-house or out-house market research.

Finally, there is the question of delivery. Prompt delivery should obviously be achieved at all times. But some witnesses also called for an improvement in other features of delivery including after-sales service. It was suggested that a 'total product' approach involving services as well as goods would help competitiveness. The reluctance of some British manufacturers to quote delivered prices may well put them at a disadvantage.

Non-price competitiveness is important and, in the Committee's opinion, the means are available to industry to improve it. Primarily it is a matter for individual firms themselves, but the Committee support the work of the CBI, BSI and other bodies to stimulate improvements in this field.

NATIONAL INDUSTRIAL POLICY

Macroeconomic Policy

The Committee considered the question of a national industrial policy under the headings of macroeconomic policy, support measures, and coordination of public policy. The Committee are convinced both from their study of competitor economies and from the evidence they have assembled from their many witnesses that government in Britain should take the initiative in formulating a national industrial policy which makes for faster growth of manufacturing. It appears to them that in France, West Germany and Japan there is, and has been over the years, a remarkable degree of consensus amongst all sections of society on the need for a strong manufacturing base and a high level of exports of manufactured goods as a means of growth. Furthermore this common understanding has in part inspired and in part been reflected in consistent policies on the part of national governments which, in contrast to the United Kingdom, have transcended party politics and, in some cases, quite radical changes in the political complexion of the governments in question.

In Japan the influence of the Ministry of International Trade and

Industry (MITI) has traditionally pervaded all aspects of commercial life
and the 'vision' of the course of future industrial growth has set the tone
of subsequent development. In Germany the Ministry of the Economy
and in France the Commissariat Général du Plan have fulfilled a similar,
if slightly less *dirigiste*, function. The influence of these institutions no
longer needs to be what it was but the legacy remains in the form of
commonly held assumptions about the importance of manufacturing and
trade and clearly articulated policies which given them effect.

In Britain this is not, and has not been, the case. The major attempts
to coordinate policies in a coherent manner conducive to growth of
manufacturing have been relatively short-lived. Some of the aims of
government at present are laudable. The Committee entirely agree with
the importance that is attached to controlling inflation, easing the
burdens on enterprise, and encouraging new businesses. But they feel
that the paramountcy of manufacturing has not been recognised in the
formulation of policy with the result that policies—or on occasion the
avowed lack of policies—have actually been inimical to manufacturing.
The Committee believe that governments of whatever political persuasion should strive for faster growth of manufacturing and in setting their
macroeconomic policy should be mindful of industry's needs. They
identify four areas of macroeconomic policy which have caused harm to
our manufacturing base in recent years.

Monetary policy
The Committee regret that a combination of tight monetary policy
under the Medium-Term Financial Strategy, as part of the government's
anti-inflation policy, accompanied by a high exchange rate, resulted in
the loss of a significant part of Britain's manufacturing base.

Exchange rate
The Committee received much evidence of the difficulties caused to
manufacturing by the exchange rate. There were two principal complaints, first that the level of sterling *vis-à-vis* other currencies has been
too high; and secondly that the rate has been too unstable. Many
witnesses stressed the adverse effect on manufacturing output of the
rises in sterling between 1977 and 1981 and its continued high level in
1981–82. The high level which Sterling attained against the United
States dollar and major European currencies made British goods less
competitive in home and foreign markets. Exports fell, import penetration rose, and for those exporters who held on to their markets, profit
margins were squeezed severely. The witnesses who complained of this
were drawn from all sectors and included the TUC, the CBI, the Bank of

England, the motor, textile, electrical, chemical, engineering, paper and furniture industries. Many also complained bitterly of the instability of the exchange rate rather than the problem of coping with any particular rate. The problem here is that long-term contracts have to be undertaken for purchase and supply and imports may have to be purchased in a currency which is rising relative to the pound while exports compete against currencies which have changed far less. This can lead manufacturers to source components in the countries to which they are selling so as to reduce currency losses. Whilst it is possible, at a cost, to hedge against some changes in exchange rates to cover future orders or deliveries, this cannot protect the domestic supplier to the home market against exchange rates which give the foreign importer price advantages that cannot be matched—hence the rapid growth of import penetration and the demise of many United Kingdom industrial concerns.

The Committee are sympathetic to these complaints. They consider that stability of the exchange at an appropriate rate is crucial to maintaining competitiveness and greater consideration should be given to this in government policy by whatever means appropriate. It was strongly felt by the CBI and some others that this could be achieved by membership of the exchange rate mechanism of the European Monetary System (EMS). The Committee concede that to maintain stability of the exchange rate might lead to greater variations in interest rates but they think that this is a price worth paying. Not all interest rate movements will, after all, be upward. The Committee urge that by these and other means the government should provide for greater stability in the exchange rate.

So far as the level of the exchange rate is concerned, the Committee feel that government should have greater regard for competitiveness of manufacturing industry in the formulation of policy. They agree with one witness who wished that 'in considering the financial policy in the United Kingdom the effect of the exchange rate on the competitiveness of British industry would be one of the factors which would be taken into account when considering matters such as interest rates, etcetera', and that the effects of any given rate of exchange upon competitiveness were better understood. In seeking an appropriate rate for sterling, government should have regard for the rate against European and other competitors' currencies rather than just the US dollar.

Interest rates

Government policy on interest rates, like that on the exchange rate, has not given priority to the needs of industry. But in the past rates have been governed by policies directed at constraining the growth of the money supply, and more recently to determining the level of sterling. It was pointed out in evidence that by long-term historical standards the real rate of interest—that is to say the difference between the nominal rate and the rate of inflation—is not 'enormously high' in this country, though it is higher than in the 1960s and 1970s. And the CBI took the view that the rate of interest is 'not a major factor in investment decisions, but it did affect the balance sheet in an unfavourable direction and therefore made one's competitiveness harder to achieve'. The CBI have more recently urged the vital importance of lower rates of interest.

It has to be borne in mind that in competitor countries loans may be obtained by large sectors of industry at subsidised rates. Cheaper money would probably lead to more investment by small and medium-sized enterprises who rely more on borrowings for their money. It would also relieve pressures on competitiveness and profitability. The Committee urge the government to have regard to the needs of industry as a borrower, and to the needs of export credit when they take a view on interest rates.

Taxes

The Committee are of the opinion that the tax regime should favour manufacturing business and investment. They are conscious that many steps have already been taken in this direction. Nevertheless, they are concerned at the government's having decided to phase out 100 per cent first-year allowances on capital investment. The government's philosophy is that this had led to a distortion of decision-making with investment being undertaken in order to reduce tax liability rather than on grounds of real return. A lower rate of tax on company profits is preferable. Nevertheless, the Committee fear the consequences of ending the concession of capital allowances, especially when the final effect of this measure is felt in 1987. While it is understandable that the government should wish to discourage investment which is inefficient the decision on allowances will also discourage innovatory investment aimed at increasing our capacity to respond to increases in demand.

Other aspects of our tax system were also thought to be inimical to growth. The motor industry felt strongly that car tax should be abolished.

Local taxes in the form of rates, also fall heavily on industry, especially if firms are not operating at full capacity or have empty premises. Liability to local rates should in some way reflect the utilisation and capacity of a plant. This can only be of long-term benefit both to the firm and to the locality in which it is placed.

Support Measures

The Committee think that government should step up their support for innovation and export and identify areas of industry which need support, and consider what steps need to be taken by them and by others for those industries and firms to develop themselves to their full potential in terms of manufacturing base and export achievement. This support should be given in conjunction with industry wherever possible. There is no doubt that, with a will, considerable achievements can be recorded as a result of positive government policy, backed up by the support of government and industry. The Committee particularly have in mind the way in which the North Sea oil resources were developed and, on a more modest scale, the manner in which the Alvey Project on fifth-generation computers has been evolved.

Having taken decisions on the areas requiring support and advice, remedial measures can be taken in a number of ways in partnership with the private sector. These include purchasing programmes which will encourage investment to increase or improve manufacturing capacity by assisting industries to undertake R&D in areas in which they are currently deficient on the lines set out in the Report of the Select Committee on Science and Technology on Engineering R&D; and by taking the initiative in education and training on the lines set out in the Report of the Select Committee on Science and Technology on Education and Training for New Technologies. Where they can be justified in terms of return on costs, infrastructure projects could also be undertaken. For example, the advantages of expenditure on improvements to the British road system in terms of the efficiency of British industry have been stressed to the Committee by witnesses. The Committee agree with them.

Coordination of Public Policy

The Chancellor of the Exchequer told the Committee that 'The Government's general philosophy is that it is industry's job to make itself competitive, it is the Government's job to provide an overall climate'. The Committee agree that the prime responsibility for industry lies with the industrial firms themselves. But it is essential for the government to provide the kind of climate in which manufacturing industry will thrive. Conditions of late years have been none too good. This is why the Committee wish to see the government adopting macroeconomic policies which favour manufacturing and trade and why they would like to see government taking a coherent view on the measures of support needed by manufacturing in general and certain sectors in particular.

A number of witnesses share the Committee's opinion that the government needs an overview of priorities backed up by measured support to achieve their aims. As Sir Hector Laing wrote, '. . . The present government has in effect made a virtue of not having a vision of the future of British industry, and a positive policy of distancing the State from the industrial sector. I think the Government should acknowledge that the nation does have an industrial problem in which it has a serious policy interest. A clear indication that the Government is ready to give a strong lead by, for example, launching an industrial priorities exercise, could prove very effective.'

Most witnesses were agreed that the widest consultation was necessary. Sir Hector Laing thought that a consultative body involving the CBI, TUC and the government—perhaps NEDO—should set these priorities. Lord Benson thought NEDO 'could be used as a basis to begin the strategy which is necessary to bring the country back into a reasonable industrial state.' The TUC also took the view that NEDC and the EDCs could be made more effective to this end. Sir Charles Villiers, on the other hand, thinks that the answer lies within the structure of government itself. He thinks that an Economic Cabinet Committee with its own staff of civil servants and businessmen should formulate a medium-term industrial strategy backed up by investment and other institutions to give effect to its policies.

The Committee are reluctant to propose the establishment of new institutions. A greater sense of common purpose will make existing organisations function more effectively. They think that the framework of the National Economic Development Office should be developed as a source of advice on these matters. The Committee are aware of the excellent work carried out by some of the sectoral Economic Development Committees and think that their advice should be more effectively followed up. However, the present National Economic Development Council has not so far proved to be an effective body in securing action on the views of the 'Little Neddies' on industrial matters nor in promoting the interests of manufacturing and trade in matters of general policy. Chaired by the Chancellor, it has to be heavily involved in macro-economic arguments.

The Committee therefore recommend that attempts be made to make the NEDC more effective in industrial matters. If this cannot be achieved, the Committee further recommend the establishment of a separate committee within the NEDC system of not more than twelve members, representative of industry, commerce and finance, and chaired by the Secretary of State for Trade and Industry to fulfil this purpose. This Committee could also keep under review legislation and policies with the aim of ensuring that priority is in fact given to the competitiveness of manufacturing industry.

BETTER MANAGEMENT

Manufacturing industry can only be as good as its managers. Without good management there can be no prospect of a resurgence of manufacturing or of trade in manufactures. The Committee think that industry is at a disadvantage in competing with the professions, the civil service, and the City. The fault partly lies with industry itself. The Committee think that industry needs to make itself more attractive to young people in terms of the career prospects it offers—in terms of pay, advancement, responsibility, job satisfaction and status. But attitudes of undergraduates in universities also need to be changed and become more positive towards industry as a career.

The Committee believe that the education system also has to give more prominence to industry and its needs than it does at present. The Committee have already alluded to the need to inculcate into schoolchildren a sense of the role and value of industry and commerce. Many witnesses have also commented on the need for universities to produce more 'industry-useful' graduates. The shortages of graduates in technological subjects have been commented upon in other studies—like the Butcher Committee and the House of Lords Science and Technology Committee. They endorse the findings and recommendations of these Committees and do not wish to go over this ground again.

But from the extensive evidence they have received, the Committee wish to draw attention to some major shortcomings. The British Importers Confederation thought that a major cause of the country's relative decline has been the lack of graduate and postgraduate production engineers. A number of leading figures in industry also thought that universities did not produce the kind of graduates which industry needed for research or for technically qualified management. This stems partly from the fact that 'industry has not told the academic world what it wants'. The Committee received heartening evidence of what could be achieved when one employer did take an interest in sponsoring sixth-formers to take up studies in textile technology. On the other hand, the Committee were also made aware of the difficulties inherent in our university system which seemed to render it difficult to steer undergraduates towards the necessary courses.

The Committee also think that the quality of management can be improved by the in-service training of people on the shopfloor for supervisory and managerial positions. The Committee noted that competitor countries' record of in-service training was better than ours in this regard.

Management also have a need to train their employees to be able to respond. The Committee know of the considerable training effort in German manufacturing firms, small and medium as well as large, and of the Japanese practice. They welcome the support given by MSC but they wish to stress their belief that in many industrial firms a larger training effort is required.

But there are some ways in which management can improve itself. It is said that British manufacturers make far less use of market research than their competitors with the result that they are ill-informed about what the markets want and the ways in which they can serve them. The Committee were also surprised to find that 60 per cent of companies rarely considered the terms on which they sold to overseas customers and that few (under 20 per cent) were offering delivered prices to customers. This can put British exporters at a considerable competitive disadvantage. Exporters are also at a disadvantage in their knowledge of foreign languages and many are afraid of quoting in local currency. These are all areas which industry itself must consider, taking advice where necessary from the CBI or BOTB.

Many of the decisions which have to be taken by management will be taken with better results if the workforce are involved in the decision-making process or at least carried along with it. Indeed, the need for better collaboration and closer cooperation between management and employees is an assumption which the Committee make in proposing a number of their recommendations—on the need for a change in national attitude; on the need for quality control; on the need to raise productivity and make appropriate investment decisions; and on the need to value profit. It is in the interest of everyone in industry—managers and workforce alike—and of the nation as a whole, that closer mutual understanding is achieved.

INVESTMENT

The success of manufacturing depends on investment, both in the right quantity and of the right quality. Britain's record of investment in manufacturing over the last twenty years has been poor. Sir Terence Beckett provided the Committee with data on the rate of net investment in all industries (except North Sea oil), and described it as 'a Cresta run, going down from 1964, right the way through to an all-time low in

1981'. Nor has investment always been of the right quality. Sir John Harvey-Jones told the Committee that Britain's problems were 'linked much to the quality of the investments that have been made and their subsequent management than to the amounts'.

There has been a recent recovery in investment, albeit from a low base. In 1984 investment stood at £6.8 billion—a 15 per cent increase over 1983 in real terms. But the Committee were concerned to find that of firms surveyed by the CBI in October 1984, 77 per cent were investing to improve efficiency but only 20 per cent were investing to expand capacity. This is a clear indication that, 'when activity is low, firms do not invest in capacity expansion'. As the Bank of England put it, 'British industry has proved itself quite good at adapting to very adverse circumstances, battening down the hatches, developing survival techniques in terms of cash conservation and so on; but that is not going to bring us the larger share of the world market in manufactured goods, which is what we are talking about here, which requires the confidence to commit resources and to invest in expanding capacity and developing new products.' Indeed, such survival measures quite deliberately look to the present rather than to the future, at the expense of R&D, investment for growth and whatever else is inessential for the short term.

The Committee think that more investment is needed first to extend existing manufacturing capacity lest industries lose their viability in international markets and secondly in innovation and developing new products. Output can only be produced if there is the capital stock to do so, and it can only be done competitively if that stock is kept up-to-date and embodies the most up-to-date techniques. The Committee have received clear evidence that not only has the capital stock been cut back sharply since 1979 but that it has not been kept as up to date as that of our competitors. . . . The exact position is obscured by the lack of statistics on the nature and quality of the physical capital of this country—a deficiency which should quickly be put right. Lack of investment itself encourages firms to invest overseas rather than at home, in order to be able to serve the 'leading edge' manufacturers, of whom all too few are now to be found in Britain. How can this investment be achieved.

The Committee wish to emphasise the close relationship between profitability and net investment in manufacturing. High profitability enables firms to invest out of retained profit—traditionally an important source of funds in British industry. At ICI, the Committee were told, there was a 'direct link between our rate of profitability and our ability to invest'. Other firms took a similar view. Of the firms surveyed by the CBI in October 1984, 42 per cent considered inadequate return as a factor inhibiting investment. Secondly, a reasonable expectation of continued profitability will itself induce investment—from whatever source. Profitability of manufacturing is higher in competitor countries than in Britain. Despite recent improvements in the profitability of British companies, there is still a long way to go.

The immediate prerequisite for increased profitability is improved competitiveness. But there are other factors too. The government must be sensitive to questions of profitability in exercising its public purchasing policies. The public, in their own long-term interests, must recognise the need for a proper return on investment by way of profit. Finally, management must break out of the constraints of low profit and low investment by making optimum use of existing resources—either by better use of capacity or by specialisation in the more profitable areas of activity.

To the extent that external finance may be necessary, there would appear to be no overall shortage of funds. Sir James Cleminson told the Committee that 'Where there is an opportunity for a good return there is every evidence that the money can be found. I have no evidence that where the investment is worthwhile you cannot find the money'. And the Wilson Committee came to a similar view in March 1979.

Bank lending to industry is considerable and for longer terms than in the past, but the Committee have heard argument from some witnesses that British financial institutions are reluctant to lend long, and that they are reluctant to lend to smaller firms and for new ventures. The difficulties in obtaining long-term credit are summed up in the evidence of the Association of British Chambers of Commerce who told the Committee that 'Every banker will tell you there is money available in all directions quite readily, but they have to, or they feel obliged to, put certain criteria on the lending which are somewhat different from our overseas competitors where the gearing is higher, banks are more venturesome, where the view of the profit and the repayment required is over much longer terms. We are under the tyranny of the immediate in our actions: we report quarterly or half-yearly.' A number of witnesses drawn from the electronics, information technology and aerospace sector complained in similar vein. . . . And it is the small and new firms who have the greatest problems.

A number of organisations already exist in Britain to help finance smaller businesses, especially those interested in new technology. The main source of such funds is the banks which, in addition to normal overdraft facilities, have introduced a variety of special schemes for the start up and expansion of small businesses, including long-term fixed or variable rate loans. Favourable interest rates are available on some loans for specific projects supported by the European Coal and Steel Community or the European Investment Bank or under the CoSira (Council for Small Industries in Rural Areas) Joint Lending Scheme and loans made under the Small Firms Guarantee Scheme enjoy a partial Government Guarantee. An indication of the total bank lending to small business is that one clearing bank provides such loans at the rate of about £1 billion per annum with a total of such advances exceeding £6 billion. In addition, there are a number of smaller providers of such finance. Some of these have government support, whilst one is owned by the Bank of England and the major clearing banks. At the other end of the scale, the development of the North Sea oil reserves and the outline proposals for funding a Channel tunnel suggest that there is no shortage of project finance from the banking system. The provision of Venture Equity Capital for small- and medium-sized businesses is a more recent development which has received considerable impetus under the Business Expansion Scheme. The Unlisted Securities Market has also opened up a new source of external finance for the expansion of medium-sized business.

There would appear, therefore, to be no shortage of money for investment for propositions that appear to be viable and that the main valid criticism relates to the cost of it and the conditions, as a number of witnesses said to the Committee. These are the difficulties which, the Committee were told, face small and new firms.

The nominal interest rates payable in the United Kingdom on investment funds have, in recent years, been significantly higher than those in some of the countries with which our industry competes. In part this is due to the lower rate of inflation in such countries and the differential in real interest rates is comparatively small. But it is the nominal rate that, inevitably, influences investment decisions and has to be carried into the costings of a business and the price of its products. The other important distinction to be noted is the extent to which some competitor countries provide substantial interest subsidies.

In 1983–84 in Germany, Kreditanstalt für Wiederaufbau invested over £1 billion and in France Crédit d'Equipement pour Petites et Moyennes Entreprises invested £1.2 billion in small and medium-sized firms at favourable rates of interest, several points below commercial rates. Although such subsidised loans usually had significant obligations attached to them, nevertheless they placed their United Kingdom competitors at a disadvantage and, not surprisingly, small and medium-sized businesses would welcome similar concessions here.

Such interest subsidy has been valuable in special circumstances such as in assisting British Steel Corporation (Industry) to develop old steel sites and for some categories of export finance. The extension of such support to providing finance to small and medium-sized enterprises at favourable rates of interest on the lines of Kreditanstalt für Wiederaufbau is an option available to government. That German institution offers favourable rates of interest for firms who would be otherwise charged about 3 per cent more. It makes the cheaper money available through the privately-owned German banks, which select the applicants for support, and which carry the risk. Kreditanstalt is enabled to offer cheap rates of interest because it has its own funds, and a government guarantee, enabling it to borrow at the finest rate, and it cross-subsidises these loans from profits on its other activities and is not subject to tax. The Kreditanstalt für Weideraufbau option is only one of a number of ways that can be found of providing money for small borrowers at below normal borrowing rates. The Committee note with interest that these questions have recently been the subject of study by the NEDC Committee on Finance for Industry. The Select Committee were impressed with the weight of evidence showing that there is a demand for some system of low rates of interest for small and new businesses.

Sir Hector Laing described another feature: 'Because institutional shareholders predominate in the securities markets, many managements have little real sense of identification with the objectives of their shareholders. Nor do fund managers have the expertise to solve problems of underperformance by the companies in which they hold shares so they resort to selling out. The takeover bid thus becomes a widely used device to cure corporate woes. While this can sometimes be a healthy process, serious problems can arise with the appearance of raiders who have no objective than to make a quick profit. Their activities can cause manangements to do imprudent things to preserve their own position.' The need to placate institutional shareholders is not conducive to long-term thinking. Although less than 20 per cent of the institutions' equity holdings are turned over in any one year, the Committee nevertheless recognise that even this constitutes a real threat to the vulnerable public company. This threat, moreover, is conspicuously absent in more successful countries like Germany, Japan and even France. The answer, in the Committee's view, is for industry to take their principal shareholders more into their confidence as recently proposed by the Governor of the Bank of England.

Export Promotion Services

The Committee consider that certain measures can be put into effect immediately to assist exports through the services which are already provided by the government. The efficacy of these services is being threatened by government cuts in expenditure—a fact which, in the Committee's view, raises considerable doubts in the minds of exporters as to the government's commitment to exports generally. . . .

Import Substitution and Foreign Sourcing

The principal means of combating import penetration is by improving competitiveness. But even with improved competitiveness positive action will be needed to facilitate import substitution—in many cases because British consumers, manufacturers and retailers have lost the habit of buying British goods.

So far as consumer choice is concerned, British industry is currently paying the price of past mistakes. The consumer has become so accustomed to looking to foreign products for superior quality, design and price, that it now takes a conscious effort to buy British. This is an effort which the Committee think must be made. As one witness said, 'A Frenchman has to make an effort of thought to buy foreign goods, the Japanese more so, and we want to perhaps aim in that direction here.' As an illustration of what could be done, evidence received from the Think British Campaign showed that if every British household increased their purchases of British goods by £3 per week on average and reduced their spending on imports by the same amount, the balance of payments would improve by £900 million, employment would rise by 350,000 and £2.5 billion more personal spending money created. All things being equal, the Committee believe that the British consumer needs to use his or her critical judgement in favour of buying British goods. It is in his or her enlightened self-interest to do so.

Retailers for their part must make a conscious effort to source the goods they buy in Britain as some already do. The Committee were very interested and encouraged to learn of the efforts of Marks and Spencer in this connection. While nationally imports represent 30 per cent of the United Kingdom clothing market, Marks and Spencer buy 90 per cent of their clothing in the United Kingdom. As Lord Sieff told the Committee, 'Much British management does not appreciate what can be produced in Britain which often represents better quality and value than the goods they are importing at the moment.' Marks and Spencer have achieved this high percentage of British content by a deliberate policy of encouraging domestic suppliers to produce goods of high quality for them. The Committee urge more retailers to do the same. They note that the Better Made in Britain exhibitions run by the Clothing, Knitting and Footwear EDC is a useful medium for promoting import substitution of this kind. They hope that further exhibitions covering a wide range of goods will be held. The Committee also believe that a requirement that large retailers publish the percentage of finished goods they import would also encourage import substitution along these lines.

Industry can also take up this principle, wherever equipment and plant, semi-manufactures or components are purchased—to the extent that the manufacturing capability still exists in Britain. The Committee wholeheartedly support the proselytising activities of Lord Sieff in this connection. But the Committee think that the government, nationalised industries and quasi-monopolies like British Telecom, could do a great deal more to help. There are three things that a purchasing body can and should do. It can help to raise standards of manufacture in the firms with which it contracts and obtain the manufactures it wants at competitive prices without having to go overseas. It can try to ensure a steady rolling programme of orders. And finally it should use its powers of specification in a way which leads to the manufacture of exportable products. As the TUC said to the Committee, 'It is not just a question of having a purchasing body which buys British all the time, though that is important . . . it is a question of seeing why it is we are not able to make the right product at the right price etc. and putting pressure on everybody, including trade unions if you wish, in order to make sense of the world market position.'

The Committee received evidence which showed that this was not always happening. The ABCC thought that not enough was done by government to encourage business through their purchases: 'This is not only in the direct purchase of their goods but also in the specifications that they demand. It has been notorious in Government Departments here that this type of specification is very often unexportable.' Other witnesses agreed. The Committee are convinced that public purchasing can be used to great advantage to stimulate the manufacture of competitive and exportable products, and they received evidence of this being done successfully from both the NCB and the CEGB. They would like to see more being done in other areas both in the public and private sector. They believe that the Ministry of Defence in their procurement policy should attach equal importance to helping the competitiveness in overseas markets of their suppliers as they do to competition. They welcome the watchdog role played by NEDO in this sphere, and would like to see its functions extend to the private sector also.

Closely allied to the question of purchasing is the separate issue of the import content of the manufactures of multinationals, whether in the form of completed products or of components to be assembled here. Where products are imported, the United Kingdom's balance of trade is adversely affected and manufacturing and employment opportunities completely lost. Where components are imported then the added value of the manufacturing process in the United Kingdom is reduced by the extent of the import content and unless production is increased and unless there are reciprocal flows of exported components then GDP and the balance of trade are adversely affected too.

The Committee find this phenomenon particularly prevalent in the motor industry. In 1972 multinational firms operating in Britain exported 229,000 cars: by 1983 they imported 305,000. Moreover the import content of those produced in the United Kingdom can be very high. A recent study shows that 'tied imports' of finished cars and imports of components rose from 4 per cent in 1974 to 31 per cent in 1984. When this is combined with the cars imported by companies with no manufacturing capability in this country, the result shows that the United Kingdom content of the United Kingdom market has fallen from 90 per cent in 1969 to 34 per cent in 1984. Some companies offend worse than others. Between 1973 and 1984 the United Kingdom content of all cars sold in the United Kingdom by Austin Rover fell from 100 per cent to 92 per cent, by Ford from 88 per cent to 46 per cent, by Talbot from 97 per cent to 42 per cent and by General Motors from 89 per cent to 22 per cent. Nor is the proposed United Kingdom content of Nissan's products at the projected Washington works very impressive: 60 per cent, rising to 80 per cent, is to be EEC 'local' content, of which only a 'majority' is expected to be produced in the United Kingdom. When Nissan's tied imports of completed vehicles are added, the percentage of total sales sourced in the United Kingdom could be quite low.

The Committee have received less detailed evidence from the IT industry which indicates a similar large volume of import content in Japanese and United States firms' products in the United Kingdom. Many factories are simply assembly plants for components produced overseas. Indeed, this seems to be the case for Japanese electronic firms generally. It is true that IBM aims to maintain a balance between imports and exports: but Hewlett Packard did not expect to balance imports against exports until the 'early 1990s'.

The Committee realise that Britain is herself in part to blame for multinationals' past decisions on sourcing. In the case of the motor industry, high costs and poor industrial relations have influenced decisions detrimentally: in the case of IT there has undoubtedly been a failure to move into new fields and meet US and Japanese competition. Nevertheless, the Committee feel the government and industry should be more aware of the real import content of multinationals' products and tailor their purchasing policies accordingly. The remedies which can be taken by government also depend on whether firms are already established here or whether they are seeking to make new inward investment.

In the case of firms wishing to make inward investment into the United Kingdom government should be less beguiled by the immediate employment opportunities they create and more concerned with the level of manufacturing and value added which is expected to be undertaken. They should be careful too in their encouragement of the import of foreign R&D to the detriment of development of new technologies by indigenous British firms. Britain's technical independence must not inadvertently be weakened.

In the case of companies already established pressure should also be brought to bear to source more manufacturing here. At present little is done. As Sir Anthony Rawlinson told the Committee: 'As regards [motor] companies which are already established here (such as Ford and so on), the Government does from time to time discuss these matters, but its powers of insistence are rather limited within the framework of current policy.' It is time for current policy to become more robust. Evidence from a wide range of sources indicated that agreements on sourcing of some kind or another need to be considered. This is a not unreasonable price to pay for continued access to a large and profitable British market. In the meantime public purchasing and purchasing by industry itself should have more regard to the United Kingdom content of what is being bought. The government can also use its support policies to encourage multinationals to turn—or return—to United Kingdom manufacture.

16. The Balance of Trade in Manufactures*

Department of Trade and Industry

INTRODUCTION

The government welcome the report of the Select Committee as a contribution to discussion.

ANALYSIS

The government agree with many of the Committee's conclusions and recommendations, though in their view they apply to the whole of the non-oil trading sector and not just, or primarily, to manufacturing. In particular, the government agree that:

—a healthy trading sector is vital to the success of the British economy. It is essential to encourage initiative and enterprise.

—the long-term decline in the relative performance of the UK economy is a matter for concern. The decline in the relative importance of manufacturing is not, of course, a recent phenomenon. The trend has been evident for most of this century and has been mirrored—at a faster or slower rate—by developments in all the other major western economies since the Second World War.

—the competitiveness of the UK economy, both price and non-price, must be improved further. It is vital to maintain downward pressure on wage costs.

—adjustment to the decline in North Sea oil production is an important issue facing the economy (though the Committee have, in the government's view, overstated the likely speed of that decline).

The government do not, however, accept the Committee's view that there is a 'grave threat to the standard of living and to the economic and political stability of the nation' which amounts to a crisis and requires a new departure in the form of an action plan.

* Cmnd. 9697, London: HMSO, December 1985.

In reaching this conclusion, the Committee have, in the government's view, paid insufficient attention to the policy changes that have already taken place. The whole thrust of government policy since 1979 has been designed to reverse the long-standing deterioration in the competitiveness of the UK economy and to create the conditions in which enterprise and initiative can flourish. Downward pressure on inflation has been successfully maintained, which has been an essential prerequisite for sustained growth in all sectors, and a range of measures has been introduced to improve the functioning of the economy. These include the reform of trade union legislation, the improvement of work incentives, the restructuring and expansion of training, the removal of unnecessary legislative and administrative burdens, steps to encourage the growth of venture capital, and the strengthening of competition. The sustained recovery of the UK economy in recent years, to which in the Government's view the Committee also gave insufficient weight, is evidence of the beneficial effects that these policy changes are beginning to have and helps to put some of the Committee's conclusions into perspective. Manufacturing output fell at the beginning of the decade as the economy belatedly adjusted to correct long-standing weaknesses at a time of world recession. But since then there has been steady growth. Compared with their troughs in 1981–82 manufacturing output has risen by 11 per cent, manufacturing investment by around 25 per cent and manufacturing productivity by 31 per cent; the volume of manufactured exports has reached a record level. Further growth in output is expected for next year.

There are also important elements of the Committee's analysis with which the government strongly disagree. Whilst the government are not complacent about the future of manufacturing industry they do not accept the Committee's call for greater discrimination in favour of manufacturing. The logical conclusion of the Committee's analysis is that economic policy should aim to increase the competitiveness and adaptability of the whole economy, not just one particular sector.

The Committee identify overall economic performance with the balance of trade in manufacturing. They state that 'sustainable growth has not been possible and will not be possible without a favourable trade balance in manufactures'. There is, however, no close link between the manufacturing trade balance and the performance of manufacturing industry, nor indeed the performance of the economy as a whole. In 1980 the trade balance in manufactures strengthened as manufacturing output fell, and the most rapid weakening in the balance has coincided with the recent period of recovery in manufacturing. The balance moved from a surplus of £4.6 billion in 1981 to a deficit of £3.8 billion in 1984 as manufacturing output increased by 7 per cent. Manufacturing accounts for just under one-quarter of GDP so that the connection between the performance of manufacturing and overall economic performance need not be a very close one.

Furthermore, the government consider that a major influence on the trade balance in manufactures has been the growing surplus in oil. An increase in the surplus on one element of the balance of payments must imply an increased deficit on other parts of the accounts. The foreign exchange earned from oil is used to purchase additional imports, both capital and current, and to invest overseas. The Committee are not consistent on this point. . . . the Committee accept that North Sea oil has contributed to the manufacturing trade deficit; but at the same time they argue that oil is masking the deficit.

The Committee concentrated, in line with their terms of reference, on the manufacturing trade balance; consequently they gave less weight to other important aspects of the problem of adjusting to a non-oil future. The UK will have to increase exports of goods and services to compensate for the reduction of the oil surplus. The greater is the level of output in the economy the easier that will be. Shifting resources into the non-oil balance of payments requires that the whole economy is sufficiently competitive and adaptable. The Committee acknowledge the importance of competitiveness but could perhaps with advantage have given more emphasis to the question of adaptability and particularly to labour market flexibility.

The government consider that the Committee's emphasis on the need to increase exports of manufactures is too narrow. With the value of manufactured exports still more than twice that of exports of services, much of the burden of adjustment will fall on the manufacturing sector. But neither is more intrinsically worthwhile than the other. No one suggests that exports of services could make good all the decline in the oil surplus, but exports of services will undoubtedly have a valuable contribution to make.

The government do not share the Committee's view that increased exports of manufactures will require increased government assistance to manufacturing. The decline in the oil surplus will put downward pressure on the real exchange rate (in the same way as the Committee accept that the build-up of the surplus put upward pressure on the rate), and, in any event, manufacturing can do much to help itself by keeping tight control of unit labour costs. The Committee's analysis also ignores the crucial wider effects of subsidies on the economy as a whole. Increased subsidies to manufacturing imply an increased tax burden on the rest of the economy, so that attempts to promote manufacturing would be at the expense of other sectors.

PART IV:
Pressure Groups

Governments formulate economic policy under a gale of advice and comment. Every daily nuance of policy and performance is subject to systematic media coverage and interest-group response. The government's economic year—built these days around its twin peaks of the budget and the autumn statement—attracts a large quantity of lobbying; and its longer-term strategy is equally subject to serious study by concerned organisations and strategically-placed individuals, each with their own bodies of expertise and sets of interests to defend. Some of those groups and individuals are closer to the state than others. There are insiders and outsiders in the world of pressure groups, and this month's flavour is not always next month's. For when governments change even insider groups find themselves rearranged in the hierarchy of influence they seek to dominate. Trade unions in particular come and go in centrality as Labour governments rise and fall, and even the institutions of the City ebb and flow in the leverage they find it necessary to deploy, and in the warmth of their welcome in the corridors of power. Moreover, much of the advice which governments receive, they receive in private, and much of the thinking of governments and parties is shaped less by specific documents than by longer-term interplays between themselves and their coterie of special interests. So what we can see and read are not necessarily the moments of greatest influence; and formal documents, if they have value here at all, are important mainly as crystallisations of arguments put less formally elsewhere. But formal statements of what is required to regenerate British industry are available in abundance; and it is possible to sample the range here in a systematic way.

We begin with the Governor of the Bank of England arguing the case for a consistent support of local manufacturing, to leave the economy capable of covering its overseas debts when North Sea oil revenues diminish. Lots of people have argued, and still argue, this case; and the Governor's statement is reproduced here both as a typical early example

of a widely-held view and also because the lecture itself is regularly cited
(not least before the House of Lords Select Committee on Overseas
Trade). Then we have taken the summary section of a discussion
document produced by the Institute of Directors in January 1985, in
which the Institute argues for a series of initiatives within the overall
framework of existing government policy: initiatives concerned to deregulate labour employment by abolishing Wage Councils and taking
away certain employment protection laws, to giving tax incentives to the
self-employed, and to extend youth training schemes as social security
payments to the young are cut. In arguing this, the Institute is expressing
one widely-held and important set of views to which ministers are
regularly subject.

Interestingly, our next entry, that of the CBI, shows the other major
employers' organisation to be slightly less enamoured of government
policy than is the Institute. While supporting the overall thrust of the
White Paper on Employment reproduced earlier in this volume, and
rejecting any large-scale increase in government borrowing, the CBI
continues to call not simply for reduced taxes on business (National
Insurance contributions, rates and so on), but also for 'some increase in
economically viable public infrastructure' and a set of measures 'to
alleviate unemployment while economic recovery continues'. As its
representatives told the House of Lords Select Committee on Overseas
Trade, the CBI remains of the view that:

> the most efficient mechanism for correcting (trade) deficits and achieving the
> optimum allocation of resources is the free play of market forces. Manufac-
> turing operations which can be made profitable in the United Kingdom will
> continue and grow, and conversely. We see the proper role of Government in
> assisting the required evolution as being to promote the supply of relevant
> industrial skills through education and aids to training and retraining: to
> ensure a favourable fiscal and financial climate for industrial investment and
> risk-taking; and to prevent genuinely unfair competition from foreign sup-
> pliers (that is that which is not merely painful but illegal under GATT rules).
> (House of Lords, Session 1984–85, 238-II, p. 48)

The CBI's detailed proposals for the alleviation of unemployment
now include support for developing the Youth Training Scheme, a
significant expansion of the Job Release Scheme, a similar development
of the part-time Job Release Scheme, the development of the Job-
Splitting Scheme, and an increase by 100,000 in the places on the
Community Programme. Yet the CBI continues to be wary of too much
government action even here, insisting that any initiatives on unemployment must be non-inflationary, conducive to improved business
performance, cost-effective in delivering help to those in need, and part

of a strategy, not just a piecemeal operation. As the CBI told the Chancellor in 1985, 'one essential message is absolutely correct: the government cannot, on its own, create jobs.' Nor, in their view, will the private sector be able to do so either, unless wages are even more severely restrained. This was what the CBI had to say on wages in 1986:

CBI members believe that the UK's poor historical performance on pay and productivity compared to our main competitors has contributed substantially to our current unemployment. The prospects for jobs will only brighten if this trend is reversed. In particular, UK firms must stop making uncompetitive pay settlements. In the immediate future, this means settlements in the coming year two percentage points lower than last—and the same two percentage point reduction is needed again the following year.

Other pressure groups attach significantly less importance to wages than that. The Church of England, for example, in its report *Faith in the City* (whose publication prompted rapid and severe criticism from certain Conservative MPs) wants action in three areas to ease the deprivation of the inner city and its inhabitants: more public sector employment and income support for the unemployed; more opportunities for education and training; and improvements in the physical environment of urban priority areas. The Church's Report also calls for greater public debate on economic policy, on the differential impact of the recession, on the definition of work itself, and on the welfare state as an institution.

The trade union movement, for its part, is already heavily engaged in that debate; and if the production of pamphlets, documents and arguments were the only determinant of policy, the number and quality of union publications in this field would already have won the day. But they have not; and trade unions under the Conservative government continue to argue from the sidelines, with policy suggestions which clash with those of the government in philosophy, analysis and detail. For as the TUC told the House of Lords Select Committee:

manufacturing is now far too weak to expect a spontaneous recovery. The severity of the recession has forced drastic reductions in manpower, loss of skills and destruction of capacity. For manufacturing to recover and fill the trade gap a key role will have to be played by government. First it will have to intervene to expand demand and output. Second, import controls will be essential in order to ensure that additional demand feeds into British industries rather than leaking overseas in the form of yet more imports. (Op. cit., p. 73)

We reproduce here, as representative of trade union opinion as a whole, sections of the TUC's argument for reflation, public investment in infrastructure, research, development and training, plus public ownership, a National Investment Bank, and widespread social reform. This is, of course, in all essentials, a moderate version of the Labour Party's alternative economic strategy; and the fuller case for that is argued at length by, among others, NALGO in a 60-page pamphlet of considerable sophistication. We reproduce here the summary section of that pamphlet, once more to indicate the flavour of public debate on the Left on how best to regenerate Britain's dwindling industrial base.

17. The North Sea and the United Kingdom Economy*

Bank of England

The basic question to which I address myself is this. Is the United Kingdom better-off because of North Sea oil? It may seem surprising to pose this question at all. Are we not accustomed to think of it as a gift of nature? The answer depends on how far back one goes: better-off than when? We are better-off than we would be if we had to import our oil at present world prices. But taking account of what we have had to pay to develop the North Sea, we are not better-off than we were ten years ago, when we imported oil at much lower world prices. Let me develop these points.

In 1970, the United Kingdom was producing negligible quantities of oil. Like most other developed countries, we imported the oil we needed—then about 750 million barrels per annum—and paid for it by exporting other goods and services. That amount of oil in 1970 cost us then about £700 million, or about 1.5 per cent of GDP. We, like the other importing countries, were getting our oil cheaply by today's standards.

With the rise in oil prices in 1973, Britain's oil bill rose sharply, and there was a major impact on the balance of payments. Even then in 1973, however, North Sea gas was already building up substantially. It was also well known that North Sea oil would soon start to be exploited on an increasing scale. As this occurred—importantly since 1976—domestically-produced oil and gas began to replace imports; and our oil import bill started to decline dramatically. By 1979–80, when the second round of price rises occurred, our overall trade account position was relatively little affected. We have become, in 1980, approximately self-sufficient in oil.

* Ashbridge Lecture, given by the Governor of the Bank of England in London, 20 November 1980.

So, what does this self-sufficiency in oil—and more generally in energy—mean for the United Kingdom? As a country, we are clearly better-off than if we had no oil, and we are better-off on this score than our major industrial competitors who now have to import high-priced oil. They, as we have seen, are indeed substantially worse-off after the oil price rises of the 1970s. In looking at the way in which Britain's own position has changed over the decade, however, it is important to make a proper allowance for the costs of oil from the North Sea. It is far from costless.

In fact, I want to argue that the costs of oil from the North Sea are now in real terms comparable with—in fact somewhat higher than—the costs of obtaining imported oil at the beginning of the decade. In 1970, we were paying about $2.20 per barrel for imported crude. Allowing for inflation and changes in exchange rates, the real price of that oil would correspond to a price of about $7.50 now. The economic cost of the North Sea oil we are consuming today is the resource cost of North Sea exploration, development and production. We know that the investment has been immense. To the end of last year, development of North Sea operations had absorbed a cumulative investment of some £20 billion in 1980 prices, taking account not only of gas but also of onshore investment in chemical plants, storage and pipelines. But much of this represents our investment in future output. It is useful to have in mind also estimates of the costs of present production. These vary widely from field to field—I understand from about $5 per barrel, to $25 or more, with an average cost of about $10 per barrel for oil produced this year. On this basis, the conclusion must be that the resource cost of the oil we are using now is somewhat greater than that of the oil that we imported in 1970.

Production on a scale to make us self-sufficient has, however, been rendered economic, and indeed highly profitable, by the relative rise in world oil prices to recent and present levels. Partly because of rising prices, but also because of recession, we are now consuming less oil than ten years ago, perhaps 650 million barrels this year. Proper allowance for earlier exploration and development, as well as for current production effort, thus suggests that we are now using rather more resources to acquire rather less oil. The resources are, of course, being used in a somewhat different way. In 1970, we produced exports to pay for oil. Now we use resources more directly in the North Sea. But even this difference is less than appears at first sight. Much of the resource cost of the North Sea is accounted for directly by imports, or by interest payments, dividends or profits paid abroad as return on the capital put in by foreign investors. Thus to a large extent we are still exporting other goods and services to meet the cost of the oil we consume.

My conclusion is that the North Sea endowment has not made the United Kingdom better-off than in 1970. We do of course appear better-off than we were in 1974 or 1975, after the first oil price increase, but before the North Sea came on-stream. We are also clearly better-off in this regard than countries with no oil of their own. But it is their position that has deteriorated, whilst ours has remained broadly unchanged. At first blush, it seems odd to be saying this at a time when our manufacturing industry is being hard-pressed by the rise in its energy costs and by the appreciation of sterling. But I am concerned here with the resource implications for the economy as a whole; and on this basis, the combination of the rising price of oil and development of the North Sea has left the United Kingdom little affected overall, while other countries that import oil are worse-off. In practical terms, this is of great significance: there is a clear difference between receiving a large windfall gain and avoiding a large windfall loss that applies to others. The economic response in the two cases should be quite different. For us as a nation, our self-sufficiency should, I suggest, be seen as a reprieve rather than as a bonanza.

The common supposition that we gain from higher oil prices only holds if the United Kingdom were likely to be a net exporter over an extended period. For a country that may not be able to count on more than approximate self-sufficiency over a run of years, higher oil prices will have little direct effect on either the balance of payments or potential living standards. More generally, the rise in oil prices has had harmful effects on world economic prospects: it has accelerated inflation both here and world wide; it has slowed world growth; and it has exacerbated international political tension. As an open economy heavily dependent on world trade, we do not avoid these injurious effects.

THE NEED TO MAINTAIN OUR NON-OIL BASE

I turn now to the relation of the development of the North Sea to the size of our industrial base. It has been suggested that because of oil it is inevitable or perhaps desirable that industry should contract. The argument is that because the growth of our oil industry involves increased output of internationally-traded goods, other parts of the traded goods sector—principally manufacturing—will have to contract, or grow less fast. In addition, it has been suggested that a high exchange rate is a desirable way of bringing about this structural change. These propositions do not fit with the analysis of the effects of North Sea oil which I have been developing.

Compare our position with that of countries who have to import oil.

They are now running greatly increased oil deficits. Their non-oil sectors are being forced to adapt, a process likely to involve an increase in the share of internationally-traded goods and services in total national production. This, as we have seen, is because oil-importing countries will have to pay for their more expensive oil by exporting more or importing less. This necessity is now generally recognised and taken for granted in the oil-importing countries themselves. For many of them the process will mean an increase in their industrial base. As shorthand, I use the word 'industrialisation' to describe this development—though I am aware that many internationally traded goods and services are not of course industrial products in the strict sense.

By virtue of our possession of North Sea oil, the United Kingdom is a country where further industrialisation in this sense is not required. But this is quite different from the proposition that it is desirable that the United Kingdom should accept a reduction in its production of traded goods other than oil—which, in practice, would mean a reduction in industrial production. This might, perhaps, have been arguable if our industrial structure had adjusted in the wake of the oil price rises of the 1970s, before we became self-sufficient. But it manifestly did not. There has not been an expansion in manufacturing since 1973–74—rather the reverse.

Since I believe it to be important, let me for emphasis put this point in another way. If the United Kingdom is taken to be an economy approximately self-sufficient in oil, in which the real costs of oil are of the same order as in 1970, it would seem that we are one of the few countries in the world where change in the size of the industrial sector is not required on account of higher oil prices. Adaptation is of course needed as industry responds to the higher cost of energy and moves from the production of exports to pay for oil to the production of capital and other goods needed to support oil output. But this takes place within the industrial sector and does not involve or require any reduction in the size of that sector. By contrast, other countries, such as Germany, France and Japan, are having to increase the scale of their industrial base within the span of only a few years to enable them to pay for higher-cost imported oil.

I thus regard the doctrine that a substantial decline in our industrial base is inevitable as needlessly depressing and misleading. What rather is true is that the maintenance of our industrial base will require substantial adjustment within our non-oil economy.

First, our endowment of oil has done nothing directly to mitigate the difficulties of many of our older industries or the problems of low productivity, weak management, indifferent industrial relations and high earnings increases that have played so large a part in the undermining of our international competitiveness in many areas.

Second, important structural change stems from the need in the United Kingdom, as elsewhere, to adapt to high energy prices. It may be objected that, if the resource cost of oil and gas is not much more now than it was in 1970, there is no reason why United Kingdom industrial and domestic consumers should pay the equivalent of world prices for their energy. But lower prices would involve the likelihood of waste rather than economy in the use of this valuable resource. We have to keep in mind that any savings of oil that can be made have a value in international trade given by the world price, not by United Kingdom costs. Higher real oil and gas prices are probably here to stay, and the insulation of British energy-users by reducing prices below world levels would slow the pace of the structural adjustment that is desirable and necessary. This is not, however, to imply that energy prices for British industrial users should be higher than those, for example, on the Continent.

The adaptations that will ultimately be required to a high relative price for oil and gas are hard to foresee with precision. I very much doubt, however, that they will involve a process of de-industrialisation. On the contrary, conservation and the development of substitutes such as nuclear power and coal will create large opportunities for industry, both directly and in terms of the investment involved.

Third, rejection of the view that the importance of our industry must diminish does not, of course, mean that all existing lines of activity should be maintained. What is important is the development of new areas of enterprise and activity to replace those that fall out in the inevitable continuing process of economic change. The needs of North Sea operations themselves are relevant here. A recent estimate made by the Chairman of Shell UK suggests that the capital expenditure that will be needed over the next fifteen years to support further North Sea development will be of the order of £40 billion in 1980 prices, with perhaps a further £15 billion over this period required for operating and maintenance. Many British companies have already acquired a considerable capability and built up substantial business in support of North Sea operations. Over the next decade and beyond, investment in North Sea and other offshore oil operations looks set to be on a very large scale, involving correspondingly large and exciting possibilities, not only in our own waters but in other parts of the world, for British companies prepared to make the necessary sustained effort.

A further major consideration is the finite life of North Sea reserves. If we fail to maintain a strong industrial presence during these years of self-sufficiency, we shall face very costly and formidable re-entry problems when the oil starts to run out. For we would not only have consumed the depleting asset, but we would also have left the next generation bereft of an effective capability to generate goods and services to pay for imported oil, when our own has run out, or for more expensive domestic substitutes. And we should not exclude that in some of the new high technology areas, prices might be raised quite sharply against us if we had no production capability of our own and thus became dependent on others. There may be a tendency to assume that, as oil runs out, our native enterprise will enable us to move with reasonable facility into whatever are by that time the new non-oil areas of activity. But we should not underestimate the scale that many modern technological processes require in order to operate efficiently. If we neglect them during our period of oil self-sufficiency, the re-entry price into such industries in terms of technology, management and specialist skills to be acquired, might be large indeed.

To recapitulate, improvement in our standard of living continues to depend, despite North Sea oil, on our success in non-oil areas of activity. Progress will depend, in a tough world environment, on a combination of improvement in our cost competitiveness in conventional areas of activity, and speed and flexibility in seizing the opportunities that will exist—massively so in support of the oil industry—to generate products and services where we are not only competitive in price but also technologically and in other non-price respects ahead of the competition.

HOW MUCH SHOULD WE CONSUME?

I turn now to the question—how should North Sea oil affect our patterns of consumption and investment? The first point I want to make is that North Sea oil is a capital asset, part of our national stock of wealth. We could raise our living standards by borrowing against it. Or, to the extent that it were technically possible, we could raise production of oil to become substantial net exporters of oil in the short term, so as to consume the extra imports that we could buy. In either case, we would be living better now, but at the expense of the future. This would, in my view, be wholly misguided. North Sea oil should not be seen as transforming the possibilities for increased living standards. These must continue to depend, as hitherto, on improvements in the performance of our non-oil economy.

As a capital asset, the North Sea endowment can be transformed, through the markets, or more generally through the economic system, into other capital assets of similar value, or can be consumed without replacement. A major question is whether we should seek to get oil out of the ground as quickly as possible, transforming the proceeds into other capital assets at home or overseas. Or would it be preferable to leave oil in the ground, or, say, to limit production to not more than our current needs? Determination of what may be termed an optimal depletion policy depends on many other factors outside the scope of this address, but it must take into account a comparison between expected real rates of return on investment in general (whether at home or overseas) and the expected development of the real price of oil. I do not myself have any confident view about what this optimal rate of depletion would be. But I feel confident in suggesting to you that, within whatever are the technical and other constraints, the rate of depletion should be determined as an investment decision, and not with a view to any particular benefit in terms of consumption in the short term.

North Sea oil is not only a capital asset: it is a wasting asset. We do not know how many years of self-sufficiency in oil lie before us, but we do know that the oil will eventually run out. We can also fairly confidently expect that the resource costs of the oil are likely to increase. Even to regard North Sea oil as a means of maintaining, but not increasing, our existing living standards, might therefore be held to involve an inadequate allocation of resources to investment and an excessive allocation to consumption. Prudence would dictate that, as we use up North Sea oil, we should to a considerable extent replace it with other assets, by greater investment either at home or abroad.

Investment abroad has increased since the removal of exchange control a year ago. But overseas investment seems unlikely to match more than a modest part of the resources that might be required to safeguard our future position. Over the longer run we need to match a substantial part of the depletion of our oil reserves by investment at home.

Industry in all countries is suffering from substantially higher energy costs. In this country, however, there is a positive side of the account—the growing tax take from the North Sea operations. Given the prospective rising revenue from North Sea oil production, the government could in principle seek to influence the pace of home investment, either through reducing its own borrowing needs—thus tending to reduce the cost of capital to corporate investors—or by fiscal easement. What is important is that choices among the available options should recognise the importance of investment to our future well-being. This points to a case for bias, over time, in the direction of favouring investment rather than consumption.

SOME FURTHER COMMENTS

I have said little so far about the effect of North Sea oil on the exchange rate—a factor which many in this audience may regard as the most important of all. This is because I wished to deal principally with the separate question of how oil price rises and the North Sea affected the need for structural change in the economy as a whole. I have argued that it is neither necessary nor desirable that the production of non-oil goods and services should fall as a proportion of our gross domestic product. But we have the fact of substantial appreciation of the exchange rate, and the possibility of a continuing strong demand for sterling; and this inevitably bears heavily on many sectors of industry.

Let me offer a few brief comments. We are fortunate in not having to expand the production of traded goods to pay for the same quantity of dearer oil, as other countries are having to do. They may therefore have to have a lower exchange rate—which means a somewhat higher exchange rate for us than otherwise would be the case. Sterling has also been affected by the immense diversion of purchasing power from oil-importing countries to the oil exporters. Even though the United Kingdom is largely insulated from these major changes by having North Sea oil, there are indirect effects. The oil exporters use some proportion of their increased revenues to buy goods and services from the United Kingdom. As part of their external portfolio management, they also acquire financial assets in sterling. Many other factors are also influencing the exchange rate, including the present recession and the strength of the present policy stance directed against inflation. Given the many factors at work, and with the world economy in substantial disequilibrium, it is difficult to disentangle and measure the effect of North Sea oil alone on the real exchange rate.

But Sterling clearly is stronger than if we did not have oil. This involves substantial potential benefit in two main respects. First, as an economy we can obtain our imports on more favourable terms, because our terms of trade are improved, and we are thus better off. Second, we benefit from the effect of lower import costs on domestic costs and prices.

On the other hand, there is the potential damage to industrial competitiveness that may be done by exchange rate appreciation. In seeking to assess the longer-run balance between such benefit and cost, the key question is whether nominal exchange rate appreciation is likely to involve comparable real appreciation or whether, as a result of compensating cost and price adjustments, the real exchange rate remains broadly stable in the long run. Because of repercussions on costs and prices, the effect of nominal appreciation in the exchange rate can be less than appears. How much less will, of course, be determined by the behaviour of inflation.

I have not been concerned in my address tonight with the immediate issue of combating inflation. We are fully engaged in that fight; and, until we have emerged successfully from it, progress towards some of the structural adjustments that we need in the longer run is hampered.

SUMMARY

Let me then summarise the main longer-run considerations to which I have sought to draw attention.

The first is that countries without oil of their own face the need for particularly large-scale adjustment. Over and above the necessity in all countries for energy conservation and substitution in the wake of higher oil prices, these countries also have to export more to pay for their oil. Thus their adjustment is likely in part to take the form of an expansion in their capacity to produce tradeable goods.

Against this background of what has to happen to other countries, the United Kingdom is obviously fortunate in its endowment of North Sea oil. It is natural to fall into the habit of imagining that we are better off because of it. A closer look suggests that this is misleading. There have been substantial costs involved in the extraction of North Sea oil—many of them arising from imported materials or capital—which must be taken into account. Looking over the decade of the 1970s, it seems that this country, favoured as it is, nevertheless uses more resources now in acquiring oil than in 1970. The combined impact of North Sea oil and international oil price rises has thus not left us better-off over the last decade; but the problem of other countries has worsened.

This is not a mere pedantic distinction. It belies the notion, currently gaining acceptance, that because of a supposed bonus from North Sea oil, Britain's production of tradeable goods will need to decline. On the contrary, the United Kingdom will ultimately have to expand non-oil production when North Sea oil tails off, or becomes much more expensive. This underlines the need to complement the depletion of North Sea assets with additions to our capital stock in other areas, and thus the case for bias, over time, in the direction of favouring investment rather than consumption.

The conclusion I draw is that this country will have to continue to rely on improvements in the efficiency and output of our industrial base—industrial base in the wider sense that I have been using in this address—for improvements in our standard of life. Having North Sea oil both enables and obliges us to take a long view of our future development. We enjoy the great advantage of a substantial insulation of real national income from higher oil prices—something not available to most of our trading partners—and we have greater time to draw on this strength while we seek to get the underlying conditions right to enable us to make best use of our endowment. If we can take the opportunities that are available to us in a responsible and disciplined way, we should be able to ensure both a sustainable improvement in our standards of living in the 1980s and also enable our successors to benefit even after the much more distant time when the flow of North Sea oil ceases to be sufficient to meet our needs.

18. Job-Creation Without a 'U' Turn*

Institute of Directors

SUMMARY

1. Lower public spending, tax cuts, removal of rigidities in the labour market and elimination of administrative and legislative disincentives to business growth represent the only viable policy for medium and long-term economic growth and job-creation.
2. Increased public spending would weaken business confidence at home and confidence in financial markets abroad; it is the primary cause of employment levels lower than the economy would otherwise generate.
3. World Bank twenty-nation comparative studies show a strong correlation between low tax and rapid economic and employment growth.
4. Tax cuts introduced by the US Economic Recovery Act 1981 have led to a massive creation of new jobs on a scale unparallelled in Europe.
5. UK academic research shows that tax cuts have a better effect on job-creation and price inflation than the alternatives of cuts in national insurance contributions, increases in public spending or marginal employment subsidies.
6. Capital spending on roads or infrastructure renewal, although desirable, is among the least effective means of increasing the number of permanent jobs.
7. Suggestions that tax cuts would be spent on imported domestic consumer goods are in many ways a counsel of despair; and the steepest rise in import penetration since 1980 has been in capital goods, bought by industry, rather than consumer items.
8. Wages Councils should be abolished because they stifle job prospects for many young and part-time workers.
9. There is a scope for a dramatic rise in self-employment.

* Published in November, 1984.

Government departments should lose the power to reclassify the self-employed as employees. There should be a £5000 tax-free starter as an incentive to move to self-employment.

10. Employment protection laws deter some businesses from taking on staff; their impact should be reduced, especially for smaller firms. Qualifying periods for unfair dismissal compensation should be lengthened to reduce disincentives to taking on extra workers.

11. All firms with fewer than 50 employees should benefit from deregulation provisions in the Employment Acts and in other legislation.

12. In the longer term many employment protection rights could be 'privatised' and left to be agreed between employer and employee; but employees should be entitled to a clear and comprehensive contract of employment without which any dismissal would be automatically unfair and subject to unfair dismissal compensation.

13. To improve work and training incentives supplementary benefit for claimants under 21 should be reduced and education and training opportunities extended at the same time.

14. Other supplementary benefit scales should be adjusted to provide a basic needs safety-net, to allow for increased spending on those in greatest need, cuts in tax to help the low paid, and improved incentives for work and training.

15. The Technical and Vocational Education Initiative should be extended to a fully country-wide, permanent scheme as soon as possible.

16. The Certificate of Pre-Vocational Education should be treated by employers as a significant job qualification.

17. The Youth Training Scheme and Community Programme should be extended so that no one under 18 need be involuntarily unemployed.

18. An early further step in trade union law reform, to link remaining union immunities to observance of agreed dispute procedures, would reduce industrial disruption and improve the opportunities for inward investment and steady job growth.

19. Small firms should be boosted by an increase in the threshold for VAT registration to £50,000, to cut compliance costs.

20. Key tax-system changes would reduce business costs and disincentives to expansion.

21. Inland Revenue and DHSS computerisation offers the chance to integrate tax and social benefit systems with significant government administrative savings and cuts in business compliance costs. It should be the subject of an early White Paper.

22. The Rayner scrutiny programme should be extended to include examination of business compliance costs imposed by government regulatory requirements; and the resources of the Enterprise Unit increased.

23. Businesses should cease to be unpaid tax and National Insurance collectors for government; the scope for the extension of rebates to businesses in return for collection work carried out for government departments should be investigated; these could be proportionally higher for smaller firms.

24. There should be a comprehensive reappraisal of company law reporting and return requirements and the development of a simplified modern business code; requirements relating to private companies in particular should be reduced.

25. Legislation reducing job prospects continues to appear. Newly-introduced proposals in the Insolvency Bill to force companies in financial difficulty to go into liquidation earlier, with increased job losses, should be dropped. All new legislation should be monitored to ensure that it stimulates rather than reduces employment opportunities.

19. Unemployment—a Challenge to Us All*

CBI

Policy objectives should not concentrate solely on the level of unemployment. They should also attempt to change the nature of unemployment by reducing the length of time people are out of work, reducing the uneven spread of unemployment and reducing the social and personal costs of being out of work.

The views that unemployment can be solved by massive reflation, general employment subsidies or rapid expansion within the framework of a statutory incomes policy should be rejected. Instead, the Group offers a comprehensive six point strategy which is realistic and practicable and could make a real impact.

- *Increasing growth in the economy* through a more dynamic and competitive economy
- *Increasing the number of jobs created by that growth* through encouragement of efficient but more labour intensive sectors
- *Increasing the number of work opportunities* by sharing a given number of jobs among more people but without raising business costs
- *Reducing the size of the labour force* and so reduce the number of people competing for work
- *Reducing the uneven spread of unemployment* by giving special help to the particular groups and areas who suffer disproportionately
- *Reducing the personal and social costs of unemployment* by making unemployment a less destructive experience.

Increasing growth in the economy will require a more dynamic economy based on improved competitiveness and attitudes.

Increasing the number of jobs created by that growth means giving encouragement to efficient but more labour intensive sectors. Two

*Summary of the first report of the CBI Steering Group on Unemployment, 1982.

major examples of this are construction and tourism, including business travel and leisure generally. In contributing to the economy, these sectors have the capacity to generate more jobs for any given level of stimulus than, say, more capital intensive sectors. Business is already doing a great deal to help the job creation process by support for local initiatives. This can be expanded.

Increasing the number of work opportunities could not be achieved by work sharing, simply reducing hours and not pay. Job-splitting, dividing a job and its pay between two people, could provide more opportunities to work without raising business costs. This should also be coupled with a scheme for phased retirement. The current Temporary Short-Time Working Compensation Scheme and the Community Programme Scheme should both be developed and extended.

The size of the labour force should be reduced by full implementation of the planned Youth Training Scheme and the extension of the Job Release Scheme as a step towards flexible retirement.

These proposals are complementary and their combined effect could be to reduce unemployment by $1-1\frac{1}{2}$ million below what it would otherwise have been in about five years.

20. Faith in the City*

Church of England

The first and still most recent comprehensive government policy statement is the 1977 White Paper *Policy for the Inner Cities*. That said that too little attention had been paid to the economic well-being of the inner cities, and to their physical environment: stress was put on the erosion of the inner area economy and the shortage of private sector investment, and on the existence of multiple deprivation. The White Paper argued for strengthened economies, improved physical fabric, alleviated social problems, and for a new balance between inner areas and the rest of the cities in terms of population and jobs. Local authorities were seen as the natural agencies for regeneration, in partnership with national government and the voluntary and private sectors. The two essentials were seen as the injection of more public resources, and cooperative and coordinated action. The key was 'bending' the main policies and programmes of central and local government to give increased help to the inner areas. The expansion of the Urban Programme was a supplement, the icing on the cake.

Since a Conservative government came to office in 1979, there has been no change in policy statements from the White Paper's emphasis on the need for regeneration. But there have been major reductions in central financial assistance to UPA [Urban Priority Area] local authorities despite a near doubling, in cash terms, in the Urban Programme. There is one exception: the one central government expenditure programme to have shown a significant growth in the inner cities in real terms since 1979 is that on the police.

The stark fact is that there has been no sustained attempt to put the White Paper's proposals into effect. Government action has been pragmatic: treating the worst evidence of economic decline and poverty by small-scale intervention.

*Reproduced from the popular edition of *Faith in the City*, published by Christian Action, 1985, pp. 14–17, 25.

The danger is that the degeneration of many UPAs has now gone so far that they are in effect separate territories outside the mainstream of our social and economic life. What is needed is an approach which adopts both people-oriented policies, promoting justice by mitigating inequalities wherever they are found, and place-oriented, area-based policies which concentrate resources to a degree which makes a visible and sustained impact, and so offers new hope.

It is now the large housing estates in the inner ring or on the fringes of the cities that present the most pressing urban problem of the mid-1980s. The official indicators used to judge the degree of urban deprivation are not adequate measures of their problems, and the Department of the Environment must take the fullest possible account of the recent research by the Centre for Environmental Studies, and the assessments by UPA local authorities. The outer estates require priority action.

Rate Support Grant

Because of the government's concern to restrain public expenditure for macroeconomic reasons, and an expressed concern for greater local accountability, the national total of RSG support has suffered a 25 per cent cut in real terms since 1977, and analysis shows that in recent years grants to deprived areas has declined in real terms. There are also inherent structural deficiencies in the distribution mechanism of RSG which work against the UPAs: the mechanism does not reflect the compounding effects of multiple deprivation, it gives much weight to school populations (in most UPAs there has been a dramatic fall in school rolls), and local authorities' resources are assessed on rateable values which are twelve years out of date. The government's own statistics show that the need for expenditure by local authorities in the UPAs has if anything increased since 1977. The remedy (financial cutbacks) chosen by the government for the perceived extravagance of some local authorities is a questionable one, given its consequences for rate levels. Rate increases could be kept down by increasing the amount of RSG, and efficiency audits carried out by the independent Audit Commission would be a direct and effective means of ensuring that wasteful expenditure is avoided.

The most severe cuts in the amount of local authority expenditure dictated by central government have been on capital works—down in 1983 by 33 per cent on the 1977 figure, in real terms. This promises serious problems in the future.

The Urban Programme

Total UP expenditure in 1985–86 is static at £338 million, marking an end to five years' slow growth. This standstill in cash terms—a cut in real terms—means parts of the UP are being cut. Rather than being, as originally conceived, a vehicle for innovation, the UP is now increasingly having to fill the gap caused by cuts in the main expenditure programmes of government. As well, the balance of expenditure is too biased towards capital schemes; the local authority component of UP expenditure is subject to the RSG penalties; no allowance is made in RSG allocations for the funding of successful UP projects to be transferred to main expenditure programmes; and there are problems on the expiry of the three-year grant period if the UP grant is not renewed. The UP—even if given greater resources—cannot be relied upon to make more than a marginal impact, when main expenditure programmes (particularly RSG, but also housing investment and other programmes) are being curtailed.

The idea of partnership in promoting urban regeneration is welcome, and needs to be developed to promote greater consultation of, and participation by, local people at neighbourhood level.

Inner city policy has seen a shift in emphasis from tackling social problems, to physical problems, to economic problems. All three are important. But a major emphasis is needed on economic regeneration: for thriving local economies to be developed which can offer employment. This will require three things:

—the public sector must provide more employment opportunities and increased income support to those who are unemployed;
—all those living in the UPAs should be given the best possible opportunities in education and skill-training;
—the physical environment of the UPAs must be improved.

The Commission considers that there is a case for greater support, from both the private and public sectors, for *neighbourhood action schemes* which enable those without jobs to undertake useful work in their neighbourhoods. This will need a partnership at local level between the public, private and voluntary sectors.

Devolution is very important. The establishment of neighbourhood offices is a way local government can improve its delivery of its services to the UPAs. The private sector, too, can provide leadership, and some form of national award might be considered to recognise achievements in this field.

The work done by the National Association for the Care and Resettlement of Offenders in setting up crime prevention schemes on run-down housing estates, encouraging residents to help to reverse a pattern of decline, is an illustration of the role the voluntary sector can play. There is a need for a new deal between the State and voluntary bodies. The central element would be recognition by the government of the need for long-term continuity and funding for recognised voluntary bodies working alongside the statutory agencies. Another feature would be respect for the independence of the voluntary agencies: both national and local government must accept the value of genuine and open debate and criticism. It is unrealistic to expect people to devote energy to innovatory projects if at the same time they are threatened that their work will be penalised if they enter into public debate about social values or priorities.

The UPAs and their people need the nation's confidence and support: if the present pattern of decline continues it will bring wider effects which will touch all our lives. Evidence of how confidence can be injected comes from the work of the two Urban Development Corporations, in the London and Merseyside docklands. They, and the New Towns, have shown how much the single-minded development agency can achieve fairly fast. But they have done so primarily because substantial direct financial support from the Exchequer has enabled them to acquire, improve and redevelop the land in their areas. This money, and the degree of central government commitment to the areas, have given the private sector the confidence to invest. Our confidence in the UPAs can be expressed through a major increase in centrally devoted resources to improve the conditions of life and encourage private sector investment. It is an inadequate response to say that throwing money at the problem is no answer. It is *part* of the answer—necessary, though not sufficient. The 1977 White Paper recognised this. Its policy proposals have not been tried and found wanting. They have not been tried.

We have lost a decade. Policy makers must return to the White Paper and to what it argued was the necessary first step:

> The first essential is a *specific commitment* on the part of central and local government to the *regeneration* of the inner areas ... both central and local government will be judged by their willingness to *implement new priorities, to make funds available, to change policies*, and *to adapt their organizations*.

POVERTY, EMPLOYMENT AND WORK

Since 1977, people in work in Britain have in general become better off. But for people in the UPAs the economic landscape looks very different.

Poverty can be relative: it exists if people are denied access to what is generally regarded as a reasonable standard and quality of life in society.

The most recent official figures show that in 1981 over 4.8 million people were dependent on supplementary benefit, and so were *on* what is reckoned as the poverty line. Over 2.8 million people were living on incomes *below* that level. Those living on an income at or less than 140 per cent of supplementary benefit level (the DHSS definition of low income) numbered 15 million.

In recent years social welfare and taxation policies have tended to benefit the rich at the expense of the poor: at the same time the tax burden to those on the highest incomes has fallen substantially, while that on the lower-paid has risen. Pay differentials have also widened sharply: in April 1983 nearly 3½ million full-time adult workers earned less than the £100 a week definition of low pay.

But it is the steep rise in unemployment above all else that has significantly increased the numbers in poverty. In 1981 just over 2.6 million unemployed people and members of their families were living in poverty or on its margins—3 out of every 10 people under pension age. And in the UPAs, a particularly high proportion of people are affected by unemployment and have to rely on state income support. In parts of estates visited in Birkenhead and North Tyneside, for example, we had evidence that 80 per cent of households had nobody in work. Unemployment hits some groups especially hard—the disabled, the young and the old, and black people, where racial discrimination is still a factor. But the main determinant is occupational class, with unskilled manual workers having unemployment rates up to ten times higher than professional workers.

The heart of the problem is the national decline in manual jobs, and the concentration of manual workers in UPAs. By 1981, there were nearly 2½ million fewer manual jobs in the UK than a decade earlier.

Policy should be as concerned with the distribution of wealth as with its creation. What seems to be lacking at present is an adequate appreciation of the importance of the distributive consequences—for cities, regions and groups of people—of national economic policies. Modern technology means that wealth creation tends not to result in job creation. And arguments that wealth will 'trickle down' are not borne out by the facts.

No Alternative?

There is a widespread—and depressing—feeling in the UPAs that nothing can be done about unemployment. The problem seems to be so baffling and the authorities apparently so unresponsive that hope has been abandoned. Do some politicians really understand the despair of many parts of Britain? While the Church cannot solve unemployment, it has a duty to question the morality of economic philosophies.

A more open debate is needed about economic policies and about the type of society present economic policies are shaping. Their main assumption is that prosperity can be restored if individuals are set free to pursue their own economic salvation. But pursuit of self-reliance must not damage our collective obligation to those who have no choice, or only forced choices. *At present too much emphasis is being given to individualism, and not enough to collective obligation.* The costs of present policies are unacceptable in their effect on whole communities and generations. The greatest burdens of economic changes are being carried by those least able to bear them.

We must use our common wealth, either to provide work for others or to provide an adequate level of income support for those without work. Small businesses can help, to a degree, and the case for setting up a Council for Small Industries in Urban Areas should be considered. Increased public expenditure on capital investment should be devoted to new infrastructure and housing construction and repair, and there also needs to be an increase in current expenditure on public services. Why should money spent on the NHS and on state education be considered unproductive, yet money spent on private clinics and schools be thought productive? The rationale is simply an accounting one: only *market* transactions (irrespective of their social usefulness) are apparently seen as adding to national wealth. This is an argument which does not carry conviction.

What are 'proper' jobs? Only those making what can be sold, whether it is useful or not? No. We need to return to a commonsense view that what matters is whether expenditure uses available resources to meet genuine needs, irrespective of whether it is undertaken in the private sector or through government provision.

The work of the Manpower Services Commission in general is to be welcomed, as is the proposed introduction of a two-year Youth Training Scheme, and the expansion of the Community Programme for the long-term unemployed. There are criticisms, however: these include the lack of jobs at the end of placements; an inadequate training element; limited eligibility rules for the Community Programme, which should be changed; and too frequent changes in the MSC's detailed rules and guidelines. We recommend that the CP should be expanded still further.

It is overtime pay that keeps many working people above the poverty line. Britain is for the most part a low-wage, long hours economy. The government should encourage public discussion of the level and persistence of overtime earnings.

In 1948, one person in 33 claimed National Assistance. In 1983, its successor, Supplementary Benefit, was claimed by 1 in 8. The rate of benefit payable to unemployed people after a year (in 1984–85 £28.05 p.w. for a single householder; £45.55 p.w. for a married couple) is too low. Child Benefit should also be significantly increased (at present it is not to be upgraded in line with inflation, let alone increased in real terms), and the earnings limits below which social security claimants are allowed to earn income without losing benefit (£4 p.w. for SB claimants, £2 per day for unemployment benefit claimants) should be raised.

There is wide recognition of the need for reform of the current framework for income maintenance. In the absence of more detailed proposals, some comment can be made on the fundamental principles for reform proposed by the government. First, high marginal 'tax' rates are still envisaged: if reducing tax rates is a government objective, it must be applied to the poor as well as to the rich. Second, a flat-rate benefit, as proposed, will produce hardship if there is no discretionary element to help those with multiple disabilities. And third, the proposed Social Fund for cases of hardship will offer loans rather than grants to claimants: the result may be to create a nation of poor people in debt. There is evidence that those in work would be ready to make real financial sacrifices to help the poor—provided that the sacrifices were shared and were equitably made. There *is* a national tradition of collective altruism.

There is a need for a major independent review body to examine the objectives and mechanisms of the welfare state across a broad canvas, including the effects of taxation and low pay. It would need to investigate a realistic poverty line income allowing claimants to take part in the life of the community—an assessment of need rather than of what can be afforded. Because of the link between benefits and tax (over 80 per cent of Family Income Supplement claimants are also income tax payers), the review would also have to look at the effects of the fiscal system.

We must reassess many of our attitudes to 'work', and recognise it as doing something useful, for yourself or others. The Church must also affirm that each of us is valued by God, in whose image we are made, for ourselves, and not for what we do. Practical measures may include providing people with tools and training to equip them to work in and around their homes. There should be a wider Church participation in local employment schemes, and industrial mission should respond by taking initiatives to appoint unemployment specialists. . . .

SUMMARY OF MAIN RECOMMENDATIONS

To Government and Nation

1. A greater priority for the outer estates is called for within urban policy initiatives.
2. The resources devoted to Rate Support Grant should be increased in real terms, and within the enhanced total a greater bias should be given to the UPAs. Efficiency audits should be used to tackle wasteful expenditure.
3. The size of the Urban Programme should be increased, and aspects of its operation reviewed.
4. The concept of 'Partnership' in the UPAs should be developed by central and local government to promote greater consultation with, and participation by, local people at neighbourhood level.
5. There should be a new deal between government and the voluntary sector, to provide long-term continuity and funding for recognized voluntary bodies working alongside statutory agencies.
6. A new impetus should be given to support for small firms in UPAs, perhaps by the establishment of a Council for Small Firms in Urban Areas.
7. There should be additional job-creating public expenditure in the UPAs on capital and current account.
8. The government should promote more open public discussion about the current levels of overtime working.
9. The Community Programme eligibility rules and other constraints, including pay limits, should be relaxed, particularly to encourage greater participation by women and unemployed people with families to support.
10. The Community Programme should be expanded to provide 500,000 places.
11. The government should extend to those unemployed for more than a year eligibility for the long-term rate of Supplementary Benefit, or an equivalent enhanced rate of income support under whatever new arrangements may be introduced.
12. The present level of Child Benefit should be increased as an effective means of assisting, without stigma, families in poverty.

13. The present level of 'earnings disregards' in relation to Un-employment Benefit and Supplementary Benefit should be increased to mitigate the effects of the poverty and unemployment traps.

14. The government should establish an independent enquiry to undertake a wide-ranging review of the inter-relationship between income support, pay and the taxation system.

15. Ethnic records should be kept and monitored by public housing authorities, as a step towards eliminating direct and indirect dis-crimination in housing allocations.

16. An expanded public housing programme of new building and improvement is needed, particularly in the UPAs, to ensure a substantial supply of good quality rented accommodation for all who need it, including single people. Each local authority's hous-ing stock should include a range of types of accommodation, including direct access emergency accommodation.

17. The Housing (Homeless Persons) Act should be extended to cover all who are homeless. Homeless people should be offered a choice of accommodation.

18. There should be further moves towards the decentralisation of local authority housing services.

19. A major examination of the whole system of housing finance, including mortgage tax relief, is needed. It should have the objec-tive of providing most help to those most in need.

20. The concept of 'care in the community' for people who might otherwise be institutionalised must be supported by adequate resources to allow the provision of proper locally-based support services for people (especially women) caring for vulnerable and handicapped people.

21. Local authorities in boroughs which include UPAs should, with other agencies, develop policies to establish and sustain commun-ity work with adequate resources.

21. Charter for Change*
TUC

THE MEDIUM-TERM EMPLOYMENT STRATEGY

A concerted medium-term economic strategy is needed to get back towards full employment. This is not an excuse for inaction or delay; immediate steps should be taken to expand the economy and bring down unemployment. But unless a longer-term view is taken the fall in unemployment may not be sustained and bottlenecks in production may arise.

The contrast between the government's Medium-Term Financial Strategy (MTFS) and the TUC's *Medium-Term Employment Strategy* (*MTES*) cannot be emphasised too strongly. The financial strategy—based on money supply and public borrowing targets—in the government's MTFS is not only irrelevant to the problem of unemployment, it is one of the causes. The reduction in inflation has only been secured at the expense of a massive rise in unemployment and a loss of industrial capacity. The *MTES*, on the other hand, would put job-creation and production at the top of the agenda and not at the bottom.

The first phase of the *MTES* would reduce registered unemployment by one million in two years. This may well mean creating more than a million jobs as some of the new jobs will inevitably be filled by unregistered unemployed workers. It is an ambitious target after seven years of decline and neglect, but it is achievable. It recognises the urgency of the need to tackle unemployment. Setting the sights any lower would simply mean condemning people to even longer periods of deprivation, a further loss of output and higher levels of spending on unemployment benefits. It has been estimated, for example, that every unemployed worker costs the Government at least £5000 a year in lost taxes and unemployment benefits. The government would therefore

* Reproduced from *TUC Economic Review*, 1986, pp. 29–35.

stand to recoup over £5 billion of its £20 billion unemployment bill by reducing unemployment by one million.

However, even when this one million target is achieved this will still leave over two million registered unemployed. This level of unemployment would have been inconceivable before 1979. So further targets will have to be set which will in part depend on the success in meeting the initial one million target but which will eventually aim to reduce unemployment below 1979 levels.

The central aim of the *MTES* would be to create jobs in all sectors of the economy. Underpinning this approach would be the need to move to a high-growth, high-productivity economy. In other words, it would not simply create jobs at any price. This contrasts with the government's lack of concern that many of the jobs created over the last three years have been in low-paid, low-productivity sectors. This will in the long run be self-defeating because creating large numbers of low-wage, low-skill jobs will depress economic growth and the rate of technological change, and hence restrict the economy's long-term ability to generate more new jobs.

The *MTES* would have three main purposes. First, it would set out those policies likely to bring about a substantial reduction in unemployment over the next two years. This reduction in unemployment would be mainly achieved by an increase in public spending, concentrated on infrastructure investment and the public services. In addition, special measures—such as an additional labour subsidy in the Assisted Areas—will directly boost private sector employment. Other sectors of the economy would also contribute to job-creation as the economy picked up.

Secondly, the *MTES* would also put in hand longer-term expansionary policies which need to be planned now, but whose effect will not be felt for some years to come. This is particularly true for some kinds of infrastructure investment, such as new road construction, and public transport, such as the railways. For example, more public spending is needed to put houses back into good repair. More also needs to be spent on new roads and replacement railway track. Planning for both needs to be started now, but in the first year or two the jobs will come from house repair because new road construction requires much more time to get underway. The *MTES* will balance public spending programmes so that new construction projects are coming on stream in a continuous flow as old projects run down. The construction programme will steadily build up, creating more and more jobs as it expands.

Thirdly, the *MTES* will need to consider how and where new jobs will be created through the technological challenge both in manufacturing and service industries in the public and private sectors. It will need to outline the policies required to bring this change about particularly on research and development and training.

Fourthly, the *MTES* will need to consider what constraints exist and what sort of policies will be needed to deal with them. Some will not become critical for one or two years into the recovery, but still require action now. For example, skill shortages in sectors such as construction are unlikely to hamper expansion seriously in the short term but could be a serious problem in the medium term. Complementary training policies will therefore be required. In contrast, the balance of payments is already in serious crisis and immediate steps will be required to deal with this problem. Policies to overcome these constraints are set out later.

THE EMPLOYMENT PACKAGE

There are four key elements of the TUC's employment package to reduce unemployment by one million: first, increased public investment, initially concentrating on repair and maintenance but gradually increasing spending on new construction projects. Secondly, expanded public services. Thirdly, expanded (and improved) special employment and training measures. Fourthly, reductions in working time.

PUBLIC INVESTMENT PROGRAMME

The TUC has carried out a major stocktake of the UK's economic infrastructure—our roads, houses and schools. This has revealed a massive backlog of repairs, especially in housing. New house building has fallen dramatically. The result is ever-growing waiting lists for decent housing. The impact is not only felt by individuals at the sharp end of the cutbacks; the national economy also becomes less and less productive as roads fall apart and the rail network becomes more and more dated.

PUBLIC SERVICES

The government has run down our public services; the standard of service offered has been reduced in many areas and the morale and status of public service workers have been undermined. This can be clearly illustrated in two quite different sectors: street cleaning and refuse collection and the health services.

Street Cleaning and Refuse Collection

This provides a perfect insight into the government's shortsightedness and double standards. The Prime Minister has recently expressed her dismay, after returning from an overseas trip, over the filthy state of Britain's streets. The PM has even gone so far as to suggest that Richard Branson should pioneer a scheme using unemployed young people to clean up the streets. The PM's proposal is remarkable in two respects—first, it suggests that the shabbiness of the streets (not to mention the holes in the roads) is a recent phenomenon; there has in fact been a progressive deterioration over the last 6–7 years. Secondly, it begs the question of why the streets are in such a state.

There is in fact no mystery about it: first, Figure 21.1 shows that local authorities have been forced to cut back cleansing and refuse services as a result of reductions in rate support grant and rate capping. Secondly, some councils have contracted out these services to private companies which has resulted in a serious drop in standards.

Merton, for example, contracted out its street cleaning to Taskmasters who undercut the council tender by reducing staffing levels and working conditions. The result has been a constant stream of complaints over the

Figure 21.1. Numbers employed in refuse collection and disposal
(whole-time equivalents)

	September 1979	September 1985	% change
England	47,770	38,146	−20.1
Wales	2,367	1,872	−20.9
Scotland (cleansing)	10,534	9,722	− 8.7
Total	60,571	49,740	−18.0

Source: Department of Employment Gazette.

level of service. Taskmasters were fined over £23,000 for poor performance in 1983 after admitting that one in five streets was not being cleaned. A more recent report in the *Wimbledon Guardian* on 1 August 1985 stated that 'since Taskmasters took over, the roads have been filthy and nobody is doing anything about it.'

The Prime Minister's proposal offers no solution to these problems and it may in addition create health and safety hazards if young people were not fully trained. The solution is in fact to restore the resources to local authorities in order to employ people permanently and to reverse the move to contracting out of these services to private companies.

The Health Service

The government claims that the National Health Service is safe in its hands on the grounds that it has increased the real level of spending since 1979. The truth is that over the last five years overall health spending has increased by a meagre 0.5 per cent a year. This is way below the 1.5 per cent a year real growth needed simply to maintain the existing level of services because of the growing cost of health equipment and the rising number of old people. Recent *Office of Health Economics* figures confirm that the UK spends less per head on health care than any other nation in Western Europe, except Italy and Ireland.

The experience on the ground provides an even more damning indictment of the government's record—this is something that many ministers, including the Prime Minister, will not be aware of as they use private rather than public health services. In Newcastle upon Tyne, for example, more than 1000 patients are waiting for orthopaedic surgery; yet cutbacks have forced the closure in April of a 30-bed orthopaedic ward at the Freeman Hospital. This has meant that a 75-year-old patient had to wait nine months in constant pain before being admitted for an urgent hip replacement operation.

An emergency employment and services package could get the NHS back on its feet by:

- improving staffing levels in the nursing, technical and support services to maintain and improve standards of care and treatment; and
- undertaking an emergency repair programme of hospital building and by increasing the number of maintenance workers to preserve the fabric of the service.

These examples—road cleaning and the NHS—highlight the great contrast between the government's and the TUC's approach to public service provision. The government is ideologically opposed to public provision in general and on top of that it takes a narrow accounting view which ignores the quality of the service offered.

The TUC on the other hand believes that an expansion of public services is vital for three reasons: first, it would be one of the most cost effective ways of increasing employment as increased resources can be quickly deployed. The 'caring' services such as health, education and social services are by their very nature highly labour-intensive as they provide individual care and attention. Secondly, public services make a direct contribution to individual and community living standards. Thirdly, it could create higher quality, more stable permanent jobs than either an expansion of short-term employment schemes such as the Community Programme or a faster growth in private services.

SPECIAL EMPLOYMENT MEASURES

Special employment measures can play a key role in reducing unemployment. They can be used to assist skill training, they are highly cost effective and they can be targeted on particular groups of workers such as the long-term unemployed. Nevertheless, they should not be seen as a substitute for policies designed to create permanent employment. Nor should they be expanded indiscriminately; for example, careful consideration would have to be given to whether the Community Programme could be expanded further without running the risk of displacing permanent jobs in local services.

A highly effective new employment measure could be a regional employment subsidy. The subsidy would be given to all firms who are able to demonstrate a net increase in employment in the Assisted Areas in the regions. The TUC estimates that if this subsidy was around a fifth of average earnings it would create between 130,000–170,000 jobs.

REDUCED WORKING TIME

Reductions in working time have a vital role to play in maximising the job-creation impact of the expansionary spending measures and in ensuring that the introduction of new technology will not lead to job losses. The TUC has campaigned for the introduction of a 35-hour basic week. Although some progress has been made—the average normal week is now below 40 hours—the process will have to be accelerated if it is to have a significant impact on jobs. Consideration should therefore be given to providing assistance to companies as they adjust working time and staffing levels. Immediate priority should also be given to reducing the current level of overtime. Although a limited amount of overtime is inevitable much of it is systematic and often reflects an inefficient use of resources. Unemployment could be reduced by around 100,000 if overtime was converted into full-time jobs.

THE POLICY MIX

The overall balance of spending between public investment, public services and special employment measures would need to be agreed at a National Economic Assessment. This would follow a comprehensive appraisal of the UK's spending priorities and economic constraints. The Assessment would include representatives from the government and all sides of industry who share the common objective of reducing unemployment and boosting production.

These discussions would need to be guided by a clear set of principles. In the medium term the level of public spending should grow at least in line with the overall growth of the economy. Within this framework:

- the first call on the nation's resources must be the creation of jobs for the unemployed;
- the second call must be the improvement of living standards for those most in need including pensioners, recipients of benefits and the low paid; and
- the third call must be the improvement of living standards for the rest of those in work.

The scale of the measures that would be needed to reduce unemployment by one million is illustrated in Figure 21.2. Three points should be noted—first, the expenditure cost is expressed in net terms, i.e. the increase in tax revenues and the reduction in spending on unemployment benefits resulting from lower unemployment are deducted. Secondly, it focuses on the reduction in unemployment which means that significantly more than one million jobs would be created. Thirdly, the year two expenditure and unemployment figures reflect the cumulative impact of both year one and two spending. In other words, public investment would be £2.4 billion higher than on current plans in year one and £5.7 billion higher in year two. This would reduce unemployment by a total of 150,000 in year one and 360,000 in year two.

This programme would boost public spending by around £4 billion (just over 1 per cent of GDP) in the first year and by £9.8 billion (less

Figure 21.2. Scale of the policy changes

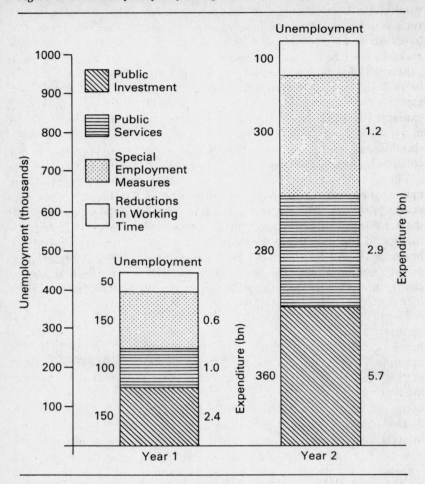

Source: Davies and Metcalf (1985), *New Earnings Survey*, CSO.

than 3 per cent of GDP) in the second. Around 35 per cent of the jobs would come from public investment; 27 per cent from public services, and 29 per cent from special employment measures. The remainder—around 100,000—would come from reductions in working time, especially overtime.

One key question that has to be answered is how the employment strategy would be paid for. First, the balance of existing spending plans would have to be changed. Resources should be diverted from sectors such as defence, which are generally highly capital-intensive and contribute little to employment or living standards, into sectors such as health and education.

Secondly, certain taxes, particularly on high income-earners, should be raised. The government has significantly cut the level of taxation on top income earners, with little or no benefit to the economy. For example, the abolition of the investment income surcharge has resulted in a loss of over £1 billion to the Exchequer each year. The government should also clamp down on tax evasion by properly resourcing the tax collection system; this could raise around £4.5 billion a year.

Thirdly, the level of government borrowing should be increased. It makes more sense to borrow now to invest in the future of the UK economy than it does to spend billions of pounds on financing the cost of three million unemployed workers. Companies borrow when they want to expand production, so do individuals when they want to buy their home. If the government adopted a balance-sheet approach—just as a private company assesses its credits and debits—it would be much clearer that the higher level of borrowing (a debit) was matched by a higher standard of infrastructure and service (a credit).

The present government claims that increased borrowing would push up interest rates. There has in fact been no evident relationship between borrowing and interest rates over the last seven years. In 1986, for example, government borrowing as a proportion of national output was at its lowest level for over a decade—at around 2 per cent—and yet real interest rates are still near an all time high. Moreover, recent TUC budget simulations on the National Institute and London Business School models confirm that spending can be increased without raising interest rates.

STIMULATING THE SUPPLY SIDE

The 'supply' side of the economy must also be improved in order to ensure that UK industry can rise to the challenge of a sustained increase in demand. The government must introduce an effective industrial strategy to increase R&D, investment, training and education, and exports—the foundations on which to build a modern technological economy. This section also shows that public enterprise can act as the cutting edge of technological advance and spur private sector companies into action.

AN INNOVATION STRATEGY

British industry has to innovate to survive. The present government's response is wholly inadequate: it has failed to understand the need for a national innovation strategy. A strategy which will ensure that research and development is effectively coordinated and directed towards meeting industries' needs. It has instead adopted a small scale *ad hoc* response which has not produced the pace of change that is required.

In comparison the TUC will be holding a major conference in July on a future innovation strategy involving trade unionists, industrialists and academics. As a start the government should introduce a new three part programme: first, a new *Innovation Council* made up of active researchers from higher education, government laboratories and from industry should be set up with trade union involvement as ACARD recommended in a recent report. The Council would help to identify the national basic research priorities. Secondly, the government should increase the funds available for the *training* of technicians, engineers and research staffs.

This would mean reversing the cuts in higher education funding which have hit science oriented universities such as Salford and Aston Universities. It also means improving the funding of Research Councils which help to train research staff. Thirdly, the level of *public funding for industrial R&D* should be boosted. To bridge the R&D gap with the UK's major competitors would mean—according to a recent House of Lords report—doubling or trebling the level of government support. This could be done in part by shifting resources from defence into civil R&D—at the moment the UK puts almost half of public R&D funds into defence compared with less than 10 per cent in West Germany and Japan. Additional resources could immediately be used to boost the 'Support for Innovation Scheme' in order to increase the use of microelectronics and the Alvey Programme for advanced information technology.

TRAINING AND EDUCATION

The UK is falling behind its major competitiors in this vital area. The process has to begin by reforming the *school* curriculum in order to increase the awareness of the contribution of industry. That is why the TUC, as part of 'Industry Year' has been involved in a number of initiatives—such as the School Curriculum Industry Project (SCIP). This has involved trade unionists going into schools to help emphasise the importance of links between education and industry. Reforms are also needed to the *higher education* system to increase its contribution to economic prosperity. Much greater emphasis also has to be given to *continuing education*. This would be directed not only at the unemployed and workers with outdated skills. It will also help individuals who missed out on educational opportunities earlier in life and those who wish to undertake further education for their personal development.

A major expansion of *training and retraining* opportunities is also required. Young people need broad-based training and relevant qualifications from an improved and properly resourced Youth Training Scheme (YTS). Improvements to the YTS should be matched by a major expansion of the industrial *apprenticeship* system. The government should provide some additional funding to 'pump prime' employers. Moreover, apprenticeships should be standards based and not time served. This will allow greater access to both boys and girls and help them to be more adaptable to technological change.

INVESTMENT

Technological change can only be speeded up if there is more investment in new equipment. Major changes are needed on two fronts:

Controlling Merger Mania

There is little evidence that the recent wave of mergers has produced an improvement in the underlying level of industrial performance. While mergers can help to build bigger and more effective UK companies to compete with overseas giants, this will not happen because of free market forces or competition. Instead, a competition policy is required which would allow mergers which boost exports, increase innovation and investment and create and save jobs; and stop those which simply represent speculative changes in ownership without benefiting the economy. An equally important reform will be to give workers in companies subject to merger or takeover rights to information and a say over the outcome. The legal safeguards on existing employment conditions should also be strengthened.

Investing in British Industry

The crucial link of the strategy is to ensure that the funds being used to finance mergers and overseas investment are invested directly in British industry. Unfortunately the major City institutions have so far been unwilling to provide industry with the long-term, high-risk funds required for investing in new capacity and technologies. This stands in marked contrast to Japan where financial institutions and industrialists have taken a far more strategic, longer-term view: this means that in order to build up capacity and markets they have been prepared to forgo high short-term returns. There is therefore a need for a National Investment Bank (NIB) which will work in tandem with local enterprise boards (LEBs) to channel public and private investment funds into industry.

The NIB

The National Investment Bank would help to redirect the funds of the major financial institutions previously invested abroad into British industry. Some of the UK's leading competitors such as Japan and West Germany are again one step ahead as they already have successful investment banks. A bank the size of the NIB—which would have assets of between £1 billion and £2 billion—can spread the risk involved in such investments, and it will be able to offer finance at below market rates.

Local Enterprise Boards

The NIB will work closely with local enterprise boards. LEBs have already been established in the West Midlands, Greater London and a number of other regions and cities facing employment problems. LEBs have also identified the need to provide high-risk, long-term funds to medium-sized companies. They have been funded from local rate money and by funds from the financial institutions. The WMEB (West Midlands Enterprise Board) has recently established a Regional Unit Trust with the backing of Lazard Securities.

Their track record in a short period of time demonstrates that they have a vital role to play in providing finance and technological expertise; the WMEB, for example, made 42 investments in 32 different companies between 1982 and mid-1985. This resulted in 4000 jobs being created or saved at a cost of less than £3500 per job. Moreover, for every £1 put in directly by the WMEB the private sector put in a further £5. Two contrasting examples of companies that have benefited are ER Hammersly and Co Ltd of Cradley, manufacturers of high quality clothing, and Enterprise Steel Products Ltd of Dudley.

The LEBs have stressed that investment should form part of a broader economic strategy to revive local economies. The WMEB for example has developed a range of specific initiatives to deal with these broader problems.

- *West Midlands Technology Transfer Centre Ltd*. This innovatory initiative has been established to increase the competitiveness of West Midlands manufacturing industry by encouraging the use of best practice new technology.
- *Tyseley Training and Community Resource Centre Ltd*. A fully equipped facility with modern technology pioneering new approaches to high quality skill training with specific attention to the needs of the long-term unemployed.
- *West Midlands Co-operative Finance Ltd*. Providing loan and grant finance to help people who would not otherwise have access to the necessary resources to create and control their own jobs in viable co-operative enterprises.
- Strategic sectoral initiatives such as the *Clothing Resource Centre Ltd*, which tackle the inter-related problems of investment, training, technology, marketing and management skills in West Midlands industries.

Through such agencies, LEBs have been developing clear principles and guidelines for economic development and investment. These include:

- the need to provide medium/long-term funds designed to assist capital growth;
- investment in human skills-training;
- promotion of equal opportunities for women, minority ethnic groups, disabled people and other disadvantaged groups; and
- promotion of good pay and conditions through good employer charters.

TRADE

The government has ignored an inescapable fact of life for the UK: a thriving healthy trading sector is critical to the long-term future of the economy. In contrast with other leading industrial economies which have used public purchasing, non-tariff barriers and other means to protect their industries, it has abandoned exporters to the vagaries of the free market and operated an exchange rate policy which had positively encouraged the flood of imports.

The UK should learn from this experience. First, the UK's exchange rate policy should be geared to the needs of industry and not the City. It is clearly more difficult to manage the exchange rate since the development of international euro dollar markets. Nevertheless, monetary and interest rates policies should be designed to achieve this objective. Secondly, much greater financial assistance should be given to exporters. The recent House of Lords report on overseas trade highlighted the need to increase the role of the Export Credits Guarantee Department. This is particularly important if the UK is to make inroads into the developing economies. Thirdly, action has to be taken to contain the flow of imports. This can be done in a variety of ways, but the most effective strategy would be to apply import penetration ceilings on a sector by sector basis. This may well be the only means of enabling companies to recapture market shares and expand with certainty in the future. The ceilings will be relaxed as soon as industrial sectors are back on their feet.

PUBLIC ENTERPRISE

An extension of public enterprise will be a vital ingredient of a successful industrial strategy. In this way the government can guarantee that growing sectors vital to the long run performance of the economy are provided with the resources to increase R&D, investment and training. The example of British Gas shows the role publicly-owned industry can play. It has a record second to none on R&D, investment, training and employment practices.

British Gas

- *R&D*. Over 1900 people employed in R&D with a budget of over £55 million. Ten per cent of budget devoted to speculative projects which provide ideas for the future but which don't yield a quick return.
- *Education and training*. Special commitment to training included in 1972 Gas Act. 173 craft apprentices recruited in 1984–85.
- *Buy British*. Policy covers 95 per cent of goods, e.g. 11,397 commercial vehicles from BL and 1701 UK made cars.
- *Equal opportunities*. Agreement covering recruitment, training, manufacturing and grievances.
- *Health and safety*. Statutory safety measures with detailed codes of practice covering all areas of its operation.

The TUC is currently examining the future role of public enterprise and will be reporting to the 1986 Congress. Nevertheless, a number of key points are already clear:

- the government should stop its programme of privatisation which is resulting in widespread job losses and in many cases an inferior service;
- new public enterprises will be needed to achieve greater economic and social progress; and
- there should be new rights for consumers and for the workers in public enterprises.

22. Alternative Economic Strategy*

NALGO

NALGO believes that monetarism and cuts in public spending since 1976 have greatly exacerbated the UK's economic difficulties, making our longer-term structural weaknesses even more difficult to overcome. As a consequence, NALGO believes that there must be a fundamental change in the direction and priorities of current economic policies.

NALGO supports an Alternative Economic Strategy based on a planned expansion in economic activity to raise output and living standards and reduce unemployment.

This expansionary strategy must be based on substantial and sustained increases in public expenditure, which represents the only way to tackle the most pressing social needs, to provide the infrastructure necessary for economic growth, and to create new jobs. In particular, attention is drawn to such areas as education, the National Health Service, leisure activities and social services where there is great scope for an expansion of employment opportunities in the public sector.

NALGO believes that the resources available for this expansionary strategy are available in the UK. A considerable expansion of public spending could be achieved at present by increasing government borrowing without any appreciable effect on interest rates or inflation. Corporation tax should be made more effective and NALGO supports the introduction of a wealth tax. Taxes from North Sea oil and gas must be mobilised for economic development. Finally, there must be changes in public spending priorities, particularly away from defence spending and towards those areas which help promote economic development.

The government must assume responsibility for managing the level of economic activity to ensure full employment. Market forces and the profit motive cannot be relied on to meet the needs of the British economy. Planning must have an essential role in laying the basis for longer-term economic prosperity.

* Reproduced from NALGO, *Alternative Economic Strategy* (1983), pp. 57–60.

Planning can be regional or sectoral; whilst regional imbalance in employment must be reduced, the success of planning also depends on the promotion of particular industrial sectors. Regional policies alone cannot solve Britain's essentially national economic problems.

The present government's economic policies have led to a collapse of output, employment and profits, and there is no sign of a revival of industry. A new government may be required to reverse the present strategy, and any effective solution to Britain's difficulties would require the government to take fuller responsibility for the national economy and equip itself with sufficient powers for the task.

Public ownership should be extended. Specific centralised planning of manufacturing industry by government would be inappropriate and government should pursue its objectives for reindustrialisation by changing the constraints and pressures to which industrial management has to respond.

A new regional policy should be designed to reduce disparities in regional employment and to provide both a sufficient number of jobs and a balance of types of employment in each region.

Manufacturing must be regenerated to raise domestic output of goods for home consumption and for export, but it will not provide the bulk of the jobs which need to be created. Creating new jobs will in future depend more on the service sector and on the public services in particular with more emphasis on government direction of jobs to the regions as well as the provision of inducements to employers.

The nationalised industries, the public services, including those run by local authorities, and central government departments themselves should all provide new jobs in the regions.

NALGO supports the TUC proposals for economic planning and believes the new institutions proposed by the TUC will be essential if a planning strategy is to succeed. Agreed development plans negotiated between company management, government and trade unions should be promoted.

A planned approach to trade must play an essential part in a coordinated economic strategy; import penetration must be controlled to give time for uncompetitive industries to recover and new industries to grow. The control of trade will be linked to the implementation of positive investment strategies to revive British industry.

To implement an alternative economic strategy the UK would have to negotiate new trade and industrial arrangements with the European Community. NALGO is committed to UK membership of the EEC and will continue to argue the case for securing suitable changes in the EEC arrangements from within. Britain should press for a much greater commitment of community resources to regional assistance and a reduction in agricultural support.

NALGO believes that planning will ultimately have to be promoted at an international level and not merely at national and regional levels. A collective international approach to the world's economic problems is vital if we are to avoid the increasing domination of the multinational corporations.

The key to the success of the alternative economic strategy is the involvement of government and the public sector in achieving higher investment, and sustaining consumer demand as a basis for successful investment. Public sector ordering, amongst other measures, should be used in the strategy. A high level of public investment and some channelling of private investments, backed by appropriate forms of planning agreement, will be necessary, and pension funds and North Sea oil revenues must make key contributions to that investment. Strict exchange controls should be imposed.

NALGO has strongly advocated the marrying of pension fund investment to the real long-term needs of the economy, and above all, the regeneration of Britain's manufacturing sector, but any pension fund monies channelled into strategic economic uses should be underwritten by government to guarantee that no detriment accrues to pension fund members. The Union has also supported the TUC view that there should be 50 per cent trade union participation in pension fund trustee bodies, including investment panels.

An expanded role for local authorities in promoting local industrial development is an essential complement to a new national industrial strategy. NALGO has welcomed the initiatives taken by some councils setting up local enterprise boards to make use of local authority pension funds for local industrial investment. The most effective action that local authorities could take in the industrial regeneration process is to expand their capital programmes. The construction industry would be the prime beneficiary but other industries would also benefit. Good planning, improved infrastructure and provision of services by a local authority can play a significant part in attracting and assisting industrial development.

The nationalised industries, which might be substantially expanded under a future government, should have a major role to play in reviving industrial activity and putting the industrial sector on a firmer basis for the long-term future.

There is a social dimension to the AES, including steps to remove inequalities, extend the social services and increase democratic involvement in economic life at all levels.

This will involve some reassessment of the respective roles of men and women and require quite radical changes in hours of work, occupational segregation, the wage system, taxation and social security.

An example of the kind of change required is provided by NALGO's response to the government's consultation paper *The Taxation of Husband and Wife* which advocated a system of genuinely individual taxation, with non-transferable allowances, for all who work to be achieved by the immediate abolition of the married man's allowance, which would finance an increase in cash benefits for those unable to work because of family or other responsibilities, including a substantial increase in child benefit.

Equal opportunity will also require other changes such as comprehensive childcare provisions, encouragement for retraining (especially where careers are interrupted), better chances for promotion and career development and massive investment in public services which will both provide job opportunities for women and free them to take advantage of them.

Sexual inequality is but one aspect of the unacceptable social divisions which must be eradicated. NALGO supports the conclusion of the suppressed Black Report which calls for more resources and better planning and allocation within the NHS and a coordinated government effort encompassing education, housing and the personal social services.

NALGO deplores government public expenditure plans which fail to take account of rising demand (e.g. from the very elderly and the unemployed) and force authorities to extend 'community care' arrangements which impose unreasonable burdens on relatives, too often women.

A major expansion of education and training would bring Britain into line with other industrialised countries and provide both economic gains, reducing the numbers seeking work to provide a better qualified workforce when growth returns, and social gains through concentrating on those with special language or literacy difficulties or encouraging changes of direction by more mature students.

NALGO rejects the cost-cutting options set out in the 'Think Tank' report but accepts that in the long run the level of social provision can only be maintained through faster economic growth. In the short run the North Sea revenues should be mobilised. Public service unions should also press the substantive case for comprehensive social provision and wide ranging public services.

NALGO has accepted that pay is an essential element in economic and social planning but that the approach advocated in *Pay Policy*, a statement adopted at the 1978 Conference and endorsed at successive conferences since then, cannot be implemented until there is a different kind of government with different priorities.

NALGO supports the new emphasis on the problem of low pay. Past measures, including equal pay legislation, achieved temporary gains and a determined policy, together with a sympathetic government and a better economic context, could see a long-term shift in unacceptable pay disparities, provided that the structure of the tax and benefit system is also reformed in favour of the lower paid. The best strategy, including the possible effectiveness of a statutory minimum wage, must be agreed as a matter of urgency.

Effective action on prices could also help the lower paid. NALGO favours a comprehensive system of price controls, again as part of a broader economic assessment and regulatory framework, operated partly by an investigatory body in the private sector and some direct subsidies within the public services.

The success of the AES, in NALGO's view, will depend on a major extension of industrial democracy not only at the level of the individual workplace but in all the vital areas of economic planning, including decisions on the level and direction of public spending.

The long-term work-destroying potential of new technology will not be overcome solely by faster economic growth. Current high unemployment is a result primarily of recession and not of technological change.

There are essentially three methods of dealing with the problem of technological unemployment: sustained economic growth; reducing the work content of each job; and creating new jobs, especially in the public services.

Reducing the work content of each job could be achieved by: shorter hours; shorter working lives (earlier retirement and longer full-time education); continuing education during working life (day release, block release, sabbatical years, etc.) and longer holidays.

An increase in part-time work and job-sharing should be promoted.

The microelectronics revolution will not be accommodated without social disruption and international economic instability unless nations agree to cooperate in mutually beneficial policies to ensure future employment for all their citizens. Economic growth and the higher living standards which can flow from that growth will only be achieved if national governments and trade unionists across the world work together and combine to restrain the growing power of the multinational corporations.

PART V:
Commentators

Policy watching is a major intellectual sport. Many of the watchers are professional economists, or journalists with some training in economics. They watch from very different positions; but through their expertise they provide us, in the end, with the best quality of arguments on which to make our own evaluation of suitable policies and parties. Evaluation will not be easy, because here, as at every other stage, choices arise—this time between commentators who think that the Conservative government is on the right lines, and if it is straying at all, is still too interventionist; those who think that the government is broadly on the right lines, but needs to intervene more at the margin; and those who see the government's policy as wholly misconceived (and within these, either because it is insufficiently Keynesian, or insufficiently socialist).

From the vast range of possible starting points, we have chosen to reproduce first the brief opening chapter of Patrick Minford's *Unemployment: Cause and Cure*. Patrick Minford has more faith in markets than economists of a more Keynesian persuasion, seeing unemployment as the result of barriers which prevent, as he puts it, 'real wages and productivity from adjusting naturally to shifts in technology, demand and industrial structure, and relocating those freed from one sector to other sectors'. The barriers which seem to him fundamental are the unemployment benefit system and trade union power. It is these which need reform if unemployment is to be significantly reduced.

This first reading from an economist who is sympathetic to government policy is then followed by the views of two who are not: Christopher Huhne and Bernard Stafford. Christopher Huhne, the Economics Editor of the *Guardian*, offers a quite different reading of how to regenerate British industry, by taking a careful look at Alliance proposals for both the short and the medium terms. That distinction is an important one because, in his view at least, any future Alliance government would have to encourage industrial expansion by a series of immediate measures which are potentially inflationary, whilst engaging in the encouragement of longer-term reforms. The Huhne (and indeed Alliance) solution to immediate job-creation without inflation relies heavily on the use of an incomes policy underpinned by an inflation tax; while the longer-term solution requires initiatives now on education and training, the relationship between industry and the City, the distribution of wealth and the reform of the electoral system.

The Stafford approach is different again. He very carefully, and in measured tones, constructs the economic thinking underpinning present policy, and then sets that against the counter-argument for demand-induced economic expansion. He argues that the latter is preferable, but demonstrates as he does so his awareness that the expansion of demand on its own will not be enough to stimulate output. Instead, Stafford argues, import penetration is just as likely to increase as demand does, unless specific action (either on exchange rates or import controls) is taken to protect the balance of payments, and unless government activity to restructure the manufacturing base is pursued in a systematic and extensive way. Economic expansion therefore, if it is to be sustained and successful, requires government initiatives in the sphere of overseas trade and domestic manufacturing investment as well as in the area of overall demand and immediate job-creation.

The Stafford conclusion takes us once more to the Alternative Economic Strategy. That strategy, as should now be clear, comes in many versions. In its moderate guise of 'planned Keynesianism' it concentrates on expanded government spending, tax incentives to firms to increase domestic investment, and a few selective and temporary controls on imports, and on capital export. Versions then become more radical as they increase in public ownership, strengthen government controls, and alter the distribution of class income and power. The 'toughest' version currently widely on offer is that from the Campaign Group, reproduced in Part II. A more mainstream version is reproduced here, from Francis Cripps and his colleagues, and it is followed by two critiques. One is David Lipsey's defence of a 'new-Keynesian' version of the AES against the Glyn-type 'new-socialist' variety (the terms are Lipsey's). The other is Sam Aaronovitch's attempt to increase the AES's electoral popularity by scaling down its ambitions to a series of discrete proposals achievable within the limits of resources likely to be available to an incoming Labour government. The Aaronovitch critique is important not simply because it demonstrates that Hattersley-type 'new realism' has spread far and wide on the Labour Left after the 1983 defeat. It is also important because it lists some of the general critiques of the 1979–83 AES—particularly its statism, its nationalism and its insensitivity to feminist concerns for which the Glyn/Campaign Group programme has also been criticised.

In fact when the Socialist Society held a conference in February 1986 on the Glyn pamphlet, these were the criticisms which were uppermost in the minds of many contributors. How to avoid creating an over-centralised siege economy without popular support? How to relate socialist initiatives in Britain to wider European and world problems, and social forces? How to respecify our understanding of work, employment and domestic responsibilities to create a non-sexist social structure in a socialist society? And how to win popular support for socialist ideas? The problem of popular support was well put by Ann Simpson:

> Despite this well known fact, Glyn who (like others in all fairness) has one eye on the popular planning lobby, says that for the wide ranging nationalisation he proposes 'of course [!] an enormous campaign must be mounted to convince first the Labour Movement and then wider layers of the population that such a plan is feasible' (p. 36, para. 5). Glyn is caught in a cleft-stick. The plans he proposes are widely opposed. Yet without popular support the plans just cannot be put into action.
>
> We could repeat his handy use of arithmetic and set ourselves a task to be completed, before the great task itself of creating 1 million jobs a year. If 1 million finance workers oppose nationalisation currently, and there are two years to a General Election, then we can pose the problem in round figures. To convert 1000 bank employees a week to nationalisation. Of course, there is always the possibility that they will refuse to be persuaded, and just stick to their own ideas. Perhaps that's where dictatorship of the proletariat comes in? But it becomes somewhat embarrassing to talk of popular planning, full consent and participation, etc.
>
> The real problem then is posing revolutionary solutions when there is in fact no revolution. The kind of mass mobilisation that would support a government suffering credit blockades, capital flight, trade sanctions, etc. is just not around. The parliamentary road to revolution is highly unlikely. What has to be discussed is a long-term strategy which makes use of a possible Labour victory in the next election to support the detailed and long-term work of building popular consensus behind radical measures. Although the heroic plan of just blasting the baddies is more invigorating ('War on unemployment must be declared, the demobilisation of the reserve army made the central objective', p. 36, para. 5) such an approach is destined to fail, above all because while recognising the need for popular support and knowing it hasn't got it, it fails to draw the necessary conclusions.

There is not space in a collection of this kind to cover all aspects of the debate around the AES in general, or the Glyn pamphlet in particular, though it will be possible to return to some of them in the final chapter. But since international action has been one theme canvassed by

Right and Centre figures in earlier parts of this book, it is important to show how left-wing thinkers on industrial regeneration approach that particular dimension of the problem. So we have included John Palmer's contribution to a *New Socialist/Spokesman* collection of essays, *Joint Action for jobs: a new internationalism*, to give some indication of the type of thinking now commonplace in Left-intellectual circles on this issue. And we also think it important to allow Andrew Glyn to defend his pamphlet against at least one of the criticisms to which it has been subject from the Left—namely the danger that his solution was 'undemocratic'. In February 1986 he said this:

> The most frequent criticism has been that the proposals contained for planning the economy are 'deeply undemocratic'. This is an extraordinary position to take. Of course central planning can be 'undemocratic' as the experience of the Soviet Union and Eastern Europe testify. But the presumption that any serious attempt to control the main levers of economic power [the pamphlet specifically says that measures of control must concentrate on the main industrial and financial companies] must be undemocratic is amazing. Of course the present nationalised industries are run in a completely undemocratic way and a major task is to develop methods of democratic accountability and control (a matter beyond the scope of the pamphlet). But the private sector companies which dominate the economy are no less undemocratic in their operation (unless, that is, you buy the idea of the market being a democracy). It is seriously suggested that for the government to require that planning in these enterprises respects national priorities (for trade, investment, training, etc.) is inherently undemocratic? Do people prefer the democracy of the monopolies?
>
> In what possible ways will the 'rights' of the mass of the population be infringed by controls over speculative movements of capital, by requirements that major financial institutions lend to the government to finance a rebuilding of the welfare services, by limitations on price increases and so forth. There is one respect in which 'consumer sovereignty' would have to be restricted, which is that foreign exchange may have to be allocated to importing necessary capital goods to rebuild industry, rather than inessential consumer goods. This poses a political task of persuading people that the expansion, which such a trade policy would facilitate, would benefit them and the community more (in terms of expanded public services, an end to unemployment, etc.) than it would cost in terms of limited consumer choice (Metros rather than Golfs).
>
> In my opinion it is quite false to pose local economic initiatives as the 'democratic' way of intervening in the economy as compared to central planning. As the London Industrial Strategy admits it is impossible to control the major companies at a local level. The job gains which could conceivably result from a national system of local intervention do not approach the number required to return to full employment (100,000 a year would be an extremely optimistic target). A major expansion of public services, which all Labour supporters would regard as a priority, could not possibly be implemented without control over the financial system. And as the LIS also

says, the experience of local intervention is that it has a far greater chance of being effected where the enterprises concerned are not left simply in private hands.

Some people may believe that it is politically impossible to win support for the policies of control necessary to allow a Labour government to move towards full employment, and that local economic intervention is the most we achieve politically. But that is completely different from posing local intervention as the solution. In my opinion local intervention, and national economic planning and controls are entirely complementary.

23. Unemployment: Cause and Cure*

Patrick Minford

Unemployment in the United Kingdom fluctuated moderately within the range of 1–2 per cent of the labour force throughout the 1950s and early 1960s. From the middle of the 1960s it began a more or less steady rise, by 1970 to 3 per cent, by 1976 to 6 per cent, and by 1984 to 13.5 per cent. Part of the current higher unemployment rate is to be attributed to the extremely severe world recession, associated with US policies to reduce inflation, while insufficiently curbing public sector deficits. Another part is the effect associated with the Conservative government's policies to reduce inflation in the UK. Both these effects are temporary in nature. In response to the government's policies at home, and as a better balance in US fiscal and monetary policies allows world real interest rates to fall, recovery from the recession will continue to occur, though at a rate and with a timing that is inherently hard to predict as world events over the past four years have repeatedly demonstrated.

However, these elements account for a limited part of the unemployment total. Precise calculations are difficult, but, assuming none of the proposals made here were to be carried out, unemployment at the next peak of the economic cycle, whenever that comes, would seem unlikely to fall below 2–2½ million (8–10 per cent of the labour force). Some would regard even the upper end of that range as optimistic, a view that would leave even more of the rise in unemployment to be explained by factors other than the recession at home and abroad.

We focus on these 'underlying' factors and remedies for them, rather than on cyclical or 'demand-management' factors and policies. We fully accept the present framework of government demand management and anti-inflation policy. . . .

* Reproduced from *Unemployment: Cause and Cure* (Oxford; Martin Robertson, 1983), pp. 1–8.

THE CAUSES OF UNEMPLOYMENT

It is a widespread opinion among economists—and one which we fully endorse—that the proximate cause of unemployment is excessively high wage costs, produced either by high wages or by low productivity. We have identified this as a strong mechanism in the UK.

However, one cannot stop at this point in the analysis and proclaim, as has from time to time been done, that government can, by direct intervention in the wage-setting process, reduce real wages or increase productivity. Such direct intervention (or incomes policy) has repeatedly failed to achieve anything of the sort in the UK, besides being inconsistent with the economic freedom that is this Conservative government's aim. The reason for this failure is that there are market forces and distortions of considerable power driving real wages and productivity to the levels we observe. In order to modify these levels and so the level of unemployment, we have to understand these forces and modify the market distortions.

We identify two major distortions in the UK labour market which prevent real wages and productivity from adjusting naturally to shifts in technology, demand, and industrial structure, and relocating those freed from one sector into other sectors.

The first, and the fundamental cause of unemployment, is the operation of the unemployment benefit system. The minimum flat rate benefit including any supplementary benefit 'top-up' is paid indefinitely to an unemployed man for as long as he remains unemployed. Such a man will very naturally expect to be re-employed at a wage after tax and work expenses which is at least as high as this benefit, and probably somewhat higher because he may not wish to 'work for nothing', whatever his personal attitude towards work. His work even at this wage may well be poorly motivated because of his lack of reward, so that productivity also suffers. Hence wages cannot effectively fall below this level for even the most unskilled worker. This level then acts as a floor under the whole wage structure, and working practices accepted at this unskilled level may similarly affect higher levels of the occupational structure. It follows that shifts in economic conditions which would warrant a fall in real wage costs, will have only a limited effect on them and unemployment will result instead. This mechanism, in other words, substantially limits the wage flexibility of the UK economic system.

The second major distortion is the power of unions to raise wages relative to non-union wages. Given the way the benefit rate sets a floor below the non-union wage, as unions raise wages for their members, the workers who then lose their jobs cannot all find alternative work in the non-union sector because wages there do not fall sufficiently; the overall effect is increased unemployment.

Though union power is a major contributory cause of unemployment, it is not fundamental, in the sense that were benefits *not* to set a floor beneath non-union wages, it would not add to unemployment. There are other factors which play a similar contributory role. They include changes in taxation, shifts in technology, adverse movements in the terms of trade and in world demand for UK products, and changes in population size and structure. Many of these are frequently cited in press and other commentary on unemployment as 'reasons' for unemployment. They are so only in the limited sense we have defined. To repeat, if wages and productivity adjusted without constraint, these factors would not alter unemployment, but would instead have their effect on real wages. Nevertheless, *given* our benefit system, such alterations in these factors as lie within our power *can* help reduce unemployment, and we give some attention to them in what follows.

POLICY PROPOSALS

Our proposals fall into three parts:

1. suggested changes in the benefit system;
2. supporting changes in tax and income supplements for those in work;
3. changes in the law and institutions regulating the labour and the closely related housing market.

Colloquially, (1) may be said to deal with the 'unemployment trap', (2) with the 'poverty trap', and (3) with union monopoly power and government regulation of wages, employment conditions, and rents. Taken as a whole, our proposals are capable of reducing unemployment very substantially over a five-year period. Politically we believe them to be well capable of implementation with public acceptance as a programme for reducing unemployment, though they will be strongly resisted by particular vested interests. They will increase incentives and get the labour market operating effectively once again.

The Benefit System

Wage flexibility is substantially reduced by the fixed ('flat rate') benefit level. This is because benefits do not vary with wage levels. Hence as wages fall, benefits do not fall in like proportion and act as a floor below wages, reducing their flexibility.

Our first proposal is therefore to introduce a maximum statutory ratio ('benefit capping') of 70 per cent for total unemployment benefits to net income in work. This is similar to the ratio used on the Continent, for example Germany, where it is 68 per cent for family men. This cap would be widely seen as fair, in view of the need to maintain minimum work incentives. It would be simple to work (Continental practice shows it to be quite feasible), and it would, according to our estimates, bring about a sizeable reduction in unemployment—about 750,000 over four years. It would also of course greatly increase the flexibility of wages, since for many workers (around 40 per cent) benefits would vary proportionally with wages.

We also propose the introduction of a jobs pool, consisting of all available vacancies and other community work specially organised, in each area (as in the US 'workfare' scheme), together with tighter procedures for denying benefit. Benefits should be conditional on acceptance of a job from the pool—after three months for workers under 25, after six months for other workers. In essence, this is an extension of the existing Community and Youth Training Schemes, but modified to increase substantially the pressure on people to take a job at lower wages, recognising that there is help *in* work for the low-paid.

Tax and the Support of Work Income

The introduction of the above measures will increase work incentives substantially for those in low-paid occupations. But a further contribution to reducing unemployment can be obtained by raising tax thresholds. This will increase incentives for those a little further up the pay scale, whose benefits will not be affected by the cap. Furthermore it will also increase the social acceptability of the cap by raising the in-work incomes of those affected by it, so both mitigating the fall in their living standards when unemployed, and implying an absolute rise in living standards if they now choose to work even at a lower wage.

Our proposals here are for substantial falls in taxation, paid for by wide-ranging reduction in the responsibilities of the state through the privatisation of virtually all state production, of state consumption of goods that are not 'public', and of some transfers (notably pensions). To protect the poor in work, we propose a negative income tax (health insurance, education and pension contributions would be compulsory). By 1990, the aim would be to double income tax thresholds and to abolish the national insurance scheme and its contributions, to raise child benefits to offset the cost of children's education and health insurance, to lower the standard rate to 25p and to eliminate the higher rates. The cost of this programme (net of tax revenue generated by higher activity) would be some £43 billion.

Laws and Regulations

Union Power

With labour legislation currently in place, though rights to restrain union actions through the courts have been substantially strengthened, enforcement of these rights is still patchy. In many cases, the public sector is involved and the government should ensure that public sector bodies enforce their rights fully. Nevertheless, private sector bodies may for various reasons, including intimidation and legal costs, be unwilling to pursue actions that it would be in the public interest to have pursued.

Furthermore, the law is by now extraordinarily complex and still fails in its original objective of eliminating labour market monopoly power. Closed shop practices are still permitted and unions still have immunity in respect of 'primary' actions. A bolder approach which goes all out to eliminate labour monopoly power is required. This should be seen to be even handed between workers and employers, for as such, charges of discrimination against workers—or 'union bashing'—would be turned aside.

Our proposals here are simple and threefold:

1. *to restore jurisdiction of the common law to all union actions* (i.e. withdrawal of all immunities);
2. *to legislate a 'status' provision* such that any contract contingent on the union status of the employee would be invalidated; this would render closed shop agreements, explicit or implicit, null and void;
3. *to institute a Labour Monopolies Commission* under the existing competition laws with independent power to investigate any apparent breaches of the public interest in labour market competition, and to bring actions under common law to obtain enforcement of the investigation's proposed remedies.

Proposal (1) would make all union strikes actionable unless expressly covered by a negotiated strike clause in a collective contract; this would give a stimulus to collective agreements, provided these were permitted by the Labour Monopolies Commission. Proposal (2) would give freedom for any person to enter into a contract with any employer; evidence of employment or dismissal because of union membership or lack of it would be actionable. Proposal (3) supplies an active agent to ensure that monopoly positions are broken up, regardless of whether the parties wish it or not, and regardless of whether the offence is by employers or unions. The activities of the Commission would build up a body of case law that should, over time, have the same effect in the labour market as the Restrictive Trade Practices Court and the Monopolies and Mergers Commission have had in the goods market under existing laws.

Minimum wages and employment protection

Wage Councils and laws to set minimum 'conditions' of work (such as restrictions on dismissal, on the work environment, and on discrimination) are extensions of union power largely brought about by the actions of unions in the political domain. Their effects are similar to union actions in raising wages in that they reduce employment. We propose here a series of steps that generally fall short of total abolition:

1. *Wage Councils and wage regulations should be suspended as their terms run out.*
2. *Small businesses should be effectively exempted from all employment protection laws* (where this does not violate treaties such as the Treaty of Rome).
3. *The qualifying period for workers to enjoy their rights under the Employment Protection Act should be raised to five years; and workers should be allowed to contract out of these rights.*
4. *Health and safety rules should be advisory, and industries should be self-regulatory on these.*
5. *Benign neglect should be shown by the executive arm of the state towards other laws in this general area.*

Housing and the Rent Acts

Mobility between regions, which would reduce unemployment, is impeded by the Rent Acts interacting with subsidies to council house rents and 100 per cent rebates to the unemployed receiving supplementary benefit. It is usually prohibitively expensive for a worker to move from a high unemployment area where he has a council house to a low unemployment area where he would need to rent on the restricted private market. *The solution to this problem lies in simultaneously liberalising the private rental market and eliminating council house rent subsidies*, while limiting (via benefit capping) the amount paid to the unemployed as set out earlier. Steps to deregulate private rentals are: include 'scarcity' as a factor in setting fair rents; allow landlords to designate *new* tenancies as being 'assured' or 'shorthold' or 'licences', effectively outside the Rent Acts; allow new tenants to contract out of their rights to go to a rent tribunal for a rent assessment; and finally allow as a new ground for eviction that 'comparable' accommodation be offered. Ultimately the Rent Acts should wither away under these alterations.

ECONOMIC EFFECTS

Insofar as the effects of these proposals can be quantified with the estimated relationships available to us, they should be sufficient to eliminate unemployment. This is one objective. But in the process, they will also substantially increase the general efficiency and wealth-creating capacity of the UK economy, which must be our ultimate objective. They should do so while maintaining protection at their current levels for the poor in work and the disadvantaged, and so achieving what we take to be the major distributional aim of society. They will finally increase people's economic freedom, which has also been a traditional objective of the British people.

24. An Overview on Economic Policy*

Christopher Huhne

It is easiest to think of Alliance policy as addressing two separate economic problems. The first problem has been largely aggravated by the Thatcher years, namely the extent to which the British economy has very considerable reserves of unused manpower (in the form of the unemployed) and machinery. Unemployment entails a human and social cost—but also an economic one. The output of the economy could be 7 per cent higher if unemployment were reduced again to 1979 levels, producing perhaps £25 billion more goods and services each year. The Alliance's budget proposals and its incomes strategy are designed to tackle this problem, and we can legitimately hope that a good part of the pay-off would be in a matter of a Parliament rather than two or three.

The second range of Alliance policies cannot be expected to produce rapid results, for it is primarily addressed to the British economic problem which has been a century in the making, namely our consistent inability over many decades to grow as quickly as our major industrial competitors. Just as relative economic decline has been a feature since the late nineteenth century, so we must expect that the proposals to reverse it will be relatively slow-acting. Most important of these measures, in my view, is a fundamental improvement in education, training and hence the skills of the British. Clearly, the distinction which I make between measures with short and longer-term pay-offs can be blurred at the edges, but I believe that is useful.

Let us take the first problem first. How are we to get as many of the unemployed back to work as quickly as we can? The essential reason why Britain has such high levels of unemployment is the fear that inflation would take off if the government attempted to reduce them. Unemployment is Mrs Thatcher's incomes policy. By holding un-employment high, the rate of increase of the price of labour—wages—is moderated. And by moderating wage growth, the most important element in costs, price rises too are moderated.

* Paper to the Tawney Society, 1986.

In essence, the Alliance budget strategy is to foster more jobs in the least inflationary manner. This is in part by ensuring that measures are targeted on those least likely to cause inflation: the long-term unemployed. Now numbering more than 1.3 million, those who have been out of work for more than a year have to all intents and purposes been sent to Australia. They are often too dispirited to look for jobs. They are 'outsiders' who exercise very little restraint on the pay claims of the 'insiders' in jobs. So if we get them back to work by doubling the Community Programme to 460,000 in the first instance, as a step towards a job guarantee for all the long-term unemployed, we shall create little inflationary pressure.

The crash programme for skills in short supply will also tend to decrease inflationary pressure, because it will provide a greater number of those people the shortage of which causes their wage rates to rise rapidly as firms bid for their services. Moreover, a large part of the Alliance's budget stimulus is designed to increase demand in the least inflationary way by cutting costs and prices. The 10 per cent reduction in all rates of employers' National Insurance contributions cuts labour costs and hence prices. Nevertheless, we can only go so far in cutting unemployment without rekindling inflationary pay claims. Hence the central need for an incomes strategy which ensures that money which the government pumps into the economy goes into more output and jobs, rather than into higher wages and hence higher prices.

An incomes strategy is also vital to handle the other most severe constraint on the faster expansion of the British economy, because it will help us to increase our competitiveness in world and home markets. The second most dangerous source of inflationary pressure in the British economy would come from the very sharp rise in import prices which would follow a collapse of the pound. If domestic demand increases rapidly, sucking in imports from abroad, the amount of foreign exchange which we would be spending on imports would rapidly exceed the foreign exchange we were earning on exports. And as we sold pounds to buy Deutschmarks, French francs, and so forth which we would need to buy imports, so too would the value of the pound fall.

This balance of payments problem has, of course, been aggravated most severely by the recent sharp fall in the price of crude oil, the increasing export of which has done much to disguise the continued loss of world market share of British manufactures (which fell from 9.7 per cent in 1980 to 7.9 per cent in 1985). Unless we can export more in order to afford more imports as demand expands at home, we shall be constrained to grow too slowly to do much to cut unemployment. Clearly, part of the answer to the problem of exporting more is to improve the world economic environment through greater coordination between governments. But a large part of the answer lies in our own hands too: we must become more competitive, both on price and other factors. Becoming more competitive technologically takes time. So in the short term, we must become more competitive on prices.

One solution is to devalue the pound, which makes our exports cheaper when priced in foreign currencies. We can pursue such a policy within the European Monetary System, with the added bonus of providing businesses with more day-to-day stability of the exchange rate as well. But increased price competitiveness cannot in the long run be achieved merely by devaluing the pound, if the consequent rise in import prices then triggers an offsetting rise in wage costs. An incomes strategy is thus also essential to make us more competitive.

The Alliance proposals for incomes strategy build on the lessons of the present and the past. It is essential in the longer term to erode the divisions between management and labour which bedevil British industry. Incentives for profit-sharing and wider employee share-ownership are designed to do just this. In the longer term, profit-sharing gives the workforce a legitimate interest in the quality of management decisions. Employees who have a stake in the company will not only feel more motivated, but be increasingly interested in the decisions taken by managers which affect their own pay packets directly. Profit-sharing can help keep management on its toes, in a way that neither the banks nor the institutions which own most of British companies' shares can ever do.

Profit-sharing may also subtly alter the options facing management over jobs, and thus also help to improve the trade-off between unemployment and inflation. If a manager has to pay a high fixed wage to a new employee, he is less likely to increase staff than if he has to pay a lower fixed wage but is also committed to paying a variable share of profits which depend on the success of the enterprise. To take an extreme case, a company hiring a new sales force is likely to hire as many people as it possibly can if they are all paid on commission.

Such a change in behaviour, though, may well take time. In the shorter run, we have to find other ways of encouraging those in work to limit their pay claims to what can be afforded without pushing up inflation. The first condition of a successful policy is that there must be a widespread understanding of the need for it. A 'green budget' each year, along the lines practised by most other European countries, would help to spread public understanding of the realistic options facing the economy.

However, it is quite possible for there to be widespread support for incomes strategy but at the same time for small but powerful key groups to decide, perhaps on the basis of a genuine grievance, that they should have a larger pay rise than everyone else. Yet if they do, self-restraint elsewhere inevitably breaks down. General threats or exhortations are ultimately ineffective, because they apply to everyone and not specifically to the people who may present the problem. A threat, for example, to increase taxes on everyone is a very ineffective way to persuade the workers at Ford in Dagenham that they should have the same rise as everyone else.

The answer of Labour's Denis Healey to this problem, supported at the time by Labour's Shadow Chancellor, Mr Roy Hattersley, was to deprive Ford of public sector contracts if it broke the guidelines. A specific sanction was required, but its failing was that it was arbitrary. It was hard to see how companies which did not sell goods to the public sector might be affected. And it did not have public or even parliamentary backing.

The Alliance's answer to this problem is, in the first instance, to give incentives to companies which settle pay within the agreed anti-inflationary guidelines for the year. They would receive a rebate of their employees' National Insurance contributions. But if such measures failed to work, the inflation tax would be held in readiness.

The principle of the inflation tax is just like any other tax, whether on petrol or tobacco. If you put the price up, you get less of the thing being taxed. If you put up the price of inflationary pay settlements, you will get less of them. Nor is it arbitrary, for it is a selective tax on that part of the pay increase which exceeds the target for the year. Those who argue that it is impractical are, in my view, misinformed. The inflation tax, levied on the increase in hourly earnings, would apply only to those large companies subject to the Pay as You Earn income tax scheme.

They already have a massive incentive to minimise their PAYE payments to the Inland Revenue through paying perks rather than cash—and by fiddling. But in the main they do not, and the whole system is policed by a few hundred inspectors. A small addition to that staff, with the inflation tax levied on the same earnings as the PAYE system, would be far from the administrative nightmare some have claimed.

Where the inflation tax has been more legitimately criticised is over the disincentive it might offer to some companies which want to encourage a sharp once-and-for-all increase in productivity, in exchange for a big pay rise. This objection can be overstated, since the tax would be levied on the average hourly earnings of large firms, on the presumption that small firms do not tend to be the source of inflationary pressure. And a large rise for 100 employees of a 1000-member firm will not push up average hourly earnings or inflation tax liability by much. The advocates of the inflation tax are entitled to point out that any small distortion introduced by their proposals would be tiny compared with the scale of the economic waste engendered by 3.4 million unemployed. It is always a mistake to allow the best to become the enemy of the good.

Even this minor potential distortion, however, can be avoided, since any increase in payments to employees due to increased profits would be exempt from the inflation tax. If a firm introduced a productivity improvement which genuinely increased profitability, it would be entitled to pay any amount of extra profit to its workforce. The only caveat is that the profit-sharing agreement would be clearly agreed before rather than afterwards, when it might merely be a disguised way of paying a wage rise. Similarly, increased payments due to increased shares of profits (rather than just increased profits) would be liable to the inflation tax.

A final point on incomes strategy: though the private sector is usually the leader in the inflationary stakes, it is essential not to allow the public sector to fall so far behind, as it has increasingly done under Mrs Thatcher, that the case in justice for a rapid period of catching up leads inevitably to an explosion similar to that of the 'winter of discontent' in 1978–79. The only sensible long-term way of handling public sector pay is through comparability with the private sector. However, it is important that each public sector group should not have its own comparability assessment body, inevitably in hock to the interests of its clients. One comparability commission for the whole public sector is the only way to avoid leap-frogging. Comparability can also be tied to no-strike deals with independent arbitration between the employer's final offer and the employees' final demand—so-called 'pendular' arbitration.

The pace at which any government might be able to cut unemployment depends crucially on the success of these ways of ensuring that money pumped into the economy by government—whether through tax cuts to encourage more private spending, government spending increases, or devaluation to encourage foreigners to spend more on British goods—actually goes into output and jobs rather than merely into an inflation of money wages and prices. Some increased borrowing of about £3.5 billion a year would be fully justified if one could be reasonably sure that national output, investment and employment were to be higher. You have to borrow some to make some. The principle applies just as well to governments as it does to firms, or indeed to households which are encouraged rightly to borrow on mortgage to buy homes which they know will provide them, like any good investment, with an assured flow of services over many years.

THE LONGER TERM

Let me now turn to those measures which might improve the performance of the British economy in the longer term. Our economic performance since 1979 has been poor whether measured by our own historical standards, or by those of other economies. However, performance until 1979 was far from ideal. The first signs of relative economic decline became apparent towards the end of the nineteenth century, when already German production of industrial goods was beginning to rival and in some cases surpass Britain's.

Indeed, Britain's growth rate in the latter years of the nineteenth century consistently lagged behind the growth rates of the United States, Germany, France and Japan. Clearly, the existence of *laissez-faire* and classical liberal policy did not ensure a 'golden age' of prosperity by comparison with competitors more prepared to recognise that the market underprovides some social goods which are essential to industrial and social progress.

Most clear was the underprovision of education and training, the relative lack of which is probably the crucial factor explaining Britain's long-run relative economic decline. Whatever a country's gifts of natural resources—whether coal or oil—ultimately it depends on the value its workforce is able to add to raw materials and other inputs through its inventiveness and skill. Switzerland is a prime example of a country endowed with few factor advantages save a canny and highly skilled population.

Moreover, it is also widely understood amongst economists that a free market will tend to provide fewer educated and trained people than is socially optimal. To show why this is the case, we need only look at the difference between the individual interest of a firm which determines its behaviour and the collective interest of all firms. It will often, for example, be in the individual interest of an expanding company to poach trained employees from another firm rather than train themselves—but socially it would be better to encourage both to train.

As long ago as 1913, Britain produced 9000 graduates from universities each year by comparison with 60,000 in Germany. The contrast was even more stark when science and technology were compared. In Germany, 3000 engineers graduated per year. In Britain, 350 students graduated in all the branches of science, mathematics and technology—including engineering. Though this enormous gap was in part filled by the expansion of higher education through the late 1950s and 1960s, it is still the case that only 14 per cent of the age group eligible for higher education in Britain actually attend some course compared to 40 per cent in Japan and 50 per cent in the United States. Clearly, the Alliance is right to be committed to a steady expansion of real funding for the universities, together with an increase in student numbers, and a bias in the expansion towards science and technology. (By contrast, the government has announced its intention of a steady 2 per cent real cut in higher education through to 1990.)

The contrast between British standards of education and training at intermediate levels is even more stark, as the work of Professor S. J. Prais at the National Institute of Economic and Social Research has done much to highlight. His work shows that, in 1977, 146,000 people graduated from the German *Berufschule* with manufacturing skills, compared to only 62,000 with equivalent City and Guilds qualifications in Britain. The shortfall since then has almost certainly become worse, in part because of the abolition of many of the Industrial Training Boards without adequate replacement and in part because training budgets tend to be hit hard during a recession.

The seriousness of this training shortfall at intermediate levels arises because of the direct impact on productivity of low skills. The less skilled are less adaptable and less able to absorb new techniques and technology. One study also showed that low skill training in Britain was a key reason for the lower productivity in a British plant than in an exactly equivalent plant with the same capital equipment on the Continent. When the production line broke down in the British plant, no one on the line had the expertise to put even simple faults right, and they had to call and wait for a special maintenance crew with the required skills before production could restart. By contrast, in Belgium the skills existed on the line to put basic faults right quickly.

A crucial condition of putting training right is that there should be common, uniform standards for particular skills throughout the country, rather than a time-serving apprenticeship system best designed to frustrate those able to learn more quickly than the norm, or award a certificate to those who merely serve their time regardless of aptitude. Secondly, employers must be encouraged through a training tax which would be refunded if they were responsible for training themselves.

A further change which is only likely to pay off in the longer run is a reform of the relationship between the City and industry. There is a good deal of evidence that financial institutions—particularly the clearing banks—apply rules of thumb in assessing whether to lend which are more conservative than those applied elsewhere. An example would be the insistence on lending only up to a limit determined by the carcass— or knock-down liquidation value—of a company. If the company is strongly asset-backed (say, a restaurant with freehold premises), it is unlikely to find much difficulty raising the money, because the banks know that it will be able to recover its cash even if the business goes into liquidation. However, a company wanting to borrow exactly the same amount not to buy freehold premises but instead to invest in capital machinery which is specifically geared to produce one product may have more difficulty, since the capital machinery is likely to have a very low resale or carcass value if the company's venture fails. This problem is avoided in other countries by banks with a tradition of and expertise in industrial lending to a far greater extent than is the case with our own clearing banks. They are able to back managers rather than rely on conservative rules of thumb because of their understanding of the marketplace in which the borrower intends to operate.

Various proposals have been put forward to build more bridges between the banks and industry, including industrial credit schemes for cheap loans to industry and special corporations such as an Industrial Investment Bank or a New Technology Enterprise corporation. My own prejudice is strongly in favour of schemes which attempt to change the existing financial institutions, particularly the clearing banks, rather than to bypass them with new institutions. For better or worse, the clearing banks are likely to remain the only presence of the financial system in large parts of the British Isles for many decades to come, even if Citibank and other American banks do succeed in creaming off some of their most profitable corporate business in selected centres. In addition, a new institution which indulges in direct lending to industry is likely in the short term to become little more than a ghetto, containing all the industrial risks which the clearing banks are unwilling to take and hence unable to build up a balanced portfolio of lending. An industrial bank could rediscount lending which fulfilled basic conditions about length of term and nature of project by the clearers, but the emphasis should be on building up the industrial expertise of the clearing banks rather than bypassing them.

Another set of measures which I suspect may have beneficial long-term effects on the supply side of the economy is the commitment to redistributive tax and benefit changes, particularly as they effect wealth distribution rather than income distribution. There is little evidence of any link between income distribution and economic growth: some fast-growing societies have low taxation and highly unequal income patterns; others have high taxation and equal income patterns. But a common feature of several of the better performing—perhaps more entrepreneurial—economies is that their wealth—the stock of assets as opposed to the flow of income—is distributed equally.

The top 1 per cent of the population owns 19 per cent of wealth in Germany; 12.5 per cent in France; 25 per cent in the United States and 30 per cent in Britain. Britain and the United States have been the slowest growing major economies since the Second World War. One reason why maldistributed wealth may affect performance is if concentration encourages risk-aversion. Arguably, a wider dispersion of wealth would increase the chances of it being loaned as venture capital to a friend, neighbour or member of the family.

There is also, inevitably, the longer-term issue of what to do about inherently anti-business and anti-industry British cultural attitudes, a compelling case for which has been made by Martin Wiener but also before him by Corelli Barnett. The easy answer is that any people which elected a government prepared to reform the education and training system in the way which the Alliance suggests would already have gone a long way to tackling the problem.

The more difficult answer is that the stress on the values of the marketplace—albeit on occasion a social marketplace—is bound over time to change attitudes to those who live from the market. The market has to be the basic paradigm from which we depart, though depart we must in areas where the market fails. In time, too, the growth both of profit-sharing and of employee share-ownership schemes is likely to do more to change the effectiveness of management than any other likely reform. Shareholders do not vet management performance: they have neither the knowledge of the business nor the expertise. Neither can the bankers be relied upon, for similar reasons. The only people who fulfill all the conditions are employees, and profit-sharing will legitimate an interest in profit-maximisation which should lead to greater efficiency and competitiveness. It is generals not foot soldiers who lose battles, but the foot soldiers may have a powerful role in keeping the generals up to the mark.

However, one other reform proposed by the Alliance may be a precondition of the sustained long-term commitment to improved performance which is needed. A move to an electoral system which proportionally represented in Parliament the votes in the country would tend to create either parties able to capture majority support by seeking the centre ground (the case, for example, with Fianna Fáil in Ireland through much of its history of using the single transferable vote) or coalition governments (on the West German model assuming that a relatively high threshold for representation was instituted). In either case, the effect would be twofold. First, the political system would accurately represent the divisions (and forces for compromise) which exist within society. By contrast, the present electoral system acts like the distorting mirrors at a funfair, grotesquely exaggerating the relative importance of some interests while minimising others. Yet if the electoral system itself presents such a distortion of reality, what chance can the political system have of performing its key social role of reconciling interests? Successful economies have successful institutional ways of promoting consensus about national objectives.

The second economic advantage of electoral reform may begin to be a renewed interest in what actually happens not just at the next general election, but thereafter too. The present electoral system offers great rewards to the party which establishes even a narrow plurality of the votes, and terrible risks for the losers. It should not come as too much of a surprise that the efforts of policy-makers tend to be concentrated on measures whose pay-off comes in the short term—even if that pay-off is in the long run illusory. Economic policy has persistently been distorted by the short-term electoral needs of the government of the day, rather than by the longer-term needs of the economy as a whole. The manipulation of demand—whether by fashionable Keynesians or by their inversion, the monetarists—has repeatedly taken priority over the reform of the supply side—the nitty-gritty of unglamorous reforms of education, training, managements and corporate finance.

Electoral reform would tend to lengthen the policy-makers' time-horizons, since the chances were that the long run—after the current Parliament had run its course—would actually arrive with the same parties actually being there when it did. They would therefore have some objective interest in ensuring that the long run looked better than it has tended to do when we have arrived there in the past.

It would be wrong, I believe, to lay too much stress on the 'inevitable' factors undermining British economic performance, whether cultural, institutional, psychological or whatever. No doubt, Britain's problems are difficult. But small shifts in emphasis and priorities may make substantial differences. After all, the economic history of the last century alone contains at least two examples of societies apparently hidebound by ancient customs and relatively poor performance but which nevertheless transformed themselves very successfully: both Japan after the Meiji restoration and France after the Second World War. Britain's problem of under-used manpower and capital, and the longer-run problem of relative economic decline, can be tackled with the application of enough determined patience. Historic declines can be and have been reversed.

25. Will Present Policy Work?*

Bernard Stafford

Although the present Conservative government came to power in 1979 with the belief that all previous administrations had misdirected the economy, its strategy for growth is in large part a development of policies first introduced by the previous Labour administration in the wake of Mr Callaghan's declaration in 1976 that 'we can no longer spend our way out of a recession'. Present policies have been interpreted in some political circles as the expression of a deranged system of thought. This is a complete misconception which impedes any serious assessment of them. The Conservative strategy is a direct and entirely coherent application of the neoclassical supply hypothesis of growth. The underlying view is that if the structure of the economy were to resemble the model of perfect competition there would be neither the need nor scope for government policy to promote growth. Allied to this is the conviction that even though perfect competition does not prevail it is not within the powers of a government to bring about a sustainable increase in the rate of economic growth. Thus, the most that a government can and should do about growth is to remove obstacles to efficiency and competition and thereby create the conditions in which a spontaneous and sustainable increase in growth can occur. The case for this strategy of *laissez-faire* has been largely made out on *a priori* grounds without detailed reference to evidence.

The identified obstacles to growth are inflation and a set of institutional and fiscal barriers to the flexible and efficient working of the market economy. The argument on inflation and growth has not been very clearly spelt out. The general idea seems to be:

1. that high and varying rates of inflation create uncertainty which makes it difficult for businessmen to plan efficiently;

* Reproduced from *The End of Economic Growth?* (Oxford: Martin Robertson, 1981), pp. 107–17.

2. that a high inflation rate requires that resources which could be more productively used elsewhere be devoted to the dissemination of information about price changes and to the rearrangement of trading activities; and

3. that the higher interest rates required to compensate lenders for higher inflation will retard investment.

The specific argument on market imperfections is simply that through spontaneous increases in efficiency the liberalised economy will naturally expand to realise the potential provided by resources. The instruments of the policy are:

1. a progressive fiscal and monetary deflation designed to reduce inflation; and

2. a wide range of measures designed to promote efficiency and competition.

Thus there are commitments to amend the legal position of trade unions, to abolish price and dividend controls, to create inner-city enterprise zones, to strengthen anti-monopoly legislation, to denationalise, to refrain from intervening in wage-fixing in the private sector, to refrain from supporting 'lame ducks' and, most notably, to reduce the burden of income tax substantially. The government's aim is to reduce the basic rate of income tax to a maximum of 25 per cent. At the time of writing the basic rate had been cut from 33 to 30 per cent, and the highest rate on earned income reduced from 83 to 60 per cent. It is somewhat out of keeping with the government's view of the nature of the economy and policy to describe its strategy in the conventional terms of targets and instruments. The government seems to expect as much from the general shift in attitudes which it hopes its policies will create as it expects from direct economic relationships between the changes it has made and economic growth.

WILL CURRENT POLICY WORK?

Does the explanation of UK growth summarised at the beginning of this paper suggest that this policy is well directed? To answer this question we must look a little more closely at the mechanisms on which the policy depends. The Conservative strategy is by design crucially dependent on the operation of neoclassical mechanisms. This can be seen most clearly in respect of the fiscal and monetary deflation. Neoclassical mechanisms are being relied on to convert the deflation of demand into lower rates of inflation at levels of activity which are depressed only temporarily and by a small amount. The transition to conditions of lower inflation favourable to growth is thus relatively quick and painless; but the less the economy works like a neoclassical system the greater will be the impact of the deflation on employment and output, and the less will be the impact on the inflation rate. Such an outcome would constitute a very serious threat to the Conservative strategy on two counts. In the first place it would make it very difficult for the government to make a significant additional reduction in tax rates. The anti-inflation policy requires a progressive reduction in the surplus of public expenditure over tax revenue; but reduced output and higher unemployment causes public expenditure to rise as the cost of supporting the unemployed grows and as nationalised industries make larger losses or small profits, and causes tax revenue to fall as the tax base contracts. Thus there is an adverse effect on the borrowing requirement of the public sector which is solely due to the slump. In this situation a government committed to pre-set fiscal and monetary targets will find that there is no scope for cuts in taxation and may indeed be forced to raise taxes. The effect of the slump on the budget means that the government can cut taxes or retain its fiscal and monetary targets but that it will be unlikely to be able to do both. The firmness of the Conservative commitment to deflation means that in this case further tax cuts will be sacrificed. The other problem is simply that the greater are the output and employment effects of the deflation the greater will be the damage to productive capacity and growth inflicted by the induced slump in investment and by the adverse effect of the recession on the growth of productivity. Thus if neoclassical mechanisms do not work the Conservative strategy will have to rely on the effects of institutional reforms (but not more tax cuts) and a slowly falling inflation rate being sufficiently powerful to (1) counteract the perverse effects of the policy itself and (2) lift the economy out of the trade-induced recession from which it is also suffering.

We can now return to the evidence. A central message of the analysis summarised above is that in its generation of growth the UK economy has not behaved like a neoclassical system. The factors which have been most powerful in governing growth have been those that would not be important in a neoclassical economy, and the mechanisms through which they have worked have been those that would not operate in a neoclassical world. The evidence is that UK growth has been strongly influenced by the expansion of demand and output actually achieved. There is no support for the argument that UK growth has been governed by the exogenously given growth of factor inputs and productivity, and also no evidence that inefficiency has been a cause of slow growth. Thus the general objection to the Conservative strategy is that it depends on the properties of a theoretical model whose account of the causes and mechanisms of growth bears almost no resemblance to what can be observed in the post-war growth record of the UK economy. The specific objection is that if the mechanisms of UK growth operate now and in the future as they have done in the past, the gains to growth from a policy of lower inflation and freer competition will be (1) small and (2) swamped by the damage to productive capacity and growth inflicted by deflation which the policy itself requires.

Many advocates of current policy would probably not disagree too strongly with this conclusion, but would insist that the mechanisms that will operate will not be those of the past. In particular they would claim (or hope) that the government's measures for liberalisation and freer competition will so transform the structure of institutions and attitudes in the UK that a neoclassical strategy for faster growth will be appropriate and effective. A difficulty with this view is that it exposes its supporters to the charge of inconsistency. How is it that the government is powerless to bring about a change in the growth of output (and even in the level of output in the short run) attained within a given economic and social structure, but powerful enough to transform the structure of economic institutions and social attitudes? There has been no explicit discussion of this question in the current policy debate. The implicit answer seems to be that the required transformation does not involve a laborious erection of alternative structures starting from scratch, but the much less demanding task of releasing powerful latent forces which will benefit all. The belief seems to be that behind the obstructions erected by trade unions and monopoly producers in the private and public sectors there is a vigorous competitive economy the release of which will bring benefits to the great majority of the population. This is not a claim which can be directly tested, and even if it could empirical evidence would not settle the matter one way or the other for there are also judgements about the conditions of political freedom and equality at stake at this level of the debate. One observation of fact is, however, worth making. This claim about the nature of the transformation implies a rather thin explanation of non-competitive institutions. If such institutions are so obviously degenerate how have.they become so prominent a feature of the structure of economies such as the UK? A more convincing interpretation, which incidentally is much more consistent with the ideas of economic theory, is that non-competitive institutions have developed as collective bodies serving interests which the relevant memberships see as legitimate but unattainable in a competitive system.

This implies that non-competitive structures are an integral part of an economy such as the UK rather than an extraneous feature of it, and that the mechanisms of growth are much less manipulable than the advocates of current policy seem to suppose. Some supporters of the Conservative strategy might agree with this but insist, as government spokesmen have repeatedly insisted, that the present policy, although difficult, is one to which there is no viable alternative.

AN ALTERNATIVE STRATEGY

The case for an alternative to the Conservative strategy based on a policy of expansion has been argued by the Cambridge Economic Policy Group. An up-to-date statement of the CEPG position can be found in Chapters 1, 2 and 3 of the April 1980 issue of the *Cambridge Economic Policy Review*. The explanation of UK growth offered here supports these arguments. The analysis of the previous chapters provides no basis whatsoever for the claim that only the policy now in force offers any prospect of success. On the contrary, this analysis points to a direction for growth policy which offers better prospects than that which is currently being followed. The requirement for faster growth is a steady and sustained expansion of demand based on a reversal of previous trends in the trade performance of the UK in manufactured goods. A policy designed to bring this about has more chance of success than current policy for the simple reason that, in contrast to current policy, it would be aimed directly at those factors which have been most important in governing UK growth in the past, and would not include measures whose direct effect on growth is adverse.

It is not difficult to describe the features and circumstances of faster growth. Improving trade performance and expanding demand will interact with the growth of actual output and potential output in a self-reinforcing relationship. The problem of policy is to know how to get there from where we are without incurring prohibitive costs. The task of policy is to map out and negotiate the transition path. As trade performance will not improve spontaneously the stimulus to demand along the transition path must first come from domestic sources, that is from a reversal of the present fiscal and monetary strategy. Only a very crude understanding of the trade–demand hypothesis would support the view that an expansion of demand is all that is required to solve the problem of growth. There are two reasons why an expansion of demand, although necessary for faster growth, would not be sufficient. First, the existing supply of resources will set a limit to the expansion of domestic production in the short-run period before induced increases in investment and productivity begin to set in motion the cumulative forces of growth. This means that the expansion of demand will draw in imports and run foul of a growing balance of payments deficit at some point in the transitional phase. Some economists would also argue that an expansionist policy will ior the same reason run straight into a problem of accelerating inflation. Whether the inflation rate would in fact be increased, unaffected or even reduced by a fiscal and monetary expansion is an extremely controversial issue which is far too large to be explored in any detail here. The greatest distance lies between those who see the excessive expansion of demand as the primary cause of inflation and those who argue that a demand expansion which provides some increase in living standards will reduce the extent to which trade unions fail to achieve their wage targets and thus ease the cost pressures which act on inflation regardless of the pressure of demand. What can be said is that it is not clear that an expansion of demand would much worsen inflation but it would sooner or later worsen the balance of payments. The second problem is that it is hard to see that the effects of an expansion of demand on investment and productivity would by themselves be sufficiently powerful to halt and reverse the strongly adverse trends in the trade performance of the UK. The effects of an expansion on investment and productivity will do something to improve the design and quality of what is already being produced, but what is required is a massive reallocation of resources into the production of new manufactured goods which will be in demand in world markets. Although such a reallocation will never be effected in a slump only an extreme optimist would expect that an expansion of demand will be sufficient to achieve it. The conclusion to be drawn from these two points is that an expansion of domestic demand will not result in a sustainable improvement in trade performance and growth unless it is supported by a set of measures designed to (1) protect the balance of payments, and (2) restructure manufacturing production.

The question of protection for the balance of payments has been given rather more attention than it deserves by the controversy provoked by the proposals of the Cambridge Economic Policy Group for import controls. The basic case for protection through import controls is that the alternative of devaluation will be ineffective due to the sluggish response of trade flows to changes in relative prices. The factors making for a lack of responsiveness are the pricing behaviour of firms and the wage resistance offered by trade unions. Many of those who reject the Cambridge proposals do so from the conviction that effective devaluation is possible. Thus the dispute about import controls versus devaluation is an argument about workable forms of protection in which no great issues of theory and principle are at stake. Indeed the Cambridge advocates of import controls would prefer the devaluation alternative if it could be made effective by a successful incomes policy, but their belief is that this is not possible.

It is unfortunate that the issue of how to protect the balance of payments has occupied such a large part of the debate amongst the expansionists. The purpose of devaluation or import controls is to protect the expansionist strategy during the transitional phase; but neither device will correct the more fundamental problem of the chronic disability apparent in the trade performance of the UK manufacturing sector. Less attention has been given to how the trend of falling exports and rising import penetration will actually be reversed. Some hope seems to be pinned on a 'demand-side miracle' whereby the trading base of the economy will be transformed by induced increases in investment and productivity; but such a result is much more than can reasonably be hoped for. This means that measures to expand demand and protect the balance of payments will only stand a fair chance of success if they are introduced in a package which includes an active industrial strategy. The industrial strategy will require:

1. a more detailed understanding than is presently available of why many UK manufacturing industries have surrendered prominent positions in world markets;
2. an identification of those manufactured goods with a high income elasticity of demand in world markets, taking into account the comparative advantage of newly industrialised economies in those manufactures the production of which can be automated on a large scale and made routine; and
3. in the light of 1 and 2 whatever combination of public finance, control and ownership will be most effective in reallocating resources in UK manufacturing.

As the reallocation will need to be highly selective, the most appropriate strategy would be one in which a central position is given to public investment in manufacturing rather than to general fiscal incentives. This will require a substantial expansion of the funding and activities of the National Enterprise Board or the establishment of a similar body. The implication of this element of the strategy is that the initial stimulus to domestic demand should be largely devoted to public investment in manufacturing.

The standard objection to proposals for public investment in the private sector is that resources directed in this way will be wasted, or at least allocated less efficiently than by the market. There is, however, often a false standard of comparison in this objection. The entrepreneur of neoclassical theory may be much more efficient than the political administrators who would implement such a policy; but this is not the choice which is available. The actual alternatives are a chronically inefficient private manufacturing sector and a less than perfect political mechanism. Any public policy may be inefficient, but the investment policy proposed here would have to be not merely inefficient but massively inept to produce results worse than those shown over recent decades in the trade performance of the UK private manufacturing sector.

An objection to the whole package of measures proposed above is that the expansion of manufacturing it envisages will be inconsistent with the changes in the structure of the UK economy made inevitable by the discovery and exploitation of North Sea oil. In fact there is very little real conflict on this issue. The apparent difficulty arises in part from the fact that a different standard of comparison is involved in the oil argument to that involved in the expansion argument. It is true by definition that UK non-oil manufacturing (and all other non-oil sectors) will account for a smaller proportion of GDP than they would have done had North Sea oil not been discovered or left in the seabed. It is also true that the mechanisms of the economy—including changes in the exchange rate—may operate in such a way as to reduce the absolute size of the manufacturing sector below what it would have been had there been no oil. As there is no reason to suppose that this outcome can or should be avoided, a policy of reflation will expand the manufacturing sector to a size smaller than that it would have attained had there been no oil. However, the manufacturing sector will in this case be much larger than it is now and much larger than it will be if present policies are persisted with. Thus the growth rate of manufacturing under a policy of expansion will be significantly greater than it has been and will be under present policies, although less than it would have been without oil. The distance between the two arguments is further reduced if the finite life of North Sea oil is taken into account. Oil production from current discoveries is forecast to fall in the 1990s, after which time the economy will become more dependent on the trade performance of the manufacturing sector. It is therefore vital for growth in the long run that the reconstruction of UK manufacturing is not seriously impaired by the economic effects of North Sea oil. The contraction of manufacturing relative to the non-oil case can be smaller rather than greater and it is important that steps are taken to see that this happens. This means that the resources and tax revenues provided by oil should be used to regenerate the domestic manufacturing sector rather than to boost private consumption or investment abroad.

It will be objected that these proposals are based on an incomplete understanding of the fundamental problem of trade performance, and that due to the world recession the scope for unilateral reflation is much less than the proposals suppose and require. It is perfectly true that the understanding of the immediate causes of UK growth offered does not provide a complete explanation of it and that there is a limit to what can be done; but these facts are not good reasons for doing nothing in the present situation and still less do they justify a policy which is likely to make things worse.

26. An Immediate Response to the Crisis*

Francis Cripps et al.

The most pressing issue in British politics today is how the crisis of mass unemployment, inflation, industrial collapse and public spending cuts can be overcome. The labour movement's claim is that a Labour government, which took powers to plan the expansion of the economy and control trade, could secure full employment, reinvigorate industry and restore the welfare state within the lifetime of a Parliament. Labour's policies are often described as the 'alternative economic strategy', and we go on to explain them in detail. The basic proposals can be set out simply:

- *expansion of the economy* to raise output, restore full employment and bring about higher living standards all round;
- *large increases in public spending* to reactivate the economy, provide jobs both directly and indirectly, and to restore public services;
- *exchange controls* to stop the City and international finance from undermining the strategy through a 'flight from Sterling' and financial crisis;
- *import controls* to prevent an immediate trade deficit and to allow Britain time to plan its trade in negotiation with the rest of the world;
- *public powers* over the investment policies of the pension funds and other semi-socialised wealth in the hands of the City institutions until such time as they can be taken into common ownership; and
- *industrial regeneration* through expansion of the economy and publicity directed investment; an extension of common ownership

* Reproduced from Francis Cripps *et al.*, *Manifesto* (London, Pan, 1983), pp. 133–46.

of large companies; and compulsory planning agreements, negotiated between the government, large companies and their workers, to bring about investment, production and employment policies in the public interest.

These proposals are a major challenge to the existing international economic system because they require the government to exercise powers of control over trade, finance and industry which are at present in the hands of the EEC, international banks and multinational companies. At the same time, it is a challenge to the British establishment, who are committed to keeping Britain within the existing framework of the international capitalist order. It also, of course, directly threatens their own interests.

Labour's strategy for developing our economy could be the first step in a long-term and profound change in the whole pattern of our society and its international relationships. The success of this first stage in meeting people's immediate needs for employment, public services and benefits, and higher living standards would demonstrate the practical advantages of Labour's perspective of continuing change. To succeed, the strategy would also have to deal effectively with opposition from those within and outside Britain who are against its development into a self-governing and more equal country. Given the huge obstacles to launching the strategy and making it effective, it is essential to be realistic about what can and what cannot be achieved at the first stage. To begin with, the strategy will largely have to operate through existing institutions. It certainly cannot rely on full implementation of fundamental reforms which would take many years to carry through. The questions we seek to answer in this chapter are therefore specific and narrow. What changes are necessary if a British government is to be able to implement a speedy return to full employment? How can the necessary changes be carried through?

THE ECONOMICS OF DECLINE

The claim is that national economic planning can succeed where the present international order patently fails. This claim is the basis of the confidence of Labour socialists in opposing not only Mrs Thatcher's policies, which are plunging Britain into hyper-recession, but also the 'consensus' policies advocated by politicians of the centre—the Tory 'wets', Liberals, Social Democrats and right-wing Labour—which hark back to the failed remedies tried in the 1970s. Before we show how the alternative strategy could be implemented, we must explain how its logic differs from that of Mrs Thatcher's policies and from those of centre politicians.

Mrs Thatcher's aim was to eliminate inflation and restore prosperity by relying on the private enterprise economy. This aim required profound changes in present society. Wages would have to be determined not by any concept of justice but solely with reference to market forces. People would have to rely on whatever they could secure individually in the private market rather than what might be provided collectively. Such changes have been enforced by cutting public spending and seeking to restrict credit to the point at which managers and workers would have no choice but to accept the dictates of the market. Implicitly, since the dominant market forces are nowadays those of the international system, this meant that our economy and society would have to adapt fully to the requirements of the EEC and multinational business. Britain would be entirely at the mercy of anarchic global competition and recession for however long the chaos of the international system persisted.

The consequences of Mrs Thatcher's policies have been incredibly damaging. Cuts in public spending and restriction of credit have not stimulated a more dynamic and competitive private sector. On the contrary, both public and private industries have contracted and investment has fallen. Millions of people have become the luckless victims of unemployment and cuts in social benefits and real wages. The government has engaged in a destructive campaign to make councils close down services and sack workers and to make nationalised industries close plants in a desperate attempt to save money. But in our interdependent economy, money cannot be saved so easily. When industries cut back or close down, their suppliers lose sales and the government loses tax revenue. When workers are made redundant, the government has to pay out more unemployment and supplementary benefit. Money is not saved, but it is used to less and less purpose. The terms for converting Britain into a viable private enterprise economy, if this could ever be done, are evidently far tougher than most people realised. The short-term price is bankruptcy, mass unemployment and increasing poverty. In the long term, the whole structure of our economy and society would come to be determined by the international market system with little scope for any independent national choice.

By contrast, Labour's strategy starts from the principle of social justice. Through public enterprise and planning, it aims to subordinate the dictates of private profitability to democratic decisions about the kind of economy and society we wish to live in. Through public benefits and services, it aims to distribute resources far more fairly and equally than can be done by market forces.

Centre politicians denounce the severity of Mrs Thatcher's policies, and express a belief in the need to reconcile social justice and the market system. But they are not willing to contemplate any major change in the way our economy is subject to the rules of the international capitalist market. Throughout the 1970s, the centre politicians who dominated the Heath and later Labour governments hoped to reconcile membership of the Common Market with prosperity in Britain, and to persuade the City of the needs of industry and the welfare state. The centre's 'consensus' approach failed time and time again. The unwillingness of the last Labour government to challenge the rules and interests of international finance and big business led inevitably to the collapse of the Labour Party's industrial strategy in 1975 and to the passive acceptance of the deflationary package and public spending cuts imposed in 1976 as the price of an IMF loan. Yet some proponents of the continuing 'consensus' approach—among them the Social Democrats who have split away from the Labour Party—appear to be ready to accept continued high unemployment and industrial decline as the price to be paid for maintaining the present form of mixed economy and remaining in the EEC. They talk sadly of the need for 'realism'. But theirs is the realism of despair.

The only firm policy of Centre politicians is their insistence on the need for a permanent incomes policy—or, to put it more bluntly, wage control. At its most negative, their purpose is to prevent inflation from undermining the prosperity of the middle and upper classes, which is periodically jeopardised by rising prices when trade unions bargain too effectively on behalf of wage-earners. Somewhat more positively, some Centre politicians argue that wage control, combined with a sharp fall in the pound sterling, would raise the profits of British exporters and help to price imports out of our market. The logic is that Britain could achieve a more dynamic position in world markets and regain employment through a shift from wages to profits. This is a rather theoretical idea. Some improvement in exports has indeed been achieved in Britain and other countries when wage control was combined with devaluation (for example, by the Labour government in 1967). But the problems of British industry today are out of all proportion to this remedy. Thus, at best, centre policies—including those of the Social Democratic Party—would make Britain's crisis less horrendous than under the present government's suicidal policies, and might slow down our continued decline.

For centre politicians, full employment is a vague and uncertain hope. The certainty is that Britain's membership of the EEC must be preserved and that our society must evolve gradually within that framework. By contrast, Labour's strategy makes full employment its first priority and seeks a new pattern of international relationships, outside the EEC, as the basis for regenerating our economy and society.

THE ECONOMICS OF PROSPERITY

Public spending is not simply a way of providing services and benefits that we need. Increases in public spending can also play a vital role in restoring full employment and industrial recovery. This is not an untried proposition. It is a return to the Keynesian policies on which our postwar recovery was founded. Increases in public spending provide jobs directly in schools, hospitals, factories, public transport, national-ised industries and other public services and utilities, and indirectly provide more business and employment for industries of every kind— large-scale manufacturing, construction, transport, shops and services in the high street. Spending on teachers' salaries, higher pensions or build-ing council homes feeds into the rest of the economy as earnings and benefits are spent and building workers and architects are employed. Reactivating the economy through higher public spending will not only provide jobs throughout the economy and raise production, but will also ease financial problems caused by the slump. As sales rise, profits will improve, bankruptcies will be reduced and nationalised industries will come out of the red; tax revenues will grow and the government will no longer have to pay out huge sums (over £2000 million this year) to maintain a growing army of unemployed people, or to prop up loss-making businesses. The benefit in terms of production and income could be large. With a rise in employment of over 10 per cent, and full use of productive resources, Britain's national income could be increased by some 20 to 30 per cent within three to four years. This is equivalent to an additional £2000 or £3000 a year for every family in the country. Most of this additional production and income would, however, have to be divided between investment in industry, transport, energy, housing and other kinds of infrastructure and improved public services and benefits. Its investment would have to be planned to match the kind of jobs and production which could be expanded rapidly and to meet the most urgent economic and social needs. There would be some rise in the private incomes of most people who still now have jobs. But the main gains would be invested in reconstruction, higher quality public services of all kinds and higher living standards for people who are now un-employed or suffering from cuts in the welfare state.

The strategy would not work miracles. It would not eliminate inflation, make industries efficient overnight or abolish low-paid boring work. But it would create employment, fund social investment, and open up the way for a longer-term development of our economy through common ownership. It could also provide the base for building a more open and diverse society with a wider range of individual and social choice than we have had in the trap of an unplanned international market.

There are many obstacles to putting this strategy into action. The government will need a strong political will and widespread public understanding and backing for its plans. The main political and institutional problem is how the government could gain sufficient control over finance, trade and the balance of payments—and, in particular, how it could negotiate workable new agreements with the EEC and other international institutions. Several economic problems have to be dealt with. Britain's industrial capacity is inadequate and out of date. Britain depends too heavily on imports not only for raw materials but for many important industrial products. Inflationary pressures, arising from low productivity, low pay and conflicts over the distribution of incomes, have accumulated.

ESSENTIAL FIRST STEPS

The immediate obstacle to a Labour government's attempting to restore full employment through high public spending and investment is the virtual certainty of a full-scale financial crisis. The unwillingness of the City and international financiers to underwrite Labour's programme would imply 'loss of confidence' in any government committed to carrying the programme out. Pressure to transfer funds from Sterling into other currencies would cause a collapse of the exchange rate. Unwillingness to lend to the government would cause a collapse of the market for government securities and send interest rates sky-high. Such a crisis of confidence could occur at any time after an election in which a Labour government came to power. It would not only make public spending difficult to finance; it would dramatically escalate the cost of imports of food, raw materials and components on which consumers and industries depend, raise the cost of working capital and threaten spiralling inflation. No government could realistically count on organising an economic recovery in such circumstances, or even with the threat of such a crisis hanging over it.

The first step which must be undertaken, therefore, from the moment any future Labour government comes into office, is to impose emergency controls on the City and the banking system to block

movements of funds out of Sterling and fix the exchange rate, to regulate
interest rates and to ensure the supply of funds to the government for
investment in the public spending increases we need. All investing
institutions would have to be prevented from disposing of government
securities and moving their money out of the country. Secondly, import
controls would be essential to prevent a massive trade deficit once an
expansion of spending got going. An emergency general tariff, except
for food and raw materials, would deter any pre-emptive rush to bring
goods into Britain. The imposition of such controls would amount to a
seizure of power over the City and over multinational business. Import
tariffs would be illegal under EEC and the articles of GATT. Blocking
the movement of funds out of Sterling could fall foul of IMF rules. It was
the difficulty and magnitude of such an assertion of our independence
which led recent Labour Cabinets to choose expenditure cuts, high
interest rates and incomes policies as, in their view, the lesser evil. This
strategy would precipitate an international challenge to the government's legitimacy—a challenge which most of the British establishment
would support. There would be immediate negotiations in which foreign
governments and international institutions sought to force the Labour
government to back down and dismantle the tariffs and financial controls it had imposed.

The essential question is whether and how the government could at
that point negotiate arrangements which allowed it to retain sufficient
powers to plan finance and foreign trade on a longer-term basis.
Without such powers a rapid expansion of public spending could not be
sustained, and hopes of achieving full employment would have to be
abandoned. The most important factor would be the attitude of the
public both in Britain and in the other western countries. The alliance of
which Britain is a member is after all one of democracies. Western
governments could not threaten direct intervention in Britain's affairs
without incalculable political risks. Indeed, the danger of 'retaliation'
and pressure for overt economic sanctions against Britain would be
tempered by the need to avoid an excessively punitive posture. Most
likely, other governments and international institutions would take
symbolic action, threatening worse unless the issues were resolved.
Therefore, the strength of Britain's position would depend first and
foremost on whether the government's actions were widely understood
to be necessary and whether they were thought to be significantly
damaging to other countries. The labour movement should begin now to
argue the case for the strategy much more widely in this country, and to
link it with struggles against public spending cuts, redundancies and
factory closures. The Labour Party and trade unions should be discus-

sing the proposals with the political Left and labour movements in Western Europe, as part of a common strategy against the recession, spreading unemployment, the power of the multinationals and chaos of the international capitalist market.

Apart from this, there would be more objective negotiating levers. The economies of Western Europe are now greatly interdependent. So far as other EEC countries are concerned, interdependence is a two-way affair. Some important British industries depend on exports to their markets. They depend on Britain, not only as an export market for their industries, but also as a source of oil from the North Sea and, more important still, as a key partner in their agricultural policy. Without Britain, they would face huge costs in disposing of food surpluses. This is not to say that Britain could get its way on all counts. Rather, once the British government had declared its intention of leaving the EEC in order to pursue independent policies, there would be plenty of scope for a realistic negotiation in which both sides took account of the other's vulnerabilities. It would be important for other EEC members, especially France and West Germany, that Britain recognised their agricultural and energy problems, just as it is important for Britain that they should recognise our crisis of deindustrialisation.

Britain's departure from the EEC need not cause a collapse of European unity. It would indicate instead the need for a more diverse pattern of development in Europe than that offered by the EEC's perspective of integration under Treaty of Rome rules. By giving up insistence on uniformity and standardisation, the differing needs of all parts of Europe—and not simply of the EEC states—could be brought into the open, and new possibilities of wider relationships would be created. Many people are concerned that we would be 'exporting' unemployment. In fact, planned growth could well be the only way of increasing our trade and, ultimately, importing more rather than fewer goods from abroad.

The United States, the IMF and the world community at large would have their own anxieties about independent policies in Britain. They would worry about the role of the City and Sterling in the international financial system, about the impact of the new policies on multinationals and on trade in different parts of the world. All these matters would have to be negotiated. But it is important to grasp that this need not be an all-or-nothing confrontation. Britain is by now in most respects a small and uninfluential country, and power in the rest of the world is diffused. As a country we are neither in the position of imposing our own will nor of being forced to accept the will of others. We are in a bargaining situation where demands can be made and the gain from insistence on some points has to be weighed against the cost of concession on others. So long as we know our own priorities and take account of the interests of other countries, there is no reason why a British government should not negotiate new trading and financial arrangements with European countries and those in other parts of the world.

FIRST STAGES OF PLANNING

Supposing that essential controls on foreign exchange, trade and international finance were in place, the main dynamic of economic expansion, creation of jobs and regeneration of industry in the first years would come from public spending through existing institutions. Local government, ministries, nationalised industries and other public enterprises would have to carry out urgent programmes to get industries on the move, restore public services hit by cuts, improve social benefits and begin new investment in infrastructure of all kinds.

If the programme of higher spending is to be creative and respond to genuine needs it cannot be laid down centrally from Whitehall but must be organised in an open and democratic manner drawing on the widest possible range of ideas and experience. Trade unions would play a crucial role.

The labour movement has already put forward proposals for open government, tripartite planning and devolved decision-making which could form the means for constructive implementation of spending programmes. The central government, apart from organising the provision of funds, would have to take responsibility for certain specific problems, which we must now consider, in the overall pattern of economic expansion.

TRADE AND INDUSTRY

Britain's industrial capacity, after years of decline, has suffered severe damage under the Thatcher government. By no means all the materials, components and machinery needed for reindustrialisation could immediately be produced in Britain. In the short term, higher imports of essential products would help to overcome such bottlenecks and less essential imports would have to be more tightly restricted to make way. At the same time, investment in new production facilities would urgently be needed to prevent worsening shortages as expansion of the economy proceeded. The government would therefore have to coordinate the pattern of imports and investment plans of companies in key sectors of industry.

The planning of trade and industry would also have to meet various specific domestic and external requirements. Within Britain, it must take account of employment problems in badly hit cities and regions. In relation to Europe and the Third World, the pattern of imports would have to take account from the start of particularly crucial needs, including those which came up in negotiations. Britain could not expect to reach a reasonable settlement with the EEC and international institutions unless its new policies gave assurance to other countries on such points. The central government would have to be hard at work adjusting import plans and negotiating investment and exports with key companies, trade unions, foreign governments and international institutions. The aim should be to achieve a clear set of principles and instruments as a basis for such negotiated planning.

DEALING WITH SPECIFIC INDUSTRIAL CRISES

In the context of rising public spending and general economic recovery there would be few of the large redundancies and factory closures which have been daily news in the past two years. But this does not mean that the government would no longer have to deal with industrial conflicts and crises. Apart from continuing difficulties in some declining sectors, companies might well run into conflict with trade unions or the government on general or specific aspects of the new policies. This need not be a question of sabotage. Companies may simply have planned their international operations on the assumption that former policies, and Britain's decline, would continue and face dilemmas as the new situation came into conflict with their pre-existing plans.

The government must have sufficient bargaining power *vis-à-vis* companies, including multinationals, to ensure a decisive change in the direction of the development of industry, and it must be able to link the energy of workers and trade unions into the new process. Conflicts and crises in industry will have to be resolved in accordance with these aims. Sometimes a solution may be found through provision of finance, through the agency of existing public enterprises or through the new instrument of import control. In other cases the government will have to be ready to change the top management or ownership of the enterprise if its existing owners or managers are not ready to follow a new approach. The formation of cooperatives or public enterprises of various forms, with workers' support, will be a valid way of responding to such

agement and ownership the whole process of recovery and reindustrialisation might be blocked by conflicts in a few key industries.

FINANCE AND INFLATION

Traditional 'reflation' of the economy, for example that undertaken by
the Heath Government in 1972–73, usually meant pouring out money
through government contracts, tax cuts and easy credit, leading to
booms in property, speculative building, consumer durables and imports
which distorted the whole process of expansion. Such pressures for
unbalanced growth could certainly not be afforded in a sustainable
recovery from the present slump.

It is evident that credit will have to be provided for investment and for
the initial expansion of public spending. Also the exchange rate for
Sterling will have to be reduced to a level at which industries have a
better chance of competing internationally and sustaining their exports.

There are specific actions the government could take to prevent the
expansion of credit and the fall in the exchange rate from feeding
accelerated inflation. For example, it could regulate the use of credit by
placing limits on funds lent by banks and other institutions for low-
priority uses. At the same time it could allocate part of the revenue from
import tariffs to subsidising basic items in the cost of living.

Apart from such specific actions, the general impact of the recovery
programme on wages, salaries, profits, rents and other incomes would be
a crucial political issue. A comprehensive, centrally determined, statutory incomes policy would not accord with the philosophy of democratic
freedom we wish to advance. But this does not absolve the government
from the need to prevent an inflationary free-for-all. Incomes policies
would certainly be necessary, including strategies for profits, pay and
taxation as well as selective price controls to prevent profiteering.

THE POLITICAL PERSPECTIVE

The success of an independent, planned recovery of the British economy
will depend ultimately on whether it is politically attractive to the great
majority of people. Success would give hope for creative development of
our own society and would beyond doubt offer an important model to
other countries, particularly in Europe, which also are suffering from
atrophy of the system under which they have developed since the war.

The best encouragement that a new Labour government could offer in terms of social and political perspectives would be to institute certain immediate reforms, including steps towards industrial democracy, procedures for open government, aid for low-income and disadvantaged groups, and so on. Such action would build and consolidate support and make sure that the new process of development was constructive. The short-term response to Britain's crisis must be related to a longer-term vision of how we want our society to develop.

27. A 'Right' Critique of the AES*

David Lipsey

What worries me is that so many advocates of the Alternative Economic Strategy . . . have adopted a frivolous approach to it. They have exaggerated its capacity for good; underestimated its capacity to make things worse; misused it; and, most culpably of all, failed adequately to refine the argument and tackle the fundamental difficulties. In consequence a Labour government which carries out such a strategy could unleash a new disillusion which would be permanently damaging to the Labour Party, the labour movement and the country. The term 'Alternative Economic Strategy' has lost precision. Used by some Labour spokesmen, it means little more than that they reject Mrs Thatcher's TINA: 'there is no alternative'. In a stronger version . . . it comprises a substantial reflation along conventional lines, with a mix of devaluation and import controls used to deal with the implications for the balance of payments. But this is still nothing like the kind of AES advocated, for example, by the CSE London Working Group, which is presented as a transitional strategy to a fully socialised economic system. In part, the difference is rhetorical. The London Group surrounds—some would say, drowns—its reflationary recommendations in a sea of phrases about the 'collapse of capitalism', the 'demise of market forces' and the rest. If this makes its broadly reformist recommendation more acceptable to its target group, never mind.

But there is a real difference too. I think we should do well to distinguish two AESs, if you like 'AES Mark One' and 'AES Mark Two'. 'Mark One' is really a form of neo-Keynesian; 'Mark Two' is neo-socialist. The first of these, a reflationary, if you like reformist, strategy, is one to which on balance I adhere. Certain problems which could arise with alternative economic strategies surely do not arise with this one. It seems to me highly unlikely to provoke the wrath of 'British

* Reproduced from *The Socialist Economic Review 1982* (London, Merlin, 1982), pp. 109–16.

capitalism', whatever that may be; indeed, given a couple of years more monetarism, industry at least will be begging for it. The City of course, won't like it. But the main weapon they have in their hands is to sell Sterling, thus depressing the exchange rate. If a Labour government does not panic before such blackmail, it is more likely to be helpful to the strategy than the reverse.

Import controls however are likely to be the main instrument in preventing the reflation from destroying the balance of payments. Unconstrained, half the impact of any conventional reflationary stimulus to the economy is likely to leak out into imports. So given the scale of reflation needed to get us back to anywhere near full employment, no devaluation which would not lead immediately to intolerable inflation is likely to enable us to do without import controls. But we would be less than honest if we claimed that there was any certainty that import controls would radically improve our economic performance.

The first problem is a technical one. Import controls, if they extend to raw materials or semi-manufactures, will require substantial changes to the factor mix in production—for example, substituting home-made energy sources for imported sources. These problems would be quite severe in the case of some industries where the production process, and not just ownership, is multinational—for example, the motor car industry. Of course, this damage could be averted by excluding semi-manufactures from controls, but only at the risk of increasing evasion.

One possible way of tackling this difficulty would be to institute a kind of 'import controls through the market' by creating a shadow foreign exchange market. The foreign currency value of our exports could be estimated; that sum (and no more) made available in foreign currency by the authorities for purchasing imports; and the price of foreign exchange would then rise to choke off any excess imports. Such a scheme would at least merit detailed examination.

The second problem is that of international retaliation. Now, it is possible to show—as Godley and Cripps have shown—that in a purely economic sense, retaliation would be an irrational response on the part of other nations. The argument goes: reflation will increase our national wealth. Though the *proportion* of it going on imports will diminish, *total* imports will increase because our GDP will increase. But which of us feels confident that we shall persuade President Reagan—or for that matter, the German Chancellor—of that fact? The problem is made more difficult by the fact that those countries with whom we run a big manufacturing deficit—not as is commonly believed Japan, or the rapidly developing countries, but those of Western Europe—are crises. Indeed, without such a perspective of possible changes in man-

precisely those where the geopolitical consequences of widespread protectionism will be perceived as most deleterious. This need not be an insuperable problem. We may know better when we have had a chance to observe how the Mitterrand government copes with the pressures that will arise from its policies. The labour movement could make it easier for itself if it conducted itself between now and the next election as if it had an understanding and a concern for our present allies, and a genuine commitment to the internationalism of the Socialist International.

The third, and to my mind the most serious issue posed by 'Mark One AES', is inflation. Directly, import controls will reduce competition at home, and thus lead to some increase in prices. Indirectly, the whole policy will, we hope, bring down unemployment very rapidly. This will restore the hideously damaged organisational strength of the unions, and could lead to a burst of wage-induced inflation. I shall say something more about this when I discuss the second form of alternative economic strategy below. But it is clear to me whether you study . . . the documents that have gone to the Labour Party–TUC Liaison Committee, that they recognise, even if they cannot yet spell out, the need for an incomes policy. I only hope that the movement will allow them to work out the details in time. The débâcle of the 1974 'social contract', 35 per cent inflation, and the rest cast a shadow over the whole term of office of the last Labour government, without doing anything whatsoever for the living standards of ordinary working people.

Even with such an agreement on incomes, I do think it important not to overestimate what 'AES Mark One' might achieve. It would be unwise for the Labour Party to go into the next election promising an economic miracle. There should be a substantial one-off benefit from the 'AES Mark One'. At the moment, the economy is clearly operating at far below its present potential capacity. A reflationary strategy should enable the economy to operate at substantially nearer that capacity, and we should have substantially less unemployment and substantially more wealth than we now do.

I used to believe that we could expect a further effect. As demand grew, I used to think, so too the underlying rate of productivity would grow. The promise of steadily increasing demand would lead to higher productive manufacturing investment. The knowledge that employment was reasonably full would enable negotiation once more to take place on productivity; unions who embarked on such measures could do so confident in the knowledge that their members would have other jobs to go to. I hope this is still the case. I fear, however, that defensive mechanisms are now very much more developed on the labour side; and I fear also that management is quite capable of reacting to reduced foreign competition and easier home markets by going back to sleep. Those elements in the programme of a future Labour government which could increase productivity are a massive programme of training and retraining. These by their nature are slow acting.

My optimistic assessment of 'AES Mark One' is that our GDP would rise quite substantially. Unemployment would fall; productivity would resume an upward trend, though a slow one, and, thanks to an effective agreement on prices and incomes, inflation would be roughly what it is now. The increase in national wealth could be substantial, but it would be one-off. The AES would not, of itself, increase the ceiling of our productive capacity; it would merely enable us to run our economy at a level closer to that capacity. Pessimists, however, are entitled to argue that the international response to our controls on the foreign balance would cause serious economic dislocation, including perhaps, some areas of physical shortages of raw materials; that the limits of our economic capacity will turn out to be lower than we hope; and that import controls will permit a wage-induced inflation to get a hold which it then becomes very hard to break. Being by nature an optimist, I would be inclined to give it a go, if only because, should it fail, the choice could lie between another prolonged experiment with monetarism—this time, *with* water cannon; or of moving to a highly controlled economy, also with water cannon; or attempting a Friends of the Earth 'solution' with more poverty all round.

There is a problem for a 'right' analyst in moving to the next stage, the examination of 'AES Mark Two'. It is a problem of language. If one chooses to conduct the argument in conventional 'bourgeois' terms, then one stands at risk of being accused of missing the point. But to conduct the argument in its chosen terms, may mean conceding points that one does not want to concede. For example, I now find it hard to give any substantive meaning whatsoever to the term 'capitalist'. How then do I debate with those to whom the supposedly 'capitalist character' of our economy is its essential feature?

This is particularly hard since 'AES Mark Two' is Janus-faced. To the present Labour Party, it presents itself as a strategy for transition to socialism. Critics can therefore legitimately question whether it adequately assesses the opposing social forces which would be brought into play in the quest for such a transition; and many conclude that it does not. But it does not partly because it has much in common with 'AES Mark One'; that is to say, it is essentially reformist, trying to make what we have work a good deal better, and founded round the non-Marxist concept of mediating conflict rather than the Marxist one of forcing it to a head out of which a new synthesis will spring.

So, to which Janus should one address oneself? Should one return to past battlefields in political philosophy? Should one take the AES for what its rhetoric sometimes suggests it is, a proposal for the transition to a society where the social conflict endemic to 'capitalism' has ceased? Or should one confine oneself to those propositions within statements of the AES which purport to be economic and empirically testable and discuss them?

Let me stick with the empirical. The first thing that strikes me is that the proponents of the AES have wholly failed to say how they intend to integrate their belief in national planning, with their commitment to workers' control at the shop floor or plant level. The London Group say: 'In the development of planning suggested [sic] by the AES, the involvement of workers at the point of production, and of workers and their families in localities, would enable planning to be democratised from the outset.' Earlier the London Group had recommended a National Planning Commission. Would someone explain how this Commission, working in London or perhaps Glasgow is going to be 'democratised' by the involvement of workers at the point of production? Either the Commission will tell the workers what to produce, in which case they are not behaving democratically. Or the workers will tell them what they will produce, in which case there is precious little planning.

The omission of this crucial link in the argument is all the more curious since it has been a central feature of all arguments about Eastern European economies. Experience suggests that such economies can evolve in one of two ways. They can be based on 'top-down' planning, with more local bodies acting as subordinate institutions to aid the fulfilment of the plan. The trade unions also become part of this apparatus of planning and control. Or they can attempt more of a 'bottom-up' approach, as in Yugoslavia, in which central institutions play a broadly indicative and predictive role. Since it is logically impossible in such a system *both* to allow local units to determine what they produce *and* to lay down national plans for the detailed use of resources, the market plays a much bigger part in such a system. We could conduct an interesting debate on the merits of these two approaches. What does not make for interesting debate is to proceed as if you could adopt both at once.

The trouble is that AES economists really have not settled what their critique of the market actually is. It is, say the London Group, 'an instrument of class power'; we need to change from 'production for profit towards production for social need'. This sort of rhetoric leaves open more problems than it answers. If we are against production for profit, where is surplus to be generated for social and other investment? If we are to produce for 'social need', who is to define this? Can we be sure that it will produce a fairer outcome than the market? Will not inequalities of political power to command resources prove worse in practice than the inequalities produced by the market which gives greater weight to the desires of those with most income and wealth? You do not make something democratic merely by saying it is democratic. Until these questions are answered—if they can be—the AES will be accused of being a strategy for a *dacha* society.

The other major sin of omission on the part of the AES is any considered approach to inflation. If the strategy is designed to be transitional, and not merely a way of heightening 'contradictions', it will have to produce an answer to the problem of inflation. In fact, it is remarkably thin on the subject. Sometimes it falls for the temptation implicit in the rhetoric of assuming that any increase in money wages can be accommodated from profit. In fact, according to the latest CSO figures, gross trading profits in the first quarter of 1981 amounted to £6026 million out of a GNP at factor cost of £51,445 million. If it were possible to transfer the whole surplus to real wages and salaries, net of tax, they would rise by about ten per cent—scarcely more than they did in the last eighteen months of the last Labour government.

An attempt has been made to avoid this dilemma by arguing that Britain has a large sector comprising multinational companies. These multinationals, it is argued, syphon off large sums of profit abroad, and therefore, if they are nationalised a much larger profit pool would be made available for popular use. That there is a problem of the control of multinational companies, I have no doubt; but I do doubt if it is sufficient to bear the weight alternative economic strategists place upon it. First, why should multinationals seek to get their profits out of the UK? It is frequently argued on the left that British taxes are unduly generous to the multinationals. 'AES Mark One' reflationary policies . . . rely on considerably higher revenues from tougher company taxation. But if our tax system is generous, then, *ceteris paribus*, firms will want to show their profits here.

Second, where the government has become deeply involved in industries, either by nationalising them or supporting them in other ways, they have never found a deep pool of profits waiting to be tapped. Indeed, it is highly implausible that they should; firms which are highly profitable want the government to step in like they want a hole in the head. Third, one only has to read company reports the world over to realise that the multinationals are not the prosperous and powerful institutions they appeared a decade ago. The reason is simple. To become highly profitable, they had to play the trick of producing cheaply in countries with low wage rates to sell dearly in countries with buoyant markets due to high wage rates. And over the decade, there have been few such easy markets.

If the AES is to have a chance of working, therefore, it must be much more forthright and honest about what this will require in terms of the planning of money incomes. This will be made easier by the fact that in the economy which the next Labour government inherits, there ought to be some scope for increasing real incomes, though the priority objectives of a socialist government should surely be to restore public spending and to increase investment. If these intellectual problems of the AES are resolved, I do not think we need to be too worried by political fears for the AES. For example, fears of military intervention have been expressed. Now it is possible that the next Labour government will run into problems with the military. If, for example, we ask them simultaneously to accept defeat in Northern Ireland, a ditching of Trident, a slashing of defence expenditure and a precipitous charge down roads that lead out of NATO, I dare say there will be more than mumbling in the barracks. But I do not think that most military men would recognise an AES if it hit them on the nose. . . .

The present economic crisis could open up enormous opportunities for socialists. I have a horrid feeling that we are going once more to pass them up by talking to each other in language that we understand, instead of talking to those whom we need to convince in language that has resonances for them. And as Bertolt Brecht wrote with savage irony of the East German regime in June 1953, it is not open to us to elect a new people because the existing one has failed to come up to our expectations. Even Labour Party conference cannot reselect its voters.

28. The AES: Goodbye to All That?*

Sam Aaronovitch

The AES was an attempt by the Left within the labour and trade union movement (in which the Communist party played an important part) to put together a credible and coherent perspective which could shift the British economy and society in a socialist direction. A Labour government committed to such a strategy would, it was believed, bring about 'an irreversible shift of power into the hands of working people'.

Though there were different versions of the AES, it had certain core ideas which can be summarised as follows:

First, to bring back full employment, improve living standards and encourage investment, the economy must grow at a faster rate. The key to this was a massive expansion in demand through increased wages, pensions and government spending.

Second, begin to move towards economic planning by way of extending nationalisation and securing planning agreements with the 200 largest firms.

Third, bringing about a major redistribution of income, attacking inherited wealth and tax evasion and reforming the tax system.

Fourth, move towards the control of foreign trade by using import controls (selective in most versions of the AES) to prevent economic growth from being blocked by balance of payments problems.

Fifth, refuse to accept any limitation on Britain's right to determine its own economic policy imposed by membership of the Common Market, which meant, on the predominant view of the Left, withdrawal.

It must be added that for some sections of the Left (though not for all), the test of a 'genuine' AES was its rejection of any constraints on 'free collective bargaining' and certainly of any form of incomes policy.

The intention was to unite the labour movement around a strategy

* Reproduced from *Marxism Today*, February 1986, pp. 20–3.

which could shape the economic and political agenda; a bid for hegemony in the field of economic policy was regarded as the key to a Labour victory which would not repeat the débâcle of 1964–70. It became the benchmark therefore against which the Left judged the 1974–79 Labour government. For the Left, the disaster was indeed repeated and the AES became part of the battleground for changing the way Labour's leadership was elected and bringing the parliamentary Labour Party to heel.

FOUR CRITIQUES OF THE AES

From the mid-1970s there has been increasing criticism from progressive and left forces of some of the assumptions and priorities of the AES. I want briefly (even at the risk of caricature) to mention four of these critiques.

The Anti-Statist Critique

The AES carried forward the strong centralising tradition in the labour movement: the people would elect a Labour government; that government would institute a system of central planning and control using the power of the state to make it work; state ownership in the form of nationalisation would be a decisive instrument.

That approach has been increasingly challenged. Workers' and consumers' experience of nationalisation as so far practised, made it a dirty word and Thatcherism has had a field day as a result. What is being questioned is the 'top-down' approach pervading the AES. How are workers, consumers and communities to decide what they need and how these needs are to be provided? How will they be involved in running their own affairs? This critique has been reinforced by the attempts of a number of left-wing councils to release local and enterprise initiatives. Cooperatives, municipal enterprise, local enterprise boards are part of the search for other forms of social and public ownership and intervention.

The Environmentalist Critique

The AES was strong on the need for high rates of economic growth, but during the 1970s an international movement began to develop, weaker in Britain than in countries like Germany, which argued that economic growth was being pursued at a high cost to the environment and to future generations; that the earth was being raped in pursuit of profit.

The Internationalist Critique

Though a caricature there was some truth in the widely held view that the AES, preoccupied with escaping from the pressures of the world capitalist economy, was really about import controls and withdrawal from the Common Market. But as industrial and financial capital increasingly operated globally and the interdependence of capitalist economies grew, the AES came under fire. The experience of the Mitterrand government since 1982 seemed to confirm the view that no second-rank state could go it alone in implementing such a strategy; or, if it did, major sacrifices would be required from working people. And the result could well be politically destabilising.

The Feminist Critique

During the 1970s also, the feminists pressed forward with their attempt to shift the very terrain itself of economic debate. They pointed out that the AES was drawn up by a group of (white) male activists reflecting the traditions of a male-dominated movement. The priorities established by the AES appeared to concentrate on restoring full employment in the male 1950s sense, to increase economic growth and so forth. In particular, it was concerned with paid work and did not recognise that capitalist society rests on a vast pool of unpaid labour, mainly by women who, in addition to any paid work they do, produce and reproduce the labour force itself.

Even if many of its proposals would have benefited women (as indeed they would), it did not see as a priority the need to deal with the needs of women as child rearers and as carers. Questions arise from the numbers of women doing two jobs (at home and in paid work); the growing number in low paid, low status, part-time jobs experiencing systematic discrimination. The needs which arise from these changes such as child care provision are not marginal but central to a left strategy.

The feminist critique however raised an even more fundamental issue: what kind of changes in human and social relations was the AES intended to bring about? What were its moral and human values?

A NEW STRATEGY

So we need a new strategy. But what kind? The changes in the balance of political forces and in the economy which have weakened the labour movement have also greatly increased the constraints to a degree not conceived of a decade ago. Though the need for radical changes is objectively greater than ever before, the Left's economic strategy must come to terms with where we are now and cannot have the 'grandeur' and ambition of the AES in its proposals for economic planning and large-scale extensions of public ownership.

However, it must take up, as a central issue, in a way hardly considered by the AES, the position of women who constitute half the population and half the labour force and who face systematic discrimination. It must also confront two problems which have emerged on a scale not envisaged a decade ago: poverty and massive unemployment.

It must recognise not just the crucial importance of modernisation but consider new forms of influence and intervention, of social ownership and control which are rooted amongst the people and provide the popular base for national action. It must recognise that economic and social divisions have grown and devise policies which help the labour movement to intervene in such a way as to recognise the unity needed for democratic and socialist advance. And one further difference is that it must be far more outward looking and open: advancing a positive project for international economic relations including the EEC.

I have argued that the constraints are now far greater than before: the question of priorities as a consequence has become more acute. The selection of those priorities helps to focus on the main thrust of the strategy.

THE NEW PRIORITIES

I would argue these priorities are:

First: adequate child care and provision; improvement in social services; the attack on poverty and low pay.

Second: modernisation and investment, revitalising British industry especially manufacturing, so that there are more resources to meet people's needs and allow the UK to negotiate its position in the world economy from some position of strength.

Third: education and training on a large scale based on equal opportunities policies.

Fourth: a programme for creating something like 2 million jobs within a parliamentary session, but with special measures for the long-term unemployed, the hard-hit regions and inner city areas where young people and ethnic communities suffer from cumulative disadvantage and discrimination.

Fifth: international initiatives (especially within Europe) to encourage coordinated expansion, tighter supervision of industrial and financial transnational corporations; practical support for Third World development and a solution to the world debt problem.

The campaign for these priorities does not only challenge the main thrust of Tory and big business policies; it asserts a different morality. And it places the Left at the head of the movement for change and modernisation instead of lagging defensively behind it.

I do not propose to discuss every one of the priorities set out above but to raise questions about how the Left should approach some of them.

The Central State

I am not concerned here with the libertarians who see the central state as marginal but with those who believe much greater weight must be put on releasing local initiatives, developing popular planning, creating new forms of social and cooperative ownership, increasing the powers of local government and the resources of community based organisations.

It does seem to me that none of the priorities set out earlier can be tackled effectively without central government using its powers. It alone can concentrate the forces needed to weaken the powers of the City and the giant multinationals; embark on the necessary fiscal and monetary policies; exercise powers of national ownership and regulation; take or underwrite major investment decisions affecting the long term development of the economy; decide international trade and monetary policy.

Those who have been developing local employment policies in Sheffield, London and the Midlands know that a single deflationary act by central government can destroy more jobs in one week than they can create in years, if at all. But even so, given the situation we are in, the forms and objectives of government intervention have to be rethought.

Nationalisation is one controversial issue. A Labour government, were one elected in 1987 or 1988, would lack support for any programme of extended nationalisation except that which could be seen by the mass of the people as vital to protect and advance their interests. In these cases, the way in which workers and consumers would be involved would be crucial to the future.

In fighting privatisation especially in the social services, the Left needs an approach which shows how these can meet the needs of users as well as those who work in them.

But I suggest that the much bigger question, in circumstances where a major extension of nationalisation is not an issue, is that of the regulation of privately owned industries as well as those owned by the state.

There is a huge area of debate on what criteria such regulation (for example of pricing, investment, location decisions) should be based; how it can be monitored and how workers, trade unions and community bodies could be involved.

Whether the phrase is used or not, the issues raised by regulation are close to those raised by Planning Agreements, advocated by the AES during the seventies and over which the Labour government sacrificed Tony Benn.

Furthermore, even though local economic initiatives already have a track record, a 'bottom up' approach needs to radically reform the way in which local authorities operate. They can be as removed from the people as central government.

Unlike a Tory government which can rely on big business support however small the electorate which voted for it, a Labour government is only as strong as its support at the grass roots.

MODERNISATION AND INVESTMENT

Modernisation has been a slogan used before as, for instance, by the Tory government in the early 1960s when the NEDC was created; by the Labour government under Wilson with its talk of the white heat of the technological revolution; by the 1974–79 Labour government with its industrial strategy; and by the Thatcher government with its policy of survival of the fittest. The slogan was used by each of these governments to try to capture the deep concern about Britain's continuing relative decline and to win agreement for the burden of any change to be borne by the mass of the people and especially the poorest.

In fact, British-owned capital has been engaged in an investment strike under both Tory and Labour governments (including the Thatcher governments). There has not been enough investment overall to maintain the capital stock, still less expand it, while the plentiful money supply finds more attractive uses in financial and allied services abroad.

A modernisation, high investment and high industrial output strategy is not an option but a necessity and the resources for it have to be found if all the other priorities are to be met. It has become more critical as the speed of change accelerates.

Most people understand this, at least in principle. The more difficult question is how a Labour government (though the question arises for any interventionist government) can pursue an active industrial policy which begins to change the shape of the British economy to meet the needs of the people into the 21st century.

Flying in the face of evidence from other countries such as Japan, the Tories insist that governments cannot 'pick winners', but since big business in Britain has failed to do so, intervention into firms and sectors is the unavoidable requirement for modernisation. The difficulty is that whereas this appears relatively simple in obvious areas such as high technology, biotechnology, aerospace, etc. it is much more complex when dealing with mainstream industries. Sweeping changes are not necessarily the best way forward; influencing and negotiating change, creating new agencies where needed may make more sense.

It is here that locally-based interventions whether through Local Enterprise Boards or Regional Development Agencies, closely linked with elected and representative bodies sensitive to the linkages in the local economy, can be important. And both central and local government, in conjunction with other public services, have hardly begun to use the leverage available to them from their combined purchasing power.

The aims of increased investment and modernisation must be to raise the level of productivity and output. It may be controversial but I believe the number of new jobs created should not be the main criteria for the Left's policy on manufacturing. The task of a revitalised manufacturing industry is to provide the additional resources which allows jobs to be created and supported elsewhere in society as well as to reduce the hours spent at work.

None of this itself solves the problem of controlling the behaviour of the multinationals. But challenges, including successful ones, have been made by less powerful states; and for many multinationals, access to the British market is an important lever which governments can use. For example, the combined use of the threat of limiting access to the UK market and of the public sector's purchasing power could compel companies like Ford and General Motors to invest and produce more cars in Britain.

DISTRIBUTION AND REDISTRIBUTION

The main concern of socialists has been the distribution of wealth as between capitalists and workers based on the ownership of capital. Redistribution between the two main classes has also been the concern of those who simply want to reduce class inequality. However, the distribution and redistribution of wealth and income between classes has become much less straightforward than it was.

A vast system of contractual saving has been created through the insurance companies and pension funds which involves millions of workers as well as the wealthy. These institutions, which have also been granted useful tax concessions, with their funds often managed by merchant bankers and big city brokers, have become the biggest owners of equity capital and the main source of new funds for investment.

In addition, the growth of welfare and social security means that the state now operates a massive system of transfer of income between those who work and those who don't or can't. And the wages and salaries of millions now employed in the public sector are financed by taxes raised by the state (apart from those who work for nationalised industries which sell their products or services).

But changes in the last decade have made the issue of redistribution more critical. In the UK, output has grown more slowly; the trebling of unemployment has not only meant loss of output but increased state spending on unemployment pay, social security and special job creation measures. North Sea oil revenues have masked the situation, but with oil revenues soon to decline and if the economy fails to revive, the question of redistribution from more limited resources must become more acute.

Unfortunately, the problem of limited resources will face a Labour government even more acutely and cannot be speedily resolved. A government which sought to carry through the priorities listed above (expanding child care, welfare etc.; tackling low pay and poverty; carrying through large-scale education and training programmes, implementing equal opportunity policies, funding large-scale investment programmes), will not find all the resources it needs by borrowing or by redistribution between capitalists and workers. Though it must attack the great inequalities of wealth through tax reform, it will be obliged to carry through substantial redistribution amongst working people.

There are other uncomfortable implications we can envisage in 1987/88 will pose acute problems to the trade union movement. Tory policy has been so oppressive for millions of workers, especially in the public sector and to millions on social security, that a Tory defeat will release an almost irresistible wave of expectations and militancy by all those who have been held down and from those who see new possibilities of advance; and they would be joined by many who could not care less about the fate of the government, and in fact, actively oppose it.

Any attempt to meet all these expectations must fail; it would provoke a new round of capitalist reorganisations and closures, attempts to pass on increased costs through higher prices, and intensify the pressure from international finance.

In the conditions of the UK a statutory incomes policy is unworkable but it is obvious that any government will have a policy with regard to its own wages bill: and a Labour government, concerned to reinvigorate the economy, will have regard to the distribution of income between consumption and investment.

It is becoming increasingly clear that the trade union movement now needs to formulate its own wages policy if it is not to become either an adjunct of government or concerned only with each union's bargaining groups. A new economic strategy calls for a wages policy which would be based on combating low pay, achieving equal pay for work of equal value—in a word, solidaristic.

To some extent, these changes are beginning to happen. The support for a statutory minimum wage has gained ground in the movement; some unions have taken the first steps to give more than verbal support to equal pay for work of equal value. Many agreements are now 'bottom-loaded', giving a bigger percentage increase to those at the bottom of the pile. There are some signs of a solidaristic wages policy; but there is a long way to go; it needs to be travelled quickly and the rhetoric of 'free collective bargaining' has not helped.

Within the private sector, restructuring and mergers are creating new concentrations of capital led by aggressive tycoons, determined to break union strength whilst the going is good. The unions will expect support from a Labour government in restoring their strength; they will benefit from expansionary policies but they need to work out their own industrial strategy if they are not to go down the blind alley of believing that the fight for wages *is* an industrial strategy.

JOBS IN A NEW ECONOMIC STRATEGY

The changes in unemployment from the 1950s to the 1980s are of extraordinary size and so also are the changes in the composition of those at work. They have made the Left itself (and that includes the writer) uncertain and troubled about any possibility of returning to the kind of full employment that existed in the 20 years after the war. Whatever the rhetoric, opinion is growing that full employment in the 1950s sense is not attainable; the economic and political conditions for achieving it are not in prospect whatever was done in the mid-1930s or wartime Britain. I am not arguing that this is a law for all capitalist states; some of them have far lower numbers out of work such as Japan and Austria.

Even to cut unemployment in Britain to 2 million would require, on some estimates, the creation of 1250 extra jobs each day for five years, taking into account the increased numbers of working age and the growing numbers of women entering the labour market. On present trends, without major changes in policy, unemployment will continue to rise. There will be fewer full-time jobs and more part-time jobs and since women take the part-time jobs, by 1990 the unemployment rate for men could be 18 per cent, and 7 per cent for women. The Left has to grapple with these changes and recognise what a new government in 1987/88 is likely to face. In spite of all the divisions that have arisen, there is a growing and widespread view that making drastic inroads into unemployment is a national priority; that the waste and degradation of human capacity is itself an obscenity.

If the priorities set out earlier are tackled boldly they will certainly create perhaps 2 million jobs within three or four years. The major increases would come in the first place from employing more in the public services—child care provision, welfare, health, education etc. In the second place from beginning to renovate the infrastructure. NEDO estimates suggest that £2 billion is needed to meet the maintenance backlog in hospitals; and £5 billion for housing construction and repairs. Maintenance programmes are extremely labour intensive.

If economic growth were sustained at even 3 per cent, employment in private services would also grow, on some estimates by 160,000 per year. Nor is it just a question of increasing the number jobs. The large-scale education and training programme would remove considerable numbers from the labour market and in the longer run improve the capacity of the economy to grow.

More problematic is the extent to which increased demand will be translated into more jobs in UK manufacturing industries. Partly, this is because increased investment will improve productivity; unless output rises faster than that, there will be no increase in jobs, there could even be fewer. But this is the medium and longer term. More immediately, the destruction of manufacturing capacity in some sectors means that even if demand improved, the equipment would not be there for workers to use. There are stratagems such as extra shift working and reduction in working hours which can help but the scale of the problem is not clear.

A NEW INTERNATIONAL POSITION

Britain cannot opt out of the international economy; nor should it. But it does not control it either. It can influence it by using such bargaining power as it has (even debtors can be influential if they unite . . .) and make useful alliances.

The guiding principle behind Left economic strategy must be that it wants the UK to play a positive role in the world economy, to develop mutually beneficial trade between countries, and enable the developing countries to grow and overcome hunger and famine. It cannot agree that the economy should be at the mercy of whatever private capital or other government, decide. It insists on Britain negotiating its place in the world economy.

The AES, as suggested earlier, had too little to say about the kind of international economic policy to be fought for. In the framework of this article I shall not deal with such problems as exchange controls, world debt policy, the UK role in the IMF, World Bank etc. I want instead to confront one particular controversial issue: Britain's membership of the EEC. I suggest that those of us who have argued for withdrawal should have second thoughts.

Within the capitalist world, economic power is now concentrated around the USA, Japan and West Germany (itself deeply involved with the EEC).

The EEC has evolved from the original six to the present twelve. Although West Germany enjoys a pre-eminent position, new kinds of alliances are now possible within it. Taken as a whole, it represents a major economic and political force; and to a degree, it presents a common interface between the EEC and the other centres such as the USA, Japan, the Soviet Union, OPEC and other developing countries.

The UK, though a fourth-rate power, still has wide international interests and concerns and must have alliances to protect them and to influence the world economy. It is not in the same position as Switzerland, Austria or Sweden for instance.

The dominant groups of British capital, and successive British governments, were, as is well known, initially hostile to the EEC; they sought to build up alliances which would provide them with an alternative power base in Britain's post-imperial phase—and failed. They were no more successful in establishing Britain as the favoured junior partner of the USA. Reluctantly for political and economic reasons, British capitalism (to some degree also encouraged by the USA) recognised that it must enter the EEC or find itself relatively isolated and confronting far more powerful groupings.

Realistically, this is the only bloc within which the UK can hope to play an important role. It would otherwise be at the mercy of EEC decisions, which would further limit Britain's bargaining position, or of the USA, notwithstanding Mrs Thatcher's deep-rooted Atlanticism. In the period of Britain's membership, a major redirection of our trade towards member countries has taken place; in the field of high technology, aerospace and weaponry, the significance of 'European' cooperation has clearly grown so as to match the competitive strength of the USA and Japan. The Westland affair is an obvious expression of this conflict.

The arguments against Britain's membership of the EEC are well known. One is the cost of the Common Agricultural Policy; but other EEC governments also find this burdensome (though less so) and the effort to change it will continue. The costs, however, are not overwhelming in the more general context. The more fundamental argument is the loss of sovereignty involved in membership. But there are two points to consider. The first is that the EEC is itself an arena of struggle between states and capitalist groupings—supranationality is a long way off. National interests, including Britain's, still have a very powerful voice in the EEC. Nor is the Treaty of Rome a sacred text as we can see from the EEC's highly interventionist industrial policies and its inability to prevent a massive extension of nationalisation by the Mitterrand government. Secondly, the UK's sovereignty will be more constrained, if my argument is right, by being outside the EEC than within it.

Two of the options available are: first to go along with the EEC as it now is; the second is to withdraw as a condition of acting independently. The first is inadequate and unacceptable to the Left. The second is mistaken for the reasons I have given.

There is a third option: to accept fully the need for involvement in the EEC and to work with all the forces available to change its policies with regard to coordinated economic expansion, industrial collaboration, assistance to the developing countries, relations with the socialist world, coordinated approach to the control of multinationals and the supervision of banking and financial systems. It could foster workers' solidarity across EEC boundaries. And of course it could seek alliances among the '12' to oppose cruise missiles and for nuclear disarmament. We cannot know how much ground would be gained but it is important to break out from the defensive position into which much of the Left is still bunkered.

29. A Common Programme for Europe's Left?*

John Palmer

It has become strikingly evident in recent decades that any socialist strategy based on an isolated national economy—particularly one so far down the path of deindustrialisation and decline as Britain is—is doomed to failure. The growing impotence of the nation-state in matters concerned with the international division of labour and the power of multinational capital is well testified. While it would be wrong to deny the possibility of any serious action by a Left government at a national level, it is important to be realistic about what purely national 'power' can achieve in current circumstances. At best it can 'buy time' and counter the most blatant external subversions of a socialist economy. But a Left government which does not have the perspective of international support will risk isolation, will be vulnerable to destabilisation and so failing in its basic objectives as to open the door to radical reaction.

There is a trend in European ruling-class politics towards an embryo 'European state'. For two or more decades it has been evident to the majority of large European capital that its interests required the developments of a stronger European economic and political executive. Although the evolution of the European Community 'Common Market' has gone some way to protect the interests of European capital this is now seriously inadequate in the face of the growing international crisis and competition from more advanced capitals based in the United States, Japan and some other countries.

There are also trends towards the 'regionalisation' of the world economy which have accentuated the need for European capital to organise itself on a comparable basis. So it is that European capital has identified the urgent need to bridge the 'technology' gap and to organise

* Reproduced from Ken Coates (ed.), *Joint Action for Jobs* (*New Socialist/* Spokesman, 1986), pp. 51–6.

production, investment and trade in ways that mitigate intense international competition. The demand of the hardest hit sectors of European capital for defence of their interests at a European level is the strongest single impetus behind the repeated attempts of some West European governments and the EEC institutions to revive progress towards economic and political union. Equally, there are forces pushing for less 'Atlanticist' and more 'European' common foreign and security policies.

The trend towards the consolidation of the power of European capital and its expression in terms of the development of a European state is, of course, subject to the deepest contradiction. At a political level the national states in Western Europe, both within and outside the EEC itself have profound bureaucratic and other interests in resisting supranationalisation. Nowhere is this more clearly expressed than in the Thatcher Tory government whose ideology towards Europe is still a strange admixture of pro-Common Market sentiments on trade and competition combined with a 'neo-Gaullist little Englandism' and a deep pro-Atlanticism in all fundamental matters affecting foreign and security policy.

A more profound obstacle to the creation of a united capitalist Europe is the obvious complicity of a large section of European big business in forms of collaboration with non-European capital. In an effort to counter the commercial and technological backwardness of European business many large European firms have preferred to strike commercial and technology cooperation agreements with American and Japanese companies rather than other European companies. This profound ambiguity will in the end have to be resolved if the political momentum towards European union is to be sustained.

There are a variety of other serious impedimenta in the way of European union. Among them are the imbalance in the development of existing European Community 'common' policies such as agriculture, budgetary disciplines, and the main provisions for an internal market under the Treaty of Rome. Because of the unevenness of benefit and contribution already evident within the ten-nation Community it will be extremely difficult to work out an acceptable new treaty which would reconcile these conflicts of interests, particularly with enlargement to twelve or more member states.

The response to these developments of the labour movement has been singularly deficient. No serious analysis has been made either of the trends towards the Euro-state nor of the mainly reactionary obstacles that still stand in its path. As a result the European trade union and labour movement has not had the ideological means at its disposal to develop a politics capable of exploiting the opportunities in Europe created by the present economic and industrial crisis. Nowhere is the labour movement suffering more under a greater parochial narrowness than in Britain. Yet any serious reading of the situation facing the working-class movement at the present time demands far greater priority to strategies designed to mobilise the European labour movement.

The striking feature of the present job crisis is that it is almost equally serious in impact throughout Western Europe. Although there are minor differences due, in the main, to variations in national economic policy being pursued by the different West European governments, these are dwarfed by the common structural crisis affecting Western European industry. On current projections the present period of economic recovery which began some three years ago will peter out at the end of 1985 or in early 1986. Yet there was no interruption of the upward trend of unemployment in Western Europe during the period of so-called recovery. Any new economic recession must risk bringing unemployment throughout Western Europe as a whole to well over 20 million by the end of the decade.

Unemployment also tends to be concentrated in and around the same structurally declining industries—notably steel, coal, vehicle manufacture, construction and textiles. There is also a common emerging pattern arising from mass unemployment in the fiscal burdens being imposed upon the West European welfare states. Everywhere governments are attempting to fund massive budget deficits induced by the enormous scale of current levels of resources being devoted to unemployment. This same fiscal constraint combined with high international interest rates means that national governments have virtually no manoeuvring room unilaterally to reflate their economies. The appalling experience of the Mitterrand government which reverted from Keynesian expansionism to Thatcherite monetarist austerity after twelve months in office is a striking testimony to these trends. Everywhere social democratic governments in office are in full-flood retreat before the goals of full employment, rising living standards, protected welfare spending and even basic civil and labour rights.

Although it will require sweeping changes made by like-minded governments throughout Western Europe to alter fundamentally the economic situation which has given rise to mass unemployment, a variety of steps can be taken immediately by labour movements in opposition. These include:

1. Support for measures to bring trade unionists working in common transnational corporations together to form a European combine of shop stewards. The GLC has been able to give direct

encouragement to this kind of work with Fords, Kodak and Philips.

2. Such combines can prepare common strategies to force the far greater disclosure of information about their companies and to lay the basis for a concerted strategy of resistance to plant closures and mass redundancies.

3. These combines, together with the wider European trade union movement, can begin to discuss and raise the issues of alternatives, particularly for those sectors most hard hit by structural decline and mass unemployment. The whole impetus of the approach to workers' plans as first outlined by the Lucas Aerospace shop stewards, taken up by such bodies as the Greater London Enterprise Board, have particular relevance at the European level.

4. Such alternative workers' plans for key sectors of the European economy will not only identify areas of unfilled market and social needs, identify, through social audit techniques, unused labour and capital resources, but will also begin to broach at least the rudimentary questions of transnational trade planning. Any strategy, for instance, for the European motor industry, devised by trade unionists in that industry would have to involve some understanding about an appropriate and planned division of labour between the different national plants.

5. Progressive local authorities and other bodies in the European Community can also be persuaded to give encouragement to twin trading agreements. This would involve preference being given in the purchasing policies of progressive local authorities to enterprises receiving the financial backing of these local authorities or their Investment Agencies throughout the European Community.

6. In the same way, a network of mutual support and twin trading can be encouraged between the burgeoning European Worker Co-operative Movement. In this way something of a partial 'sheltered economic environment' can be developed both for worker co-operatives and for enterprises backed by the Left local authorities which would go some way to enable them to survive in the present economic climate.

7. Conferences of all those engaged in this work should be held to discuss wider issues raised by their work, notably what demands are appropriate to place upon their respective national governments and what demands should be placed upon the institutions of the European Community. As far as the latter is concerned there should be a concerted programme of demands to expand the European Social Fund and to encourage the development of an

EEC Enterprise Board to mobilise public sector resources at a European level to be put behind worker cooperatives and other such enterprises.

8. There should be coordinated pressure for national strategies to be adopted by incoming Left governments which maximise European cooperation and minimise the dangers of nationalistic confrontation within Western Europe. One key priority here should be the future of the European Monetary System which could provide the basis for the European planning of exchange rates and currencies in ways that did not subordinate employment and living standards to the hegemony of bankers. Equally, there should be concertation of measures to extend public ownership, to impose controls on foreign trade and on capital movements to maximise reciprocity and mutual interests between like-minded governments.

9. There should be a concerted campaign to introduce European Community 'best practice' in welfare provisions, trade union rights, the contractual conditions for labour, as well as redundancy and social benefit rights. If we live in a Common Market where the same rules governing the movement of capital or free trade apply we should also live in a community which has West German level unemployment pay, French level social security payments, or Dutch payments to single parent families. At the same time measures should be advanced to campaign for a common programme of equal rights for women and 'guest workers'.

10. Particular and immediate attention should be given to the demand for a shorter working week and the related demand by the trade unions for 'liberated time' that is the diversion of a part of 'excess production' in firms benefiting from new technology to enable them to extend output to socially useful areas outside the market.

11. The whole question of conversion from the arms industries and from nuclear based power must be integrated into any such strategy. Urgent work needs to take place to devise a common European workers' energy programme and a common programme to switch employment from arms to socially useful production.

These are only some of the issues which are possible to raise and to win support for in the perspective of a common European Left political stragegy. None of this is to accept either the present Rome Treaty or the present boundaries of the European Community. To the contrary, the above demands are clearly incompatible with the Rome Treaty as it is currently framed and this demands an ultimate programme to replace the Rome Treaty with a new treaty between West European socialist governments enshrining cooperation and coordination towards an ulti-mately common socialist United States of Europe. Such a United States of Europe could not but challenge the Iron Curtain which divides Europe down the middle. It goes without saying that every effort should be made to establish contact with the oppositional trade unions and peace movements in Eastern Europe with whom common cause in the struggle against nuclear alliances and bureaucratic despotism should be established. Finally, at least the beginnings of a dialogue with the labour and trade union movements outside Europe must begin, particularly in the Third World. A European transnational strategy is itself only an interim towards a global internationalism to pose the fundamental question of worldwide socialism. In the meantime Left governments which obtain office must be placed under the maximum pressure to extend public ownership and to make radical changes in the whole character of state power so as to permit the growth of the embryonic institutions for a socialist economy and for democratic working-class power.

30. The Nature of the Choice Before Us

David Coates

The choice of policies which we are asked to make emerges from a particular debate between professional economists on the role of the state in the creation of economic growth, full employment and price stability; and though the choice is new, the debate itself is not. It stretches back at least into the 1930s, to an earlier Depression, to one moreover in which, as now, the official Treasury view was that increases in government spending were likely to make unemployment worse. If people were out of work, so the argument ran, that could only be because the price which they were asking for their labour was too high. If wages fell, employment would in the end pick up automatically. Government spending could only delay that process, and get in the way. Money available for public bodies to spend could only come from the stock of private money available to the rest of us in our roles as consumers and lenders. Far from reducing unemployment, all that government spending could hope to do was to move it about; shifting it from the public sector into the private. And in fact, government spending was likely to make unemployment grow, through the disincentive effects experienced by private enterprise when subject to excessive government intervention and taxation. If full employment was the target of public policy, it would come soonest if public spending was cut and wages allowed to fall.

That view was challenged in the 1930s by John Maynard Keynes. His argument then, and that of his followers since, is that output and employment are affected less by the level of wages and public spending than by the level of total demand in the economy. According to Keynes, there is nothing in the 'free play of market forces' to guarantee economic growth and full employment; and certainly wage cutting, or the withdrawal of public spending, is no solution to mass unemployment. Cutting wages will reduce costs of course, but it will also—and in a much more immediate way—reduce the purchasing power available to the economy as a whole. For workers are also consumers. Cut wages and you cut demand. This cannot help business confidence to flourish; and without that confidence in their capacity to sell the goods they make, businesses will not feel able to make the investment in new plant and equipment which is the ultimate guarantor of jobs and prosperity. Politicians in pursuit of full employment, according to Keynes, must not spend less. They must spend more; and they must encourage the banking system to extend credit on attractive terms. Then businesses will invest, and jobs will come, and the economy will be able to move into a 'virtuous circle' of high demand, high investment, growing productivity, full employment, high wages and high demand. Unregulated capitalism, Keynes thought, would not automatically produce that virtuous cycle, but a managed capitalism could—if the political will was there to bring it into existence.

Keynesians have never entirely agreed, however, on just how much spending governments should do, or just how managed capitalism needs to be. There are 'right-wing' and 'left-wing' Keynesianisms, differing on whether all that is required is 'quite limited state intervention, where the state simply influences private investment indirectly by managing aggregate demand' or instead, and because private capital is seen as inadequate to this task, 'state expenditure itself supplants private investment as the principal driving force behind economic activity' (Schott, in Held *et al.*, *State and Societies*, Martin Robertson, 1983, p. 340). So far at least, moderate Keynesianism has held centre stage, and certainly for a generation after the war its prescriptions moulded the economic policy of western governments of various political persuasions. Politicians used fiscal and monetary techniques to keep the economy as near full employment as they could. They altered levels of purchasing power through tax changes and credit controls. They superintended an unprecedented peacetime growth in government spending, and allowed the public sector to become a major source of employment and a major consumer of the products of private enterprise. They even persuaded their electorates, as inter-war politicians had never tried to do, to judge them on their performance as Keynesian managers of employment and growth.

Latterly of course, all this has changed. The economic difficulties of western capitalism in the 1970s brought with it a major reconsideration of the adequacy of Keynesianism. In 1974, for the first time since 1948, the volume of output and trade in the capitalist bloc actually fell; and in the years since rates of economic growth have been lower, less evenly distributed, and harder to achieve, than they were in the boom years of the Keynesian ascendancy. Instead of sustained growth and full employment, joblessness has returned on a massive scale; and within this generalised crisis the competitive position of British manufacturing industry (which had already weakened significantly in the 1950s and 1960s) suddenly diminished in a quite dramatic way. Once the 'work-shop of the world', Britain by 1983 was importing more manufactured goods than it was managing to sell abroad. What was perhaps even worse, governments seemed impotent to prevent this decline or to reverse the enormous amounts of unemployment which accompanied it. In spite of repeated promises (by Conservative and Labour governments after 1961) that economic growth and competitive strength could be achieved by indicative planning, tripartite consultation, and large amounts of state aid, the relative decline of British manufacturing industry went on apace; and the coincidence—not just in Britain but throughout the capitalist bloc—of inflation *and* unemployment further immobilised governments which had been led by Keynesianism to expect these as alternatives. Politicians had come to realise in the 1950s that full employment could produce rising prices, and so had already had to run their economies at levels which traded off low rates of un-employment against equally low rates of inflation. But suddenly in the 1970s they found themselves faced with *high and rising* levels of both, and could no longer vary levels of aggregate demand to appease one without accentuating the other. This arrival of 'stagflation' precipitated a monetarist counter-revolution to Keynesianism in the chancelleries and universities of the entire western world; and the intensity of inflation in Britain (it reached 30 per cent in 1975) and the visible decline of the competitiveness of British manufacturing industry, gave that counter-revolution a particular potency here. It brought to power in 1979 a Conservative government determined to leave Keynesianism far behind.

Monetarists drew attention to what they saw as serious errors of analysis in the Keynesian account of growth, employment and inflation. From their point of view, the preoccupation of Keynesian economists with job creation through *demand* management led them to ignore problems on the *supply* side of the economic equation. Keynesian economists were prone to assume too readily that spare capacity existed for quick reflation, that machines and skilled labour were available for immediate mobilisation, and they were prone too to discount the existence of what monetarists called the 'natural level of unemployment' in an economy—a level fixed not by government spending, but by the character of the labour force, the level of technology, the degree of unionisation, and so on. If politicians insisted on inflating economies beyond this 'natural' level, they would produce not jobs but inflation; and they would miss the importance of acting on the supply side of the economy, to reduce the impact there of social and economic processes which keep the natural level of unemployment unnecessarily high. Inflating demand was no substitute, according to monetarists, for policy which reduced trade union power, removed welfare barriers to work, and took away subsidies and controls which protected industry from the invigorating impact of market competition. In fact Keynesian demand management was another of the things which actually kept unemployment levels high. Keynesianism meant 'big government', and big government got in the way of private wealth creation—by over-taxing, over-regulating and over-subsidising business and by allowing strong trade unionism to consolidate itself in the cosseted labour markets of an over-expanded economy. Britain was a prime case of too much Keynesianism, according to monetarists both here and abroad. Its unions were too strong, its public sector too large, its welfare system too generous, and its industries too subsidised. Therefore the route back to competitiveness and full employment did not lie through yet more state intervention and welfare provision. It lay instead in a return to a more limited role for the state and to a greater reliance on private initiative and market competition. The job of politicians in Britain, on this view, was to create the conditions in which private enterprise could flourish again: and that meant guaranteeing price stability through the control of the money supply. It also meant cutting back the public spending which fuelled money supply growth; and cutting the tax barriers to private wealth-creation (taking limits off high earnings and capital movements at the top, and taking away welfare benefits and wage council protections which stopped people working for low wages at the bottom). It also, of course, involved reducing trade union power and moving large chunks of the public sector back into private ownership.

This debate between Keynesians and monetarists has occupied the public stage for over a decade, and will no doubt go on doing so. Charge and countercharge are, and will continue to be, exchanged, as the collection of views here indicate only too well. Keynesianism was so vulnerable to monetarist criticism in the 1970s because monetarism itself was untried; and Keynesianism is in some kind of ascendancy again because seven years of Conservative policy still leaves the dole queues appallingly long and the manufacturing base desperately weak. Just as once Keynesian economists used to explain policy failures in terms of the inadequate application of their theory, so now monetarists have to do the same: either denying that there is a crisis, or explaining it by saying that the government is not monetarist enough, or by pointing the finger still at union power and high wage settlements as in the 1970s. It may well be that somewhere in that cacophony of claim and counterclaim you will find a position which still makes some sense: but as you search for that position you might do well to remember that beyond the debate a third set of positions are also available, ones which—because they are more radical—are less publicly heard or generally understood. The ecologists have one such position—as we have seen; and the Marxists have another.

Marxism is of course a dismal science. It offers no easy, gradual or piecemeal solution to Britain's economic decline. The crisis of capitalism of which Britain's decline is a part is, on a Marxist argument, structural and endemic, the result of a set of contradictions and associated interplays of class forces, which are visible at both the national and international level. Marxists, like Keynesians and monetarists, come in many shades and sizes, but they all tend to agree that capitalism suffers from a central clash of position and interests between capitalists and workers: a basic incompatibility between wages and profits, machinery and labour. The capitalist class (understood as the owners of capital and their senior managerial personnel) needs workers both to produce commodities and to consume them in the form of wage goods. It needs to pay them wages as workers, and to receive income from them as consumers. Yet here is one contradiction: capitalists cannot pay their workers too much without experiencing problems of capital *accumulation*, since high wages erode profits and competitiveness. Yet equally they cannot pay them too little without being unable to *realise* their profits through the sale of commodities to the workers as consumers. This contradiction at the heart of capitalist economies can never fully be resolved, and remains instead a source of perennial crisis within the system as a whole. It is only the form of the crisis, never the crisis itself, which varies. The form the crisis takes depends on the strength of the class forces surrounding production—manifesting itself as a crisis of realisation if the workers are too weak, as in the 1930s, or as a crisis of accumulation if the workers are too strong, as in the 1970s. Nor can capitalism extract itself from the logics it sets up by its own combined but uneven development. Capital is accumulated through competition between capitalists, first on a local, then on a national and ultimately on an international scale. In that competitive struggle, advantage accrues to the technologically sophisticated; and that in its turn introduces into capitalist economies a propensity to replace labour by machinery, to create unemployment and to erode profits. Counter-tendencies exist of course—as unemployment grows, labour becomes cheaper and so slows the propensity to mechanise people out of production. But capitalism rarely generates full employment. The prosperity of the long postwar boom was the exception, not the rule, for capitalism. Marxists see no way in which capitalism can permanently guarantee jobs for all, and no space for one capitalist economy easily to free itself from competitive pressures to perpetually innovate, mechanise labour away, and destroy old skills and traditional ways of working.

Thus, many Marxists agree with Keynesianism that government spending was an intelligible response to an under-consumptionist crisis in the 1930s which derived from the defeat of the labour movements in the intense struggles of the 1910–26 period; and they are equally willing to share with monetarism that sense of Keynesianism's failure as post-war full employment altered the balance of class forces in favour of trade union strength and working class wages. They are also broadly tolerant of monetarism's observation that the competitive edge of particular national capitalisms will weaken fastest where Keynesianism is most pronounced—for in such circumstances (and Britain is a case in point) the labour movements are strong enough to protect wages longer, and the welfare state more extensively, than was the case in economies where the balance of class forces, even in the long boom, was more favourable to capital. Where Marxists and monetarists part company is when the latter offer trade union strength as the major or even the only reason for Britain's economic decline. For behind the 'market forces' to which monetarism perpetually refers Marxists see the persistence of class power and privilege. If capitalism is weak here it is primarily because of the character of the local capitalist class—of the domination within it of fractions geared to accumulation on a world scale—tied, that is, to financial transactions which are only tangentially and accidentally connected to local industrial investment. British manufacturing industry is weak less because trade unions are strong than because national industrial capital is itself subordinated to multinational interests and to financial institutions with large overseas portfolios. That is why there is no 'market' solution to Britain's industrial decline, according to Marxists. No government will 'persuade' capitalist interests to reindustrialise Britain when its industrial base is now so weak. Capital will go where the profits are greatest: and they are greatest elsewhere. On this view the logic of market forces under private ownership must continue to de-industrialise Britain—and to do so at an ever-quickening pace; and full employment and economic growth will never be permanently guaran-teeable while the contradiction of capital and labour remains. If full employment and economic regeneration are to be the targets of public policy, the weight of the Marxist analysis suggests that they require—not government spending or trade union reform—but rather the replacement of the power of private capital.

It is from this debate that the policy range we have experienced emerges. People just disagree on whether economic growth is desirable at all, and if it is, whether it is best achieved through the free play of market forces, through tinkering and talking, through government spending and intervention, or through various government attacks on the existing distribution of wealth and power. That leaves us with a number of strategic routes from which to choose: to alter the distribution of power and wealth by increasing or reducing welfare provision, tax handouts and trade union power; to increase or reduce the 'weight', 'burden', 'control' or 'ownership' (the choice of words is itself an argument) of government over business; to add to or to reduce government involvement in the provision of infrastructure, research and training: and whether to extend or to reduce government control over, planning of, and interference with patterns of foreign trade, capital movements and corporate ownership. The debate has its parameters because there seems a consensus that these are the issues. It has its longevity because there is no consensus on how those issues are to be resolved. The choice at the moment seems to be like Figure 30.1.

The privilege of editorship normally takes two forms. The first is to choose the extracts and their organisation. The second is to have the last word. It would be nice to be able to claim that the two privileges are unconnected, but of course they are not. We have attempted throughout to let each position speak for itself, untrammelled by editorial intervention, and to speak in as clear, coherent and sophisticated a form as the position can generate. What we have imposed is only a structure, a movement within each section broadly from Right to Left. That is not, in our view, either an arbitrary or an idiosyncratic way of ordering things, nor one that is excessively loaded in political terms. The government in power is a Conservative one, and the dialogue is largely with its initiatives. So there is point in placing its views, and its apologists, first. Things placed last just come at the end. They have no necessary superiority just because they are the last thing presented. Yet we are aware that not everyone agrees. Some highly intelligent political commentators doubt the adequacy of the division of Left and Right. Samuel Brittan is one such. Other reviewers of our earlier collection seem to feel it is biased to include Marxist positions at all: and if it is, then we are biased again. And of course by taking you each time to left-wing arguments we imply they have an importance which you may not feel they deserve. Our view on that is that we discharge our editorial responsibility by drawing your attention to the danger, and by making clear our own reading of the debate we have gathered. Of course what we think is of no particular importance in itself: but by making it clear in

Figure 30.1.

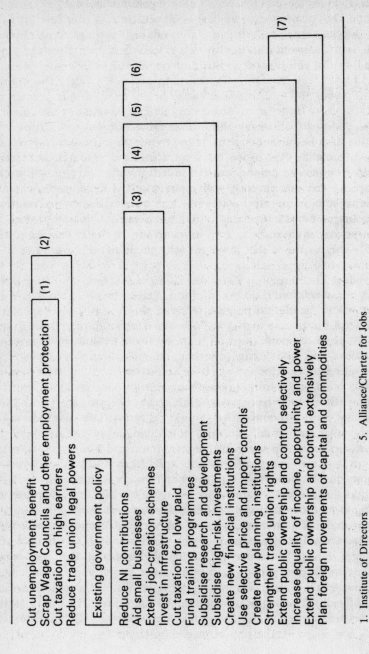

Cut unemployment benefit
Scrap Wage Councils and other employment protection — (1)
Cut taxation on high earners
Reduce trade union legal powers — (2)

Existing government policy

Reduce NI contributions
Aid small businesses
Extend job-creation schemes
Invest in infrastructure
Cut taxation for low paid
Fund training programmes
Subsidise research and development
Subsidise high-risk investments
Create new financial institutions
Use selective price and import controls
Create new planning institutions
Strengthen trade union rights
Extend public ownership and control selectively
Increase equality of income, opportunity and power
Extend public ownership and control extensively
Plan foreign movements of capital and commodities

(3) (4) (5) (6) (7)

1. Institute of Directors
2. Patrick Minford
3. Confederation of British Industry
4. Tory Reform Group
5. Alliance/Charter for Jobs
6. Labour Party
7. Campaign Group of Labour MPs

these final pages there at least can be no legitimate feeling that anything underhand has gone on here. If left-wing positions do not interest you, you have no need to read on. But if they do, or if you are still politically curious and intellectually open, as we hope, then let me indicate one possible way of resolving the nature of the choice before us.

Monetarist positions seem to me to have the following two major problems.

1. The market forces and private capitalist interests on which they place such importance as the prime movers of economic activity do not seem to be working with sufficient speed, or on a sufficient scale, either to restore employment to all who want it or to significantly improve the overall competitive position of British manufacturing industry. Nor are they likely to. For once an economy becomes under-capitalised the logic of market forces, unless disturbed by purposive intervention, will keep it so. If there was only one economy in the world, it might all right itself in the long term— though as Keynes said, in the long term we are all dead. But there is not just one economy, there are many, and profit rates and other key economic indicators settle at different levels in each. To get behind in the capitalist competitive struggle is, unless something is done about it, to stay behind. The productivity rates of an under-capitalised industrial economy will be lower than those of its competitors, its rates of return less, its next round of investment surpluses more difficult to generate or attract, and its future productivity and profitability correspondingly low again. And since its competitors will be experiencing a parallel process of virtuous growth, a weak economy is likely not simply to stay behind, but to drop ever further behind. Of course it is always possible—in the statistics issued by the ministry—to create the illusion that productivity is increasing if you are prepared to shut down, and to leave shut down, vast tracts of industry which had previously been under-capitalised. A shiny new factory in the middle of an otherwise empty field can be highly productive. But I can see no reason why British fields should be chosen as the site for large numbers of those factories when there already exist greener and fuller pastures elsewhere. On the contrary, to take just one instance, the director of a pension fund is under massive short-term commercial pressure to export capital, and not to take risks here. That, after all, is what has happened. The export of capital has gone on at unprecedented levels since the Chancellor removed controls in 1979, and the rates of return from all that overseas investment, as he never tires of

telling us, help to balance our external account. So they do; but what they do not do is develop manufacturing capacity here, or generate jobs. They help to build a *rentier* economy in Surrey and in Kent; but they do not—and they will not unless they are forced— redevelop the industrial economies of the northern river valleys.

2. Moreover, and associated with the first problem, there is a definite *class* dimension to the monetarist case. Monetarist arguments have a hardness, an insensitivity and a selfishness about them which are quite intolerable. When Margaret Thatcher can tell the CBI, as she did in May 1986, that 'yesterday's overmanning has become today's unemployment', she ducks her own responsibility for the enormous human waste and suffering brought by joblessness on this scale. It is just not enough, as her description implies, to place the blame for unemployment on trade union power and weak management. Edward Heath saw that very clearly a year before, when he said:

> Falling apart is what is happening. It is no use trying to pretend that all the unemployment we have seen since 1980 has been getting rid of overmanning. I would support any move to curb overmanning. But we have seen whole industries destroyed . . . billions of pounds worth of industrial capacity that could quite easily have been rehabilitated have been lost. (*Guardian*, 13 March 1985)

To argue for ever greater cuts in welfare (always other people's, of course) and for greater tax concessions to the well-paid (including oneself) may have a crazy market rationale. But it is also selfishness masquerading as truth. The society it would create is a profoundly immoral one, built on greed and inequality, on suffering and deprivation. Selfish people can invest abroad. The North-East can be turned into an industrial wasteland. Inaction can be covered by platitude and rhetoric. The poor can be blamed for their own poverty. The desperate can be taught patience by those too powerful to have to wait. But the bankruptcy of the philosophy which underpins all that cannot be denied. In 1979 we were told that inflation was the cause of unemployment. Well, inflation is now 3 per cent; and unemployment is 11 per cent. The Prime Minister talks of private wealth-creation, the Chancellor of popular capitalism. There is little popularity for it among the unemployed, and little wealth-creation there. If there is an indictment to be made, it is not of the unemployed, but of the system which made them so. Private capital is failing in its public duty. It is not reindustrialising Britain on a scale, and in a manner, which can guarantee even minimum standards of living to us all. And because it isn't, no amount of political double-talk can persuade me that monetarism has anything to offer. It is part of the problem; and it, and the government which espouses it, must—and must quickly—go.

So will *Planned Keynesianism* be any better? As far as I can tell it will be an improvement, but it will not itself be enough.

1. It will be better because it will bring employment to some people quickly. People will be trained in great numbers, and jobs will reappear in construction, railways and housing. The social capital of this society is steadily in decline. Our housing stock, our transport systems, our public utilities are all in need of extensive renovation; and any renewed public investment programme can only stop their further degeneration—if only for a while. The great strength of Centre–Left policies (of both the Alliance and the Hattersley kind) is that they recognise this, and are set on doing something about it. They don't expect the unemployed to wait for the market to get round to job-creation, and they don't ask them to wait for the revolution either. They act now—and bring benefits now—and they deserve our support for that.

2. My problem with them is their temerity in the face of private capital. Monetarists always criticise Keynesians for ignoring supply-side problems, and I hesitate to do the same. Monetarists, after all, are highly selective and self-indulgent in their specification of what those problems are. It always comes down in the end to the workers, their unions and their welfare benefits, and not to middle class privilege and upper class power. Yet the biggest supply-side problem is that privilege and power. The biggest supply-side problem is the capitalist class itself—its concerns, its privileges, its arrogance, and its dependence on immediate profits. It is true that there are other supply-side problems which capitalist domination has brought in its wake: not least the collapse of industrial training, the difficulties of funding high-risk investment, the high cost of borrowing and the volatility of exchange rates in an unplanned capitalist world, the lack of coordination in economic activity, and the appalling imbalance of resources between core capitalisms and the Third World which they dominate. But as you move along that list, what Keynesianism and its contemporary protagonists have to say diminishes—both in quality and certainly in effectiveness. Both the Alliance and the Labour Party are good now on industrial training and on industrial funding. They have proposals for exchange rates and (in the case of the Labour Party) for attempts at planning. They all publicly subscribe to the *Brandt Report*. At least their intentions are good here. But they have no convincing solution to the anarchy

and power (in the market and in the wider society) of private capital, either internally or on the world scale; and because they do not, it seems to me that their ability in practice to implement their high ideals, even on areas as relatively modest as training and industrial funding, is likely to be undermined whenever they are in office.

3. For there are contradictions in capitalism which block its easy management and reform. The current Labour Party programme is very similar to that on which the Party won two elections in 1974; and the disappointing experience of the government which followed has since been repeated in Mitterrand's France. Any rapid expansion of government spending will meet internal bottlenecks (in the absence of spare capacity in skills and machines) and will push up prices and costs, and draw in imports, just as quickly as it will generate greater output and jobs. The Labour Party promises a complex package of planning, power sharing, state aid, and selective price controls to get round that. But multinational corporations threatened with nationalisation and planning agreements will move their capital elsewhere: and it is hard to see what incentives governments can create to attract them back in, even if those controls are, as with the Alliance, not there in the first place. Expansion too will strengthen working-class industrial and political power. That will frighten private capital more, to give the Alliance one set of problems; and it will block even Labour's industrial restructuring, unless the Party comes good on its promise to involve workers and their representatives in the planning of that reconstruction to such a degree that the labour movement genuinely comes to identify with it as its own. But that identification can be forged only through a shift in class power—and it is precisely that shift which private capital fears the most, and which it will resist with the greatest intensity. There is a class contradiction here, and though the Alliance can hope to tax it away (through inflation taxes) and the Labour Party talk it away (in national economic forums) neither will manage to remove it and its impact. In all previous reforming governments, the talk in opposition of cooperation between classes has, in power, fallen foul of the clash of classes; and as a result income policies have quickly generated into state wage-cutting, social priorities in investment and planning have given way to market forces and profit requirements, and foreign capital and the City have only been appeased by trade union restrictions and welfare cuts. All that is on the horizon again, and the Hattersley solution to the danger of underperforming on promises seems to be to plan to underperform

as usual but to promise less. It may be better than Thatcherism, but it is not likely to win the enthusiasm of a cynical population, or ease quickly or on a sufficient scale the desperation of the deprived.

That is why more *socialist* solutions are needed if reconstruction is to come. I find Andrew Glyn's arguments convincing that the private ownership of large companies and financial institutions will have to go, and will have to be replaced by a new system of industrial decision-making linking workers, unions, management and government in a permanent and democratic dialogue. I see too that if economic expansion here is not to be blocked by balance of payments problems and the flight of multinational capital, foreign trade will have to be controlled, the export of capital banned, and the import of foreign commodities geared to the requirements of a coherent reindustrialisation strategy. Moreover, if economic reconstruction is not to be blocked by working-class resistance and sectionally-inspired wage militancy, wealth and income will have to be redistributed in an egalitarian way, with the bulk of public social provision being directed in the first instance to the renovation of decaying cities and regions. And it seems obvious too that if these changes are going to be genuinely socialist ones, then things are going to have to alter fundamentally in the relationship between paid and unpaid work, and in the distribution of social tasks and rewards by gender and by race. The need for all this seems to me to derive from the severity of our present difficulties and their uneven distribution by class, race and gender, from the origins of all this in the history of British capitalism and the contemporary character of its ruling class, and from the associated inability of more moderate programmes of reform to address themselves to the awesome nature of the changes required.

For they are truly awesome. They do involve very considerable short-term dislocations. They will meet quite massive opposition; and they do not yet command more than the tiniest amount of popular support. All this means that they are not to be canvassed lightly. If there are easier things to do which will work, then those must take precedence in their claims on our loyalty and support. I just cannot see what these easier things are. I wish I could. But if this is the scale of the task before us, then it too has to be approached realistically, with due recognition of the stages to be gone through and the problems to be faced. The radical alternative lacks detail and precision yet. Those details have to be filled in, by discussion and planning on the Left now. The radical alternative is not sufficiently known to, or accepted by, people within the labour, womens and peace movements who would be called upon to implement it; and so there is a major job of education and propaganda to be undertaken too. Both those tasks are urgent, not because such a solution is a genuine runner at this election, but precisely because it is not. Whether I care for the situation or whether I don't, I cannot get around the fact that the immediate choice before us is between monetarism and Keynesianism, with the latter on offer only in its moderate forms. To my mind, Labour's Keynesianism is preferable to the Alliance's, and both are streets ahead of the Conservatives when measured against the touchstones of jobs, growth or even underlying morality. So the Left will need to work for the return of Labour now while preparing the ground for better choices at elections to come. The political forces necessary for the successful implementation of socialist change will not appear overnight. The tragedy of our current situation is that political coalitions (both in Parliament and among the wider electorate) exist only for programmes which will fail. We are at a point at which the forces of the Right command the state, those of the Centre–Left increasingly command the support of the electorate, and the Left has the makings of a programme. Our job now is to develop the programme, win the electorate and eventually capture the state. For if we do not, and when Keynesianism (as it must) once more discredits itself in office, then Thatcherism will rise again in still more strident form. The job of the Left now is to win an audience for the argument that the limits of Labour in power should carry us on to a more radical socialism. Last time, the legacy of Labourism was Thatcher. We must never let that happen again.

Suggested Further Reading

D. Aldcroft, *Full Employment: the elusive goal* (Brighton, Harvester Press, 1984).

K. Coates (ed.), *Joint Action for Jobs* (London, Spokesman, 1986).

D. Coates and J. Hillard (eds), *The Economic Decline of Modern Britain* (Brighton, Wheatsheaf Books, 1985).

House of Lords Select Committee on Overseas Trade (1) Report: House of Lords Papers 238-I (London, HMSO, July 1985).

J. Keane and J. Owens, *After Full Employment* (London, Hutchinson, 1986).

R. Layard, *How to Beat Unemployment* (London, Oxford University Press, 1986).

J. Tomlinson, *Monetarism: Is there an alternative* (Oxford, Basil Blackwell, 1986).

Glossary of Abbreviations

ABCC	Association of British Chambers of Commerce
AES	Alternative Economic Strategy
BL	British Leyland
BOTB	British Overseas Trade Board
BSC	British Steel Corporation
BSI	British Societies Institute
CBI	Confederation of British Industry
CEGB	Central Electricity Generating Board
COCOM	Coordinating Committee (of NATO)
CP	Community Programme
DE	Department of Employment
DEIP	Department of Economic and Industrial Planning
DHSS	Department of Health and Social Security
DoE	Department of the Environment
DTI	Department of Trade and Industry
EAS	Enterprise Allowance Scheme
EC	European Community
ECU	European Currency Unit
EDC	Economic Development Council
EEC	European Economic Community
EMS	European Monetary System
Fed	Federal Reserve Bank (U.S.A.)
GATT	General Agreement on Tariffs and Trade
GDP	Gross Domestic Product
GLC	Greater London Council
GNP	Gross National Product
HMSO	Her Majesty's Stationary Office
ICFC	Industrial and Commercial Finance Corporation
IMF	International Monetary Fund
IT	Information Technology
LEB	Local Enterprise Board
LIS	London Industrial Strategy
MITI	Ministry of International Trade and Industry
MSC	Manpower Services Commission
MTES	Medium Term Employment Strategy

MTFS	Medium Term Financial Strategy
NALGO	National Association of Local Government Officers
NATO	North Atlantic Treaty Organisation
NCB	National Coal Board
NEB	National Enterprise Board
NEDC	National Economic Development Council
NEDO	National Economic Development Office
NHS	National Health Service
NI	National Insurance
NIB	National Investment Bank
OECD	Organisation for Economic Co-operation and Development
OPEC	Organisation of Petroleum Exporting Countries
PESC	Public Expenditure Survey Committee
PSBR	Public Sector Borrowing Requirement
R & D	Research and Development
RPI	Retail Price Index
RSG	Rate Support Grant
SCIP	School Curriculum Industry Project
SDA	Scottish Development Agency
SDP	Social Democratic Party
SEM	Selective Employment Measures
SERPS	State Earnings Related Pension Scheme
SFIC	Small Firm Investment Company
SKIP	Skills Improvement Programme
SPC	Statistical Process Control
TRG	Tory Reform Group
TUC	Trades Union Congress
UNCTAD	United Nations Conference on Trade and Development
UPA	Urban Priority Area
VAT	Value-added Tax
WDA	Welsh Development Agency
WMEB	West Midlands Enterprise Board
YTS	Youth Training Scheme

Index

Note: Italicised entries indicate proposed institutions, policies and so on.